ARKANSAS WILDFLOWERS

DON KURZ

TIM ERNST PUBLISHING
CAVE MOUNTAIN, ARKANSAS

Front cover photo by Don Kurz: Turk's Cap Lily, page 141

Copyright © 2010 by Tim Ernst Publishing
www.TimErnst.com
All photographs and descriptions copyright © 2010 by Don Kurz

All rights reserved.
No part of this book may be reproduced in any form or by any electronic or mechanical means, including information storage and retrieval systems,
without the permission in writing from Tim Ernst Publishing and Don Kurz.
Printed in Korea.
Library of Congress Control Number: 2010906539

ISBN: 9781882906710

Book designed by Tim Ernst, Pam Ernst, and Don Kurz

All photos are by Don Kurz

Wild plant uses for medicine or food described in this book are for information purposes only, and should not be read as promotions for medical or herbal prescriptions for self-healing or for nutrition.

To order autographed copies of this guidebook, and to see the complete line of other Arkansas guidebooks for hiking, waterfalls, scenic areas, plus maps and other outdoor publications, contact:

Tim Ernst Publishing
HC 33, 50-A
Pettigrew, Arkansas 72752 (Cave Mountain)
Toll–free order line: 800–838–HIKE
See everything in color on the web (secure online store): www.TimErnst.com

New dealers always welcome!

This book is dedicated to Carl G. Hunter (1923-2005), author of several books on the trees, shrubs, woody vines, and wildflowers of Arkansas. His tireless work in promoting the conservation and appreciation of the state's flora is very admirable and he will long be remembered for his groundbreaking efforts.

Passion Flower, page 195

Table Of Contents

Introduction, How To Use This Guide 6

Arkansas State Map with Counties and Regions 9

White Flowers 10

Yellow Flowers 80

Red and Orange Flowers 134

Pink Flowers 143

Blue and Purple Flowers 166

Green Flowers 219

Brown Flowers 229

Selected Reading 241

Glossary 242

Index 244

About The Author 256

Ruler .... back cover

Purple Prairie Clover and friend, a Hoverfly, page 195

Color Tab Index

To aid in quicker identification the wildflowers in this book are arranged in chapters by color and then season of bloom. Simply determine the flower petals' color and find the matching colored tab located along the outside edge of the chapter pages. The first part of each chapter will contain spring-blooming wildflowers and progress through the season with fall-blooming wildflowers towards the end. There will sometimes be variations in color, so refer to the start of each chapter for suggestions on where else to look.

White Flowers Page

Yellow Flowers Page

Red & Orange Flowers Page

Pink Flowers Page

Blue & Purple Flowers Page

Green Flowers Page

Brown Flowers Page

Introduction

Arkansas is very diverse, with a part of the state having hills so great in relief that they actually qualify as mountains, to the lowland cypress swamps on the eastern side of the state that are reminiscent of traveling through Louisiana bayou country. And, in between, there occurs a variety of landscapes that support beautiful, clear-flowing streams, majestic cliffs, Ozark springs, extensive forests and woodlands, desert-like glades, and patches of tallgrass prairies. Although much of Arkansas has undergone vast metropolitan and agricultural expansion, there are still a variety of public and private lands where one can observe and enjoy a vast array of plant life. One example is the Arkansas Natural Heritage Commission, which protects and manages 66 natural areas. These special areas serve as living museums that provide habitat for plants and animals that were once more common during presettlement times. (Visit the following website to find a natural area near you: http://naturalheritage.com.) Other places that offer great opportunities to observe and photograph wildflowers in Arkansas are: state and national parks, nature preserves owned and managed by The Nature Conservancy, national forest lands, and Arkansas Game and Fish Commission areas. If you would like to learn more about Arkansas' native plants, there is an organization, the Arkansas Native Plant Society (http://www.anps.org), that promotes the preservation, conservation, and study of the wild plants and vegetation of the state. They hold two general meetings per year, conduct numerous field trips, and produce an informative quarterly newsletter.

HOW TO USE THIS GUIDE

Within the large and varied landscape of Arkansas, there is a great diversity of plant life. According to Edwin B. Smith (1994), at least 2,518 species are known to occur in the state. Within this diversity of plants, there is a lesser number that are considered wildflowers, a term that lacks a precise definition but it is generally understood, however, that certain plants have flowers that are attractive because of their color, shape, and/or size. Maybe half of the plants encountered in Arkansas easily fit this description, but not all are often encountered, plus some are so closely related that one representative example is often sufficient for the average wildflower enthusiast. There are books listed in the back of this guide that can be used to gain a more technical and detailed understanding of the flora of the state.

Photographs and descriptions of 400 species of wildflowers are included in this book. These include wildflowers that are more commonly encountered in Arkansas as well as a few uncommon species that are particularly showy and indicative of certain habitats that may be declining. Closely related species are described in the Remarks section; this adds another 131 species to this guide. Exotic or weedy plants, those brought in and established from other countries, are also included. Although their flowers are sometimes showy, it is important to distinguish them from the native flora so one can gain a better understanding and appreciation of native plants and the habitats in which they are found.

For ease and speed in identifying plants, wildflowers with similar color are grouped together. This is not a perfect method, however, since some wildflowers vary in color shades, especially where lighter pinks and blues sometimes grade into white. When a plant has flowers with two colors, the most noticeable color is the one determining its placement in this book. Within each color group, plants are arranged by their flowering sequence so that spring-flowering plants are first and fall-flowering ones are last. Flowers will not always bloom in the exact same sequence as presented in this book. There will be some variation depending on the climate fluctuations from year to year and in what part of the state the plant is growing. For example, compared to an individual of the same species of wildflower growing in northern Arkansas, a spring-flowering plant will bloom earlier and a fall-flowering plant will bloom later in southern Arkansas, due to the longer growing season.

Each photograph is accompanied with text, beginning with the plant's **common name**. Often, a wildflower has several different common names, so an attempt was made to select the name most widely used in Arkansas. Because of the general confusion surrounding multiple common names, the **scientific name** is also presented. These names, rendered in Latin or Greek, are more reliable and universally accepted. The scientific name consists of two words. The first word, the **genus**, is the name of a group of plants with similar general characteristics-such as the goldenrods, which are in the genus *Solidago*. The second part of the scientific name is the **specific epithet** or **species**, which identifies the particular species of a plant. The name may honor a person who may have first discovered the plant, it could refer to a geographic location, or it could describe some characteristic of the plant. The plant's scientific name is correctly written in *italics* with the first letter of the genus name capitalized and the first letter of the species name in lower case, for example: *Solidago rigida*.

In a few instances, a plant has a scientific name with a third part, preceded by **var**. the abbreviation for the word **variety**. This is added when a set of plants differs slightly but consistently from other plants of the same species; these often have distinct ranges. An example would be: *Baptisia bracteata* var. *leucophaea*. Less frequently, the term **subspecies**, abbreviated **ssp**., is used. It is similar to a variety, but used to denote a discreet portion of the range of a species. The scientific and common names used in this book are for the most part from the Arkansas Vascular Flora Committee's, 2006, *Checklist of the Vascular Plants of Arkansas*.

Next, the **family** name is listed. For example, the evening primrose family has the scientific name of Onagraceae. (Family names now always end with the suffix –aceae.) Families are grouped according to similarities in their structure and biology. As one becomes more familiar with plants, this grouping by family characteristics becomes more obvious.

Each plant has a brief **Description** section that provides information on size and shape of the plant and important characteristics of leaves, flower, and sometimes fruit. It is not intended to describe a plant completely but to provide those features that readily distinguish it from other plants without getting very detailed. Sometimes identification, especially when examining flower parts and hairs, can be aided by the use of a magnifying glass or hand lens, preferably with a magnification of 10 times.

As mentioned earlier, flowering periods are approximate and may vary slightly according to seasonal climatic conditions and at what latitude or elevation in Arkansas the plant is observed.

The **Habitat/Range** section provides information on where the plant occurs. A plant is considered a native to Arkansas unless otherwise noted. Many of the plants selected for this book have a wide range of distribution. There are a few, however, that are found only in a particular part of the state, especially those that may be on the edge of their range and are found more commonly elsewhere.

Finally, the **Remarks** section provides an opportunity to describe closely related species and mention alternative common and scientific names the plant may have once been known by. Also, to increase interest and appreciation of plants, historical information on how plants have been eaten or used as medicine is presented. This information is based on written reports and should not be read as promotions for nutrition or as medical or herbal prescriptions for self-healing. Those interested in historical or modern herbalism, homeopathy, or flower essences should check the reference section in the back of the book.

The theme throughout this book is to reduce or eliminate technical terms. Whenever possible, more user-friendly terms are substituted. For example, instead of describing a leaf as "obovate," the term "broadest above the middle" is used.

ARKANSAS NATURAL REGIONS

Overall, Arkansas is divided into two broad categories: uplands and lowlands. These two landforms are easily distinguished by drawing a line from the northeast part of the state to the southwest part and that area above the line would be the uplands while the lowlands occur below the line. This is a simple, generalized demarcation that few other states can exhibit. The state is further divided into natural regions, which are described below:

Ozark Mountain Region: Or simply the Ozarks is an uplifted plateau where rivers and streams have cut deep valleys into the landscape. Some of the wildest looking views in the Central States can be found here. Dense forests of oak and hickory with scattered pine provide habitat for a wide variety of wildlife and plants. The bedrock is primarily composed of sandstone interspersed with shale along with some outcrops of dolomite (a type of limestone) in the northern part.

Ouachita Mountain Region: Or the Ouachitas is composed of a series of east/west trending mountains that were squeezed, uplifted, and folded over on themselves like an accordion millions of years ago. Some of the most far reaching views between the Rocky Mountains and the Appalachian Mountains can be found here. The south-facing slopes of the mountains are dominated by pine while the north sides contain oak and hickory. The bedrock is primarily sandstone, shale, and novaculite (a type of chert). For the purposes of this book, the Ouachita Region also includes the Arkansas River Valley.

Gulf Coastal Plain Region: A large area that was once underwater and part of the Gulf of Mexico. Today, the landscape varies from level ground to low, rolling hills interspersed with bottomland containing swamps and marshes. The trees range from pine, oak, and hickory on the uplands to bald cypress in the lowlands. Along with forests and wetlands, prairies occupy the drier sites.

Delta Region: Also known as the Mississippi Alluvial Plain, this is a relatively level landscape with rich bottomland soil that was deposited during the massive melt water floods from numerous ice age periods. Massive bottomland forests and swamps dominated the landscape and, on slightly higher ground, a section known as the Grand Prairie, hosted many species of prairie plants and animals. Also in this region, a north-south ridge known as Crowley's Ridge stands record to the scouring effects of the ancient Mississippi River as it eroded away a once higher landscape. Crowley's Ridge is a unique landform and contains several plants that are found more commonly eastward but are now isolated on this ridge.

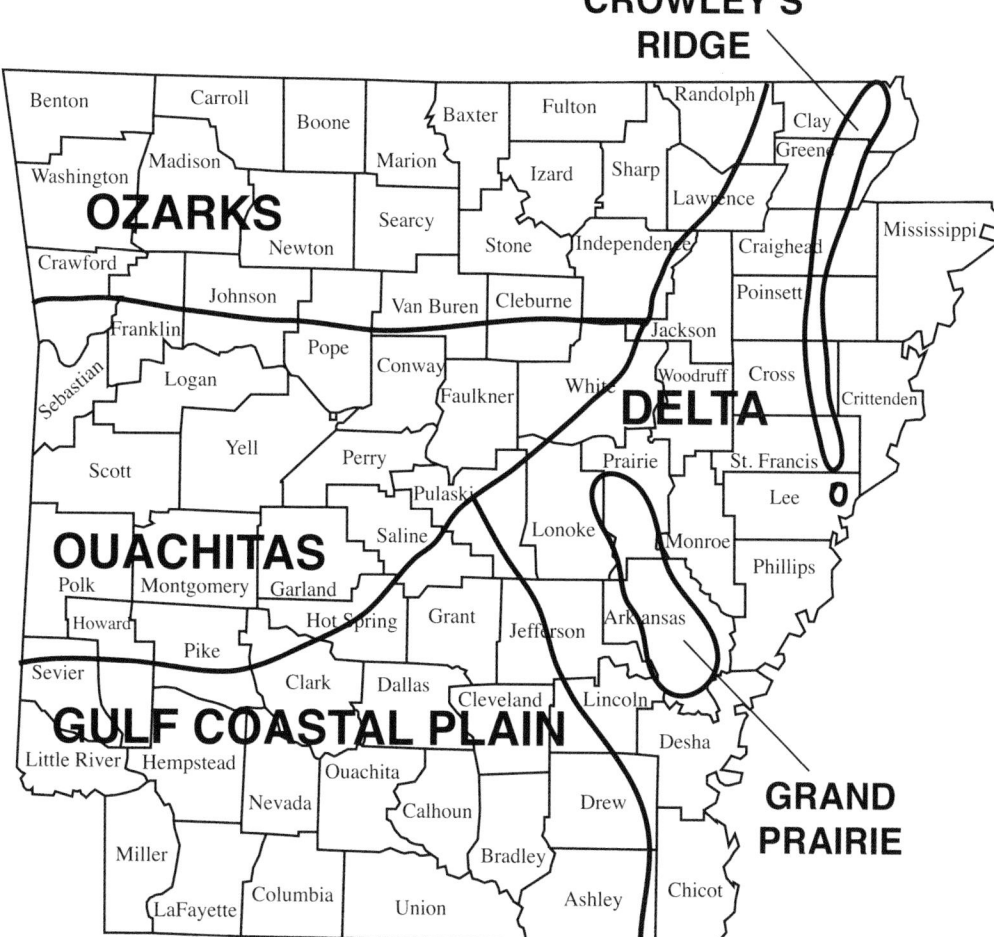

White Flowers

This section includes flowers that are mostly white.
Off-white flowers can grade into light colors of
yellow, green, pink, and blue,
so those sections should also be checked.

Northern Spiderlily, page 55

SMALL-FRUITED WHITLOW GRASS
Draba brachycarpa
Mustard Family (Brassicaceae)

HARBINGER OF SPRING
Erigenia bulbosa
Carrot Family (Apiaceae)

Description: A small, delicate plant with flowering stems to 6" tall. The fernlike leaves are divided into numerous small lobes and may not appear until after flowering has started. The flowers are in clusters at the end of stalks with white petals and dark reddish anthers giving it another common name, Pepper and Salt.

February—April

Habitat/Range: Moist woods on slopes, in ravines and on terraces along streams; occasional; found primarily in Ozark Region counties.

Remarks: True to its name, this is one of the first native wildflowers to bloom in spring. It may often be overlooked because of its small stature and partial concealment by fallen leaves.

Description: A winter annual, its seeds germinate in the fall and its leaves overwinter. The hairy flower stalk appears in early spring with leaves clustered at the base and a few along the stem. Leaves are hairy and up to ½" long. Flowers white, with 4-notched petals, each about ¼" long.

February—April

Habitat/Range: Found along ledges of bluffs and glades, woods, lawns, fields, and in sparse areas with little competition; found throughout the state.

Remarks: The name *whitlow* derives from the ancient belief that some species could cure "whitlows," which are sores that develop around nails, or in the hooves of horses. The common name erroneously implies that this plant is a grass. Another species, Whitlow Grass, *Draba cuneifolia*, has hairy leaves, up to 1" long, clustered at the base of a bare stalk; found on ledges of bluffs, glades, and rocky open woods, primarily in the Ozark Region.

WHITE DOGTOOTH VIOLET
Erythronium albidum
Lily Family (Liliaceae)

Description: A single-flowering plant with a stalk up to 6" tall. Flowering plants have a pair of flat to slightly folded leaves emerging from the base, while the more numerous nonflowering plants produce only single leaves. The leaves, up to 6" long, are mottled with brown and resemble the pattern on a trout, hence the other common name, Trout Lily. The 3 sepals and 3 petals are similar and curve backwards as the flower ages. The flowers are about 1" wide, with large yellow stamens.

February—April

Habitat/Range: Lower wooded slopes and valleys where soils are moist, usually in colonies; found primarily in the Ozark Region.

Remarks: Dogtooth Violet is named for the shape of its underground corm (a swollen area at the base of the stem). Large colonies often can be found with few plants in flower. The deeply buried corm has the ability to send out side shoots to produce new plants, each with a single leaf. Native American Indians used root tea for fevers, and a warm mass of leaves was applied to the skin for hard-to-heal ulcers. A similar species, Prairie Dogtooth Violet, *Erythronium mesochoreum*, has strongly folded leaves lacking mottling and spreading flowers that do not bend back; found mostly in prairies; rare.

SPRING BEAUTY
Claytonia virginica
Purslane Family (Portulacaceae)

Description: Plants arise from bulbs with flower stalks to 6" tall. One pair of opposite, grasslike leaves occur about halfway up the stem. A single, strap-like leaf up to 7" long is produced at the base. Not all plants flower in a year, but their single leaf identifies their presence. Flowers, usually less than ½" across, vary from white to pink, with distinctive darker pink veins running the length of the 5 petals. There is a pair of green sepals below the petals. The 5 anthers are typically pink.

February—May

Habitat/Range: Moist woods and lawns; common throughout the state.

Remarks: Both Native American Indians and early settlers dug the small, round tuberous roots and ate them raw or boiled as a potato substitute. Their bland flavor has often been likened to that of chestnuts. The succulent leaves were used in salads. Deer are known to browse on the leaves when they first appear, and wild turkeys and rodents eat the tubers.

FALSE RUE ANEMONE
Enemion biternatum
Buttercup Family (Ranunculaceae)

Description: A delicate plant with branched, smooth stems to 10" tall. The leaves are compound, divided into 3 leaflets with each leaflet with 3 lobes. The leaves at the base are on stalks, the upper leaves nearly stalkless. The flowers have 5 petal-like sepals about ½" across with numerous stamens; there are no petals. The sepals are always white.

March–May

Habitat/Range: Moist woods on lower slopes and valley floors; found in the Ozark Region and a few southern counties.

Remarks: The white flowers of false rue anemone are among the earliest of spring. Petal-like buds give the plant an unusual beauty even before the flowers open. Formerly known as *Isopyrum biternatum*, it is similar to Rue Anemone, *Thalictrum thalictroides*, but the latter occurs on drier sites in woods, grows more solitarily, has a whorl of 6 leaflets below the flowers, has 5–9 petal-like sepals, and varies in color from white to pink to lavender.

RUE ANEMONE
Thalictrum thalictroides
Buttercup Family (Ranunculaceae)

Description: A plant with upright, smooth, unbranched stems up to 8" tall. The leaves at the base are compound, divided into 3 divisions, with each division divided into 3 leaflets; a whorl of 6 leaflets occurs just below the flower stalks. Each leaflet is smooth, 3-lobed, and up to ¾" across. There are usually 1–4 flowers, each about 1" across, occurring at the end of a stalk; each flower has 5–9 petal-like sepals and numerous stamens; there are no petals. The sepals vary in color from white to pink to lavender.

March–May

Habitat/Range: Dry to moist open woods; found primarily in the Ozark and Ouachita regions.

Remarks: Formerly known as *Anemonella thalictroides*, Rue Anemone is sometimes confused with False Rue Anemone, *Enemion biternatum*, but the latter occurs in moister sites in valleys, grows in colonies, and has leaflets more numerous on the stem with their lobes more deeply cut.

CAROLINA ANEMONE
Anemone caroliniana
Buttercup Family (Ranunculaceae)

Description: Plants arising from rhizomes, each with a single flower and up to 16" tall. There are usually 3 basal leaves on long stalks and 2 to 3 stalkless leaves along the stem. The lower part of the stem lacks hairs. All the leaves have 3 deep lobes and appear as narrow segments. Flowers are 1½" across with a central cone-like structure and numerous white (rarely violet or purple) sepals, there are no petals.

March—April

Habitat/Range: Prairies, glades, open areas; scattered across the state, scarce in the Delta Region.

Remarks: A similar species, Southern Anemone, *Anemone berlandieri*, differs by plants solitary from a tuber, not a rhizome, and hairs along the entire stalks. Occurs in prairies, sandy areas, and open ground; Gulf Coastal Plain and in a few Ozark counties

COMMON CHICKWEED
Stellaria media
Pink Family (Caryophyllaceae)

Description: A highly variable annual plant with weak stems up to 18" in length. The leaves are opposite along the stem, smooth, variable in shape but generally rounded from ½–1½" long. The small flowers are divided into 5 white petals with deep lobes giving the appearance of 10 petals. The petals are shorter than the 5 green sepals below them.

March—December

Habitat/Range: Disturbed sites, especially fields, lawns, and gardens; native to Europe; common throughout the state.

Remarks: The plants are usually compact at first but later grow loose branches in dense masses. Young shoots have been used as edible greens, either eaten raw in salads or cooked, although there is little taste.

TOOTHWORT
Cardamine concatenata
Mustard Family (Brassicaceae)

Description: A plant with an unbranched, smooth, upright stem up to 10" tall. The leaves appear in whorls of 3 about midway up the stem, each leaf with 3–5 deeply cut segments with teeth along the margins; young leaves are often tinged with purple. Another set of leaves develops at the base of the plant after flowering. Nonflowering plants produce a single leaf. The 4-petaled flowers are up to ¾" long and are sometimes tinged with pink as they get older. The flowers are often nodding and only partially open on cloudy days.

February—May

Habitat/Range: Moist woods; found primarily in the Ozark and Ouachita regions; also Crowley's Ridge.

Remarks: Formerly known as *Dentaria laciniata*. The common name may come from the toothlike shape of the fleshy root; it was also used as a folk remedy for toothaches. Pioneers gathered the little tuberous roots in early spring and used them throughout the year for seasoning soups, stews, meats, and other dishes. Eaten raw, the little tubers have the flavor of a radish or mild horseradish.

SPRING CRESS
Cardamine bulbosa
Mustard Family (Brassicaceae)

Description: A smooth, sparingly branched plant to 18" tall. Leaves at the base are round, to 1½" long, sometimes toothed, and on long stalks; stem leaves are scattered, mostly without stalks, longer than broad, and toothed. Flowers are small and 4-petaled; appearing in clusters at the end of a stalk.

March—June

Habitat/Range: Low wet woods, margins of spring branches and streams and along roadsides; occasional to common throughout Arkansas.

Remarks: Also known as *Cardamine rhomboidea*. Pioneers used the young shoots and leaves of Spring Cress to give a peppery-pungent taste to salads and as cooked greens. The base of the stem and the roots were used as a mild horseradish.

BLOODROOT
Sanguinaria canadensis
Poppy Family (Papaveraceae)

Description: This showy, low-growing plant produces a single flower that normally blooms for only a day. A single, light green leaf, paler underneath, emerges from the ground wrapped around the flower stalk. The leaf may open with the flower or shortly after to a width of 3" with 3–9 lobes. The fragrant flower opens to 1½" wide and usually has 8 petals, 4 of which are slightly longer; 24 yellow stamens surround the single pistil.

March—April

Habitat/Range: Lower slopes of moist woods and in moist wooded valleys; common in the Ozark and Ouachita regions.

Remarks: The large, fleshy root emits a red sap, as does the rest of the plant. Native American Indians used Bloodroot as a dye for fabrics, tools, and war paint. The red sap was mixed with oak bark, which is a source of tannin, to set the color, making it more permanent. The plant was used by Native American Indians and settlers to treat hemorrhages, fevers, rheumatism, poor digestion, colds, and coughs. Today, Bloodroot is used commercially as a plaque-inhibiting agent in toothpaste and mouthwashes.

SMOOTH ROCKCRESS
Arabis laevigata
Mustard Family (Brassicaceae)

Description: A single, leafy stem, up to 3' tall, arises from a cluster of leaves at the base. The smooth leaves clasp the stem by their eared bases and are somewhat toothed along the margins. The small white or yellowish-white flowers have 4 petals, each about ¼" long. The fruit forms pods, up to 4" long, which spread outward and downward.

March—June

Habitat/Range: Moist woods, slopes and rocky areas; found primarily in the Ozark and Ouachita regions.

Remarks: The overwintering leaves at the base of the plant are often purplish. A similar species, Sicklepod, *Arabis canadensis*, has hairy leaves along the stem, which lack the eared flaps at the base. Sicklepod occurs in moist woods and with a similar range as Smooth Rockcress.

DUTCHMAN'S BREECHES
Dicentra cucullaria
Fumitory Family (Fumariaceae)

Description: A perennial with smooth, slender, often leaning stems to 10" long. The gray-green fernlike leaves are finely dissected and emerge from the base on long stalks. Single leaves appear on flowerless plants. The 4–10 flowers appear on leafless stalks and hang in a one-sided cluster. The V-shaped or "breeches-shaped" petals are up to ¾" long and sometimes tinged with pink.

March—May

Habitat/Range: Moist woods near the bases of slopes and in wooded valleys; common in the Ozark Region.

Remarks: The Iroquois used Dutchman's Breeches in an ointment to make athlete's legs more limber. Settlers used a tea from the scaly bulb as a diuretic to treat urinary problems and to promote sweating. It is poisonous and can cause skin rashes. The plant, especially the bulb, contains an alkaloid toxic to cattle.

PALMER'S SAXIFRAGE
Saxifraga palmeri
Saxifrage Family (Saxifragaceae)

Description: A shallow-rooted plant to 12" tall. The bare, unbranched, flowering stem is hairy and arises from a basal rosette of oval leaves that are entire or slightly toothed. The small white flowers, each about ¼" across, are in an open cluster at the top.

March—May

Habitat/Range: Moist wooded rocky areas, along protected bluffs and streamsides; occurs in the Ozark Region while less frequent in the Ouachita Region.

Remarks: A similar species of Saxifrage, *Saxifraga texana*, is sparsely hairy, up to 10" tall, with a relatively tight flower cluster at the top. Found on sandstone glades, moist wooded ledges, and bluffs. Occurs in scattered counties in the central and northwest part of the state; also Drew and Bradley counties.

OZARK WAKE ROBIN
Trillium pusillum var. *ozarkanum*
Lily Family (Liliaceae)

Description: A showy spring wildflower with white flowers that turns pink to purple with age. The single stems rise up to 12" tall and spread a whorl of 3 narrow leaves each about 3" long and about 1" wide. A single white flower is attached to a 1" stalk. Each flower has 3 green sepals, up to 1½" long and 3 white petals usually about 1" long, with crinkled margins.

March—May

Habitat/Range: Moist woods on gentle slopes and in valleys; occurs in a few northwestern counties; also Montgomery, Polk, and Pulaski counties.

Remarks: Also known as Ozark Trillium. Another species, White Trillium, *Trillium flexipes*, is up to 2' tall, with 3 broad leaves that are up to 5" across and as about as long. A single nodding white flower, about 3" across is attached to an arched stalk up to 4" long. Found in moist woods on lower slopes and ravines; very rare, only found in Stone County.

WILD STONECROP
Sedum ternatum
Stonecrop Family (Crassulaceae)

Description: A low spreading succulent with creeping stems that forms a mat. The leaves are in whorls of 3 with each leaf about ⅜" across. Each plant produces several leafy, sterile shoots and one leafy flowering stem up to 7" tall. The flowers are clustered on top, each with 4 spreading, white petals, about ¼" long.

March—June

Habitat/Range: Moist wooded ravines; in a few scattered counties in the Ozark and Ouachita regions.

Remarks: Although relatively uncommon in Arkansas, Wild Stonecrop is the most widespread native *Sedum* species in eastern North America. The low growing plant makes an attractive ground cover and can be propagated from cuttings that will root when in contact with the ground.

MAYAPPLE
Podophyllum peltatum
Barberry Family (Berberidaceae)

Description: This distinctive plant has extensive underground rhizomes and can grow to a height of 2'. The large, umbrella-like, usually smooth, paired leaves are each up to 14" across and have 5–9 deeply cut lobes. Plants with single leaves are young and do not flower. At the base of the leaf stalks, a single slightly nodding flower is produced with 6 sepals and 6 petals, all cream colored. The flower is up to 2" across and has 12 yellow stamens. The large green fruit turns yellow when ripe and is up to 2" wide.

March—May

Habitat/Range: In low moist or dry open woods and in pastures at the edge of woods, usually in colonies; common; statewide.

Remarks: The Cherokee used a root tea for treating constipation, deafness, rheumatism, sores, and ulcers, and for expelling intestinal parasites. The Osage used an infusion as an antidote for poisons. Early settlers used the powdered rhizomes in an infusion to treat a wide range of common diseases. The active component, podophyllum, still is the most widely used treatment for venereal warts. Ripened fruits lose their toxicity and are edible, but the rest of the plant is considered a powerful intestinal irritant, acting as an emetic and purgative. If misused, it can be fatal.

FALSE GARLIC
Nothoscordum bivalve
Lily Family (Liliaceae)

Description: A slender plant that grows from a bulb, producing leafless stems to 12" tall. The smooth, grass-like leaves that emerge from the base are long and narrow. The 5–12 fragrant flowers, each less than 1" wide, are on stalks that arise from a common point on top of the stem. There are 3 petals and 3 sepals, all about the same size and white to slightly yellow in color.

March—May; also in fall

Habitat/Range: Dry woods, bluffs, prairies; statewide.

Remarks: False garlic is related to the onion, which it resembles, but there is no characteristic onion odor.

WILD CHERVIL
Chaerophyllum procumbens
Carrot Family (Apiaceae)

Description: A low-growing annual with stems weak, spreading, and branched, to 15" long. The base of the stem lacks hairs. The leaves are so deeply cut, they appear fernlike. Minute white flowers occur at the ends of stalks.

March—June

Habitat/Range: Moist woods, along streams, floodplains, along railroads, and highways; Ozark and Ouachita regions.

Remarks: Wild chervil sometimes forms a nearly solid mat of fernlike leaves, sharing the forest floor with more showy spring wildflowers. A similar species of Wild Chervil, *Chaerophyllum tainturieri*, differs by being taller, up to 26" tall, with stems hairy towards the base; occurs in similar habitat; statewide.

PALE VIOLET
Viola striata
Violet Family (Violaceae)

Description: Several flowers and leaves arise from the elongated stem up to 10" tall. The stems are smooth and angular. The leaves are round, heart-shaped at the base, smooth, with round teeth along the edges, and about 1½" across. The flowers emerge solitarily from the axils of the leaves on long stalks. The flowers are white or creamy white, about 1¼" long, with 5 petals, some with purple lines.

March—May

Habitat/Range: Moist woods; occasional in the Ozark and Ouachita regions.

Remarks: A similar violet, called White Violet, *Viola primulifolia*, has flowers and leaves arising from the base of the plant; leaves somewhat more elongated; found in moist areas; and occurring in the southern Ouachita Mountain and Gulf Coastal Plain regions.

CORN SALAD
Valerianella radiata
Valerian Family (Valerianaceae)

Description: Although a native plant, this small, succulent annual often occurs in disturbed soil and is somewhat weedy. The much-branched stem is angled, has sparse hairs, and grows to 15" tall. The leaves are opposite on the stem, stalkless, and slightly toothed on the lower margins. The white flowers are packed tight at the ends of the branched stalks, forming a flat top with the stamens extending just beyond the petals.

April—May

Habitat/Range: Low woods, wet fields, disturbed areas; statewide.

Remarks: The young tender leaves gathered before the flowers appear have been used in salads or prepared like spinach.

OZARK CORN SALAD
Valerianella ozarkana
Valerian Family (Valerianaceae)

Description: An annual plant around 10" tall that branches at the top with numerous small flowers. Leaves are narrow, opposite, and smooth. Flowers are lilac or rose-purple, each less than ½" long on slender tubes.

April—May

Habitat/Range: Rocky wooded slopes, glades, roadsides; mostly northern Ozark counties; also reported from Perry and Pulaski counties.

Remarks: A similar species, Long-flowered Corn Salad, *Valerianella longiflora*, is difficult to tell apart. The fruit of Ozark corn salad is broadest near the tip with three lines of hairs along the capsule while long-flowered corn salad has a more circular shape and lacks the three lines. Also found in similar habitat as Ozark corn salad; southwestern Ozark counties and most Ouachita counties.

PUSSYTOES
Antennaria parlinii
Aster Family (Asteraceae)

Description: A slender plant spreading by underground runners to form large colonies. The stems, which reach to 15" high, are covered with a dense mat of woolly hairs. The leaves at the base are somewhat oval, about ¾" or wider, with 3 prominent veins and woolly underneath. The leaves along the stem are much narrower and very hairy. The woolly flower heads are either male or female. The male flowers are in low, rounded heads with reddish yellow stamens. The female flowers are more elongated and sometimes have a pinkish color.

April–June

Habitat/Range: Open woods, pastures, fields; statewide.

Remarks: The woolly flower heads account for the plant's common name. Early folk medicine sometimes prescribed a tea of Pussytoes leaves taken every day for two weeks after childbirth to keep the mother from getting sick. An extract from the plant was once used to treat stomach disorders, and the flowers have been used to make cough syrup. Also known as Ladies' Tobacco.

ROBIN'S PLANTAIN
Erigeron pulchellus
Aster Family (Asteraceae)

Description: This plant often forms small colonies by sending out leafy runners at its base. The stems are unbranched, to 15" tall, hollow, with long, soft hairs. The leaves at the base of the stem are very hairy and spoon-shaped with shallow lobes; the leaves along the stem are scattered, smaller toward the top, and clasp the stem. The flower heads are loose and showy on long stalks and about 1" across. The flower heads have 50–75 threadlike white or lilac ray flowers surrounding a circle of densely packed, yellow disk flowers.

April–June

Habitat/Range: Open woods, clearings; occasional throughout the state.

Remarks: A similar species, Philadelphia Fleabane, *Erigeron philadelphicus*, differs by lacking leafy runners at the base of the plant and having 150–200 threadlike white ray flowers; fields, disturbed areas; common throughout the state.

THIMBLEWEED
Anemone virginiana
Buttercup Family (Ranunculaceae)

Description: A long-stalked plant up to 3' tall. The leaves are divided in 3, with deep lobes and large teeth along the margins. Both of the basal and stem leaves are on stalks. There are 1–3 flowers, about 1" across with 5 white to greenish white sepals; the petals are lacking. The fruits develop on a dense cylinder, less than twice as long as wide, in the center of the flower, which resembles a thimble, hence, the common name. The fluffy, white mass of seeds often remains on the stalk through winter.

April—July

Habitat/Range: Open, typically dry woods; common throughout the state.

Remarks: Also called Tall Anemone. Native American Indians boiled the roots to produce a liquid for treating tuberculosis, whooping cough, and diarrhea. Smoke from the seeds was blown into the nostrils to revive an unconscious person.

ONE-FLOWERED CANCER-ROOT
Orobanche uniflora
Broomrape Family (Orobanchaceae)

Description: Several branchless hairy stalks emerge from this plant to a height of 8". Brownish scales, which are actually rudimentary leaves, are found at the base of the stalks. The flowers, which are about 1" long, are solitary at the tip of the stems. The petals are united below into an elongated, curved tube with 4 yellow stamens found within. The flowers range from white to lavender.

April—June

Habitat/Range: Woods; found in a few scattered counties in the western half of the state.

Remarks: This plant lacks chlorophyll (the green pigment associated with photosynthesis), so it must rely on other plants for its food. It parasitizes the roots of oaks, asters, goldenrods, and others; the name, One-Flowered Cancer-Root, probably comes from its having been used as a folk remedy for cancer.

SWEET CICELY
Osmorhiza longistyllis
Carrot Family (Apiaceae)

Description: An upright, branching plant with white hairs along the stem and up to 3' tall. The large, hairy leaves, as much as a foot across on lower parts of the plant, are divided into three parts and then either further subdivided or deeply lobed to appear somewhat fernlike. The tiny white flowers are carried in loose, umbrella-shaped sprays. The 5 petals are curved at the tip. The 5 stamens may extend just beyond the petals, but the styles (female stalk) are longer than the petals.

April—June

Habitat/Range: Moist woods in valleys and along streams.

Remarks: The carrotlike root contains anise oil and has been used as a flavoring for cookies, cakes, and candies. The Illinois-Miami Indians used sweet cicely to treat eye ailments. The Ojibwa used a root extract for treating sore throats. Settlers used the root to relieve colic, gas, indigestion, and to improve the appetite. Another species of Sweet Cicely, *Osmorhiza claytonii*, differs by having the styles (female stalk in the flower) slightly shorter than the petals; a determination that is often difficult to make; reported from Hot Spring County.

WHORLED MILKWEED
Asclepias quadrifolia
Milkweed Family (Asclepiadaceae)

Description: A slender, single-stemmed plant with whorled leaves to 18" tall. The long-pointed, smooth leaves are usually in 1 or 2 whorls of 4, plus 1 or 2 pairs along the stem. The flowers are in 1–4 clusters at the end of the stem, often causing it to bend. The flowers are about ¼" across on slender stalks up to 1" long, causing them also to turn downward. The 5 petals are white to pink and turned back, displaying the 5 cuplike hoods characteristic of milkweeds. The seed pods are smooth, slender, and up to 5" long.

April—June

Habitat/Range: Dry or rocky open woods; occurs in the Ozark and Ouachita regions and northern Gulf Coastal Plain Region.

Remarks: This is the first milkweed to bloom in Arkansas. Like most milkweeds, the sap is milky.

LONG-LEAVED BLUETS
Hedyotis longifolia
Madder Family (Rubiaceae)

Description: Low slender plants with several stems arising from the base to a height of 8". Leaves at the base of the stem are narrow and long; leaves along the stem are opposite, narrow, and smooth, to 1" long. The flowers are white but sometimes tinged with pink, small, about ¼" across, and clustered at the tops of leaf axils. The 4 small petals are hairy on the inside and the stamens extend just beyond the petals.

April—July

Habitat/Range: Rocky open woods, glades; statewide except for the extreme southern counties.

Remarks: Long-Leaved Bluets was formerly known as *Houstonia longifolia*.

WILD STRAWBERRY
Fragaria virginiana
Rose Family (Rosaceae)

Description: This low ground-hugging plant spreads by runners, often forming large colonies. Along the runners, hairy stalks up to 6" long support leaves, each of which are divided into 3 leaflets with teeth along the margins. The flowers, about 1" across, are in small clusters, shorter than the leaves, and contain 5 white petals, 5 green sepals, alternating with 5 leaf-like bracts, and numerous stamens. The fruit ripens June—July, to an attractive scarlet color and grows to about ½" in length.

April—June

Habitat/Range: Woods, prairies, fields; common in the Ozark and Ouachita regions.

Remarks: Some say wild strawberries are sweeter than the typical garden-variety strawberries, which are hybrids between the wild strawberry and the Chilean strawberry. Wild strawberries were greatly appreciated by Native American Indians and later, early travelers and settlers.

STAR OF BETHLEHEM
Ornithogalum umbellatum
Lily Family (Liliaceae)

Description: These showy plants with their star-shaped flowers and grass-like leaves colonize disturbed sites. From underground bulbs the leaves emerge to a length of about 12". The margins of the leaves are curved inward with a white strip down the middle. The flowers are on stalks up to 12" tall, with each stalk bearing 3–7 flowers. The flowers are about 1" across and have 6 petals with a green stripe down the back of each petal.

April—May

Habitat/Range: Along roadsides, lawns, fields, open woods; native to Europe; found throughout the state.

Remarks: This exotic plant is very aggressive, producing bulbs at a rapid rate, and is very difficult to eradicate once established. The leaves and bulbs are poisonous, containing toxic alkaloids, and should be kept away from children and domestic animals.

fruit

DOLL'S EYES
Actaea pachypoda
Buttercup Family (Ranunculaceae)

Description: This stately plant is bushy in appearance and grows to about 2' tall. The large leaves are divided twice, ending in 3–5 leaflets that vary in shape. The leaflets, especially the end ones, may have 3 irregular lobes. The leaf margins are sharply toothed. The flowers appear in a tight rounded shape on the end of a stout stalk. The petals fall away early, leaving a mass of creamy white stamens, giving the flower its basic color. The fruits are a loose cluster of oval, shiny, white berries marked with a dark purple spot at one end, which accounts for the common name.

April—May

Habitat/Range: Moist woods; northwestern counties and Crowley's Ridge.

Remarks: Also called White Baneberry. Both Native American Indians and settlers made a tea of the root for relieving pain of childbirth. Settlers also used the plant to improve circulation and to cure headache or eyestrain. The plant is poisonous and all parts may cause severe gastrointestinal inflammation and skin blisters.

fruit

GOLDENSEAL
Hydrastis canadensis
Buttercup Family (Ranunculaceae)

Description: The attractive, coarsely textured leaves easily identify this woodland wildflower. Hairy, unbranched stems to 10" tall support a pair of broad, 5–9 lobed leaves. Younger plants do not flower and only produce a single leaf. The leaves, up to 6" across, are hairy and irregularly toothed along the margins. One leaf, about 9" across, is found at the base. A small single flower emerges at the top of the uppermost leaf. The flower, about ½" across, has 3 whitish sepals that fall away early; there are no petals. The numerous white stamens give the flower its color. The distinctive red fruit, resembling a red raspberry, persists for some time.

April—May

Habitat/Range: Moist woods; often forming large colonies; scattered across the Ozark Region and Crowley's Ridge.

Remarks: Goldenseal is declining throughout its range due to root diggers; the plant can be cultivated for commercial use. The perennial rhizome, with its distinctive yellow sap, was used by Native American Indians and settlers as a tonic, stimulant, and astringent. The plant has a wide use with herbalists today.

RATTLE WEED
Astragalus canadensis
Pea Family (Fabaceae)

Description: Sturdy plant to 5' tall, with compound leaves alternating along the stem. The leaves are divided into 11–31 leaflets that are narrowly oval, smooth along the edges, and each 1–1½" long and ⅜–½" wide. The creamy white, ½" long flowers are crowded along a stalk that emerges above the leaves. The pods are numerous, crowded, erect, up to ¾" long.

April—July

Habitat/Range: Rocky open woods; Ozark and Ouachita regions.

Remarks: Also known as Canada Milk Vetch. Young Omaha-Ponca boys used the stalks with persistent dry pods as rattles in games where they imitated the tribal dances. Milk vetches, in general, had a reputation for increasing a cow's or goat's milk yield.

FLY POISON
Amianthium muscaetoxicum
Lily Family (Liliaceae)

Description: A slender wand arises up to 3', with a cluster of white flowers that turn yellowish green with age. The leaves are mostly basal, up to 16" long, narrow, and somewhat pleated. The flowers are on stalks about ½" long, which are longer than the flowers.

April—May

Habitat/Range: Mesic upland forest on level ground or lower slopes of ravines or valleys; Ozark and Ouachita regions, also Hempstead County.

Remarks: The plant has been used to kill flies by crushing the bulb and mixing it with sugar to attract the flies. A similar looking species, Death Camas, *Zigadenus nuttallii*, differs by having a more rounded cluster of flowers, flower stalks shorter than the flowers, and 2 black glands at the base of each petal; dry, open areas; eastern and southern Ozark Region, also Little River, Logan, and Sevier counties.

FALSE SOLOMON'S SEAL
Maianthemum racemosum
Lily Family (Liliaceae)

Description: The slightly zigzag stem stiffly arches to a length of up to 3'. The firm spreading leaves alternate along the finely hairy stem. The leaves are 3–6" long, 3" wide, with smooth margins, and very short stalks. Tiny creamy white star-shaped flowers with 6 petals are borne in a branched cluster at the end of stems. Clusters are up to 4" long. The fruits are ruby red berries about ¼" across and often speckled with brown or purple.

April—June

Habitat/Range: Moist woods; nearly statewide except for the extreme eastern and southern counties.

Remarks: Formerly known as *Smilacena racemosa*. The Mesquakie tribe burned the root as a smudge to quiet a crying baby and to return someone to normal after temporary insanity. They also used the root with food during times of plague to prevent sickness. The plant was also used for its internal cleansing effect.

SOLOMON'S SEAL
Polygonatum biflorum
Lily Family (Liliaceae)

Description: A gracefully arching plant with alternate leaves; it may reach to 5' in length. The stems are smooth, unbranched, and stout, supporting several leaves each up to 7" long and 3" wide. The leaves have parallel veins and pale undersides. The greenish white flowers are about ¾" long and hang from slender stalks in clusters. The fruits are dark blue berries about ½" in diameter.

April—June

Habitat/Range: Moist woods; nearly statewide, less common in the Gulf Coastal Plain Region.

Remarks: Native American Indians used the rhizome of Solomon's Seal in a tea for treating internal pains. Externally, it was used as a wash for poison ivy, skin irritations, and hemorrhoids. Settlers used root tea for rheumatism, arthritis, and skin irritations. The young shoots, when boiled, are said to taste like asparagus, while the starchy rootstocks have served as a substitute for potatoes.

COLIC ROOT
Aletris farinosa
Lily Family (Liliaceae)

Description: A smooth, single-stemmed, wand-like plant, up to 2½' tall. The leaves are clustered at the base of the plant, with each strap-like leaf up to 8" long. The flowers are clustered at the top of a mostly bare stem. The white tubular flowers are about ¼" long, with 6 lobes and covered with a rough surface.

April—June

Habitat/Range: Open woods, pinelands; mainly in central and southeast counties.

Remarks: The root was used to make a bitter tonic to treat indigestion and colic, and to promote appetite; also for rheumatism, diarrhea, and jaundice.

SLENDER SANDWORT
Minuartia patula
Pink Family (Caryophyllaceae)

Description: A slender-stemmed winter annual that provides numerous spreading branches from the base to 12" tall. The leaves at the base form mats of cedar-like soft foliage with linear needlelike leaves that are opposite; the stem leaves are also soft, opposite, and very narrow. The white flowers are ¼" across with 5 notched petals, 5 sepals, and 10 stamens.

April—June

Habitat/Range: Occurs on thin, sandy, or light soils; primarily in the northwestern part of the state.

Remarks: Formerly known as *Arenaria patula*. As a winter annual, the seeds germinate in the fall and overwinter as threadlike minute leaves on the ground.

GARLIC MUSTARD
Alliaria petiolata
Mustard Family (Brassicaceae)

Description: A biennial plant, up to 3' tall with few branches. The leaves, when crushed, have the odor of garlic. Leaves are alternate on the stem, up to 2½" long, broadest at the base, narrow at the tip, and coarsely toothed along the margins. The flowers have four white petals, each up to ½" long. Fruit pods are narrow, 4-sided, up to 2½" long.

April—June

Habitat/Range: Moist woods and wood margins; native to Europe; scattered across the state.

Remarks: Garlic Mustard spreads rapidly with each plant producing thousands of minute seeds. Once established, this aggressive weed forms dense stands that smother spring wildflowers and lowers the diversity of woodlands. The first year's growth produces a single heart-shaped leaf that overwinters. Hand pulling is the easiest way to eradicate this exotic pest through successive visits.

FALSE TOADFLAX
Comandra umbellata
Sandalwood Family (Santalaceae)

Description: A creeping underground rhizome sends up yellow-green stems to a height of 12". The smooth stems produce alternate narrow leaves up to 1½" long that lack stalks. Flattened clusters of flowers emerge at the top. Each flower is about ¼" long with 5 sepals; petals are absent. The fruit is urn-shaped, green, maturing to a chestnut brown or purplish brown. The flowers and fruits persist for some time.

April—June

Habitat/Range: Dry or rocky open woodlands; occasional in northern counties and a few eastern counties.

Remarks: Formerly known as *Comandra richardsiana*. Like other species in the sandalwood family, False Toadflax is parasitic on other plants. However, it may be considered only partially parasitic since the plant has its own green leaves that photosynthesize and provide energy for growth. Like mistletoe, it may only need its host plant for water. Native American Indians ate the fruits, which are sweet, but consuming too many could produce nausea.

ARKANSAS BEARDTONGUE
Penstemon arkansanus
Snapdragon Family (Scrophulariaceae)

Description: Slender, clustered, mostly smooth, reddish-stemmed plants typically to 2' tall with opposite leaves. The leaves are thin, olive-green, hairy, and randomly toothed. The leaves partly clasp the stem at the base and taper to a point on the end. The flowers are in clusters at the end of the stalk. Each tubular flower is about 1" long and marked inside with fine purple lines. The front of the flower has a 2-lobed upper lip and a 3-lobed lower lip. At the mouth of the flower is a large sterile stamen with bright yellow hairs.

April—June

Habitat/Range: Dry or rocky woods, glades; found mostly in the Ozark and Ouachita regions.

Remarks: Another, Pale Beardtongue, *Penstemon pallidus,* differs by having solitary green stems, hairy, not clustered, with thicker, pale green leaves. Flowers are 1" long; occurs in the northern part of the Ozarks. Various members of the genus *Penstemon* have been used by Native American Indians in the form of root tea for treating chest pains, stomachaches, and to stop vomiting. Parts of the plant were used by the Navahos to treat, burns, toothache, snakebite, eagle bite, and backache.

HORSETAIL MILKWEED
Asclepias verticillata
Milkweed Family (Asclepiadaceae)

WHITE MILKWEED
Asclepias variegata
Milkweed Family (Asclepiadaceae)

Description: This attractive large-flowering milkweed has a stout purple stem up to 3' tall. The leaves, about 5" long, are opposite on the stem but some may be whorled. The leaf base tapers to a stalk, and the leaf margins are smooth but often wavy. The large vein running the length of the leaf is yellow and sometimes red. The flowers are in clusters of 1–4. The 5 white petals are turned back, revealing purple markings at their base. The 5 cuplike hoods in the center are characteristic of milkweeds. The sap is milky.

May—July

Habitat/Range: Dry or rocky woods; nearly statewide except absent from the far northwestern part of the state.

Remarks: Also called Variegated Milkweed. The bright white flowers with purple centers make this a particularly showy milkweed.

Description: Slender plants, sparingly branched, up to 2½' tall, with milky sap. The soft, threadlike leaves, up to 2" long, are mostly in whorls along the stem. The flowers are arranged in clusters of 2–14, with less than 20 flowers in each cluster. There are 5 greenish white petals and, in the center of the flower, 5 white hoods. The seedpods are smooth, narrow, and about 3" long.

May—September

Habitat/Range: Dry open woods, prairies, fields, pastures; found mostly in the Ozark and Ouachita regions.

Remarks: A tea from the whole plant was given to Lakota mothers unable to produce milk. The theory behind this practice is similar to the medieval concept of the doctrine of signatures, the belief that certain characteristics of a plant signify its uses. In this case, the milky sap was thought to signify that the milkweed would promote the production of milk. This milkweed is poisonous to cattle but is rarely taken in enough quantity to cause problems.

RAGGED ORCHID
Platanthera lacera
Orchid Family (Orchidaceae)

Description: A smooth, slender plant up to 2' tall with up to 40 white to greenish-white flowers. The leaves are 2 to 5, from 3 to 10" long, lance-shaped, longest near the base of the stem and reduced in size upward. The flowers are less than 1" long with a lip that has 3 lobes that are deeply divided into thread-like segments.

May—July

Habitat/Range: Prairies and open woods, usually in damp ground; western and central counties, also Drew County.

Remarks: As for other orchids in the genus *Platanthera*, sphinx moths are the main pollinators. This is the earliest to flower of the 7 species of *Platanthera* in Arkansas.

SPIKENARD
Aralia racemosa
Ginseng Family (Araliaceae)

Description: A bushy looking plant up to 5' tall and nearly as wide, with broad spreading leaves divided into large leaflets, each up to 6" long. Flowers are arranged in branched clusters. Each flower is about $\frac{1}{8}$" wide with 5 greenish-white petals and 5 protruding stamens. Fruit in clusters of dark purple berries, each about $\frac{1}{8}$" across

May—July

Habitat/Range: Moist woods and wooded ravines; scattered across Ozark Region and Crowley's Ridge counties.

Remarks: Spikenard can send rhizomes long distances, up to 50', to initiate new plants. Native American Indians used the spicy-aromatic roots to improve the flavor of other medicines. The unusual name, Spikenard, comes from the Latin *spica*, a spike and *nardus*, an aromatic root.

HORSE NETTLE
Solanum carolinense
Nightshade Family (Solanaceae)

Description: An upright, branched plant with spiny stems up to 3' tall. The leaves, up to 6" long, are alternate, pointed at the tips, and tapering at the base. The leaf margins are wavy with deep lobes and spines along the veins on the underside and along the leaf stalk. The flowers are few, loosely clustered at the end of stalks, and about ¾" across. The 5 petals are united at the base. There are 5 large, bright yellow stamens. The fruit, about ⅔" in diameter, is a smooth yellow berry, like a tiny tomato, which persists through the winter.

May—October

Habitat/Range: Open woods, waste ground, cultivated fields, and roadsides; in every county.

Remarks: Horse Nettle and other nightshades are closely related to tomatoes and eggplant. However, the attractive bright yellow berries are toxic, and fatalities have been reported in children. Native American Indians gargled wilted leaf tea for sore throats, applied wilted leaves to the skin for poison ivy rash, and drank tea for worms.

WHITE SWEET CLOVER
Melilotus officinalis
Pea Family (Fabaceae)

Description: This legume, depending on conditions, grows as an annual or biennial. The branching, smooth stems can be found up to 7' tall. The leaves are alternate, divided into 3 leaflets, with each leaflet about 1" long, oval, rounded at the tip, and finely toothed. The white flowers are fragrant and clustered on 4" stalks, and each is about ⅜" long.

May—November

Habitat/Range: Disturbed ground, especially along roadsides; can invade prairies and glades; native to Europe; likely spread to every county.

Remarks: Formerly known as *Melilotus alba*, the white and yellow forms have been combined under *Melilotus officinalis*. (See p. 101.) This weedy plant is highly drought resistant and has spread from its intended use as hay, pasture, and green manure. It is also a popular honey plant by beekeepers. The leaves have a sweet vanilla-like odor when crushed. The young leaves, before the flowers appear, can be added to salads or boiled for 5 minutes and used as cooked greens. The pea-like fruits can be used to flavor soups and stews. The dried leaves can be used as a vanilla-like flavoring for pastries.

WILD CARROT
Daucus carota
Carrot Family (Apiaceae)

Description: A biennial with a large taproot and stout, branching, hairy stems to 4' tall. Both basal and stem leaves are large and finely divided on long hairy stalks. Tiny white flowers are tightly grouped in clusters, which in turn form a larger umbrella-shaped cluster about 4" across. In the center, there is often 1 purple flower. As the flowers fade, the featherlike stalks curl into a tight bird nest shape supporting numerous oval, bristly, dried fruits that are up to ⅛" long.

May—October

Habitat/Range: Fields, waste ground, roadsides, and disturbed prairies; native to Europe; nearly statewide, less common in southeastern counties.

Remarks: Another name, Queen Anne's Lace, refers to Anne of Denmark, wife of James I, who loved fine clothes and lace. Wild carrot is the ancestor of the cultivated carrot. Its root is white, instead of orange, due to a lack of beta carotene. It does, however, contain provitamin A carotene and vitamins C and B complex. The first-year roots have been eaten raw or boiled as a vegetable, but care must be taken not to mistake the leaves for that of Poison Hemlock, which has smooth leaf stalks. (See p. 40). Root tea has been used as a diuretic, to prevent and eliminate urinary stones and intestinal worms.

FOG FRUIT
Phyla lanceolata
Vervain Family (Verbenaceae)

Description: These moist-soil-loving plants mostly creep along, rooting at the nodes (point of leaf attachment to the stem), up to 1½' long. The leaves are opposite, up to 2" long, broadest near the base or towards the pointed tip, and coarsely toothed along the margin. Several flowers, less than ¼" long, are clustered on small heads that emerge from the axils of leaves on long stalks. The 4 petals are more or less united into a pair of 2-lobed lips. The flowers are white, with some showing pink or purple.

May—September

Habitat/Range: Wet soil of ponds, ditches, low meadows; common; in almost every county.

Remarks: This plant is also known as Frog Fruit. The small seeds are a source of food for waterfowl.

MOTH MULLEIN
Verbascum blattaria
Snapdragon Family (Scrophulariaceae)

Description: A biennial plant with a slender form up to 5' tall. The stem is either single or branched, and is smooth on the lower part with round gland-tipped hairs above. The leaves at the base are large, tapering to the base, and toothed along the margins. The leaves along the stem are smaller, alternate, and somewhat clasping or simply lacking a stalk. The flowers, about 1" across, are loosely spaced along the branch. The 5 petals are either white or yellow with 5 stamens displaying woolly filaments that are violet to reddish brown.

May—September

Habitat/Range: Pastures, fields, roadsides and other disturbed sites; native to Europe; scattered throughout the state.

Remarks: Both white and yellow-flowering moth mulleins appear equally as common. Looking at the flower, with some imagination, one may see a moth, hence the common name; others say it is because the flowers attract moths.

HEDGE BINDWEED
Calystegia sepium
Morning Glory Family (Convolvulaceae)

Description: A twining vine that creeps along the ground or climbs with branching stems up to 9' long. The leaves, up to 4" long, are alternate along the stem and triangular with 2 squarish lobes at the base. The long-stalked flowers arise singly from leaf axils. The flowers are funnel-shaped, large (up to 2½" across), and white to pink in color.

May—September

Habitat/Range: Moist soil, fields, roadsides, disturbed ground; mostly in the northern half of the state.

Remarks: Formerly known as *Convolvulus sepium*. On sunny days the flowers close by midday. The pulpy roots have historically been used as a purgative–a medicine stronger than a laxative; also to treat jaundice and gall bladder ailments.

WILD POTATO VINE
Ipomoea pandurata
Morning Glory Family (Convolvulaceae)

Description: A trailing or climbing vine 10–15' long. The leaves are alternate, heart-shaped, smooth, and up to 6" long and nearly as wide. The leaf veins, margins, and leaf stalk are often purplish. There are 1–7 flowers on long stalks that emerge at the junction of the leaf and stem. The flowers are funnel-shaped, about 3" wide, with red or purple centers. The flowers close about midday.

May—September

Habitat/Range: Fields, low ground along streams, borders of lakes, roadsides, fencerows; statewide.

Remarks: The large root, which can weigh over twenty pounds, was used as a food source by Native American Indians. The root was heated and applied to the skin to treat rheumatism and "hard tumors." Root tea was used by settlers as a diuretic and a laxative, and for treating coughs, asthma, and the early stages of tuberculosis. Since the root is a strong laxative when eaten raw, it was often boiled like a potato to neutralize its effect before consuming. The taste is said to be somewhat bitter.

POISON HEMLOCK
Conium maculatum
Carrot Family (Apiaceae)

Description: A robust biennial with large, highly dissected leaves, reaching a height of up to 9'. The branching, furrowed stems are smooth with purple spots and hollow centers. The leaves are up to 14" long, highly dissected into numerous leaflets, and almost fernlike. The numerous flowers are produced in loose, flat-topped clusters 4–5" across.

May—August

Habitat/Range: Disturbed soil, low ground, pastures, fields, roadsides; native to Europe; mostly in the northwest part of the state.

Remarks: This is the infamous plant that was used to put Socrates to death in 399 B.C. All parts of the hemlock, especially the green, almost ripe seeds, are deadly poisonous and may also cause contact dermatitis.

GOAT'S BEARD
Aruncus dioicus
Rose Family (Rosaceae)

Description: A bushy plant with showy branching plumes that reaches a height of 6'. The single stalk is smooth with few but very large leaves to 20" long. The compound leaves are divided into 5–7 leaflets. The lower leaflets may be further divided. Each leaflet is pointed at the tip and finely toothed along the margin. The flowers are numerous, small, about $1/16$" across, and appear in plume-like clusters. The male and female flowers occur on separate plants. All flowers have 5 petals and 5 sepals, but the male flowers have 15 or more stamens, and the female flowers have 3 pistils and 15 or more incompletely developed stamens.

May–June

Habitat/Range: Moist woods, along lower wooded slopes, at the bases of bluffs; Ozark Region and Crowley's Ridge.

Remarks: Although the male and female flowers are on separate plants, they are easily distinguished by the showier stamens on the male plant. The foliage turns yellow in the fall. The somewhat scraggly appearance of the spikes of flowers account for the plant's common name. The Cherokee applied pounded root on bee stings. Root tea was used to diminish bleeding after childbirth and to reduce profuse urination. Tea was also used externally to bathe swollen feet.

SENECA SNAKEROOT
Polygala senega
Milkwort Family (Polygalaceae)

Description: Several stems emerge from one base, up to 20" tall. The leaves are alternate along the stem and up to 3½" long and less than 1" wide, the lower progressively smaller. The small, white flowers, about ⅛" wide, are clustered along the upper part of the stem.

May–July

Habitat/Range: Wooded slopes and valleys; occasional in the northwest quarter of the state.

Remarks: Seneca Snakeroot was used by North American Indians to treat snakebite, hence the common name. A root tea was used for respiratory ailments.

NEW JERSEY TEA
Ceanothus americanus
Buckthorn Family (Rhamnaceae)

Description: A small shrub, up to 3' tall, with spreading branches. The stem is woody with greenish-brown bark that becomes brown and flaky on older stems. The upper branches are mostly herbaceous, often dying back in winter. The leaves are alternate, up to 4" long and 2½" wide. The leaf margin is toothed, the upper leaf surface is hairy, and the lower leaf surface is gray and velvety hairy. The leaf stalks are about ½" long. The flowers are on branched clusters arising on long stalks from the base of leaves. The 5 white petals are hooded, usually notched, each resembling a miniature ladle. There are 5 white stamens.

May—June

Habitat/Range: Woodlands, moist to dry prairies; statewide.

Remarks: The leaves were used by Native American Indians to make a tea. Tribes along the Atlantic Coast probably taught the colonists the use of New Jersey tea, which was used as a patriotic substitute for black tea during the American Revolution after tea was dumped in Boston Harbor. Native Americans also used a root tea for treating colds, fevers, snakebites, stomach disorders, diarrhea, lung ailments, constipation, and as a blood tonic.

BLACK SNAKEROOT
Actaea racemosa
Buttercup Family (Ranunculaceae)

Description: A stately plant with a skirt of finely cut, fanlike leaves and a tall-flowered stem to 7'. The leaves are divided 2 to 3 times to produce numerous small leaflets that are shallowly lobed and coarsely toothed along the margins. At the top of the wand-like stem, 1 to 3 branches produce a cylindrical spray of showy white flowers. The flowers actually lack petals; it is the numerous stamens that account for the color.

May—July

Habitat/Range: Moist woods on lower slopes, bases of bluffs, and ravines; found in the Ozark Region.

Remarks: Formerly known as *Cimicifuga racemosa*. Black snakeroot, also called Black Cohosh, was an important medicinal herb to Native Americans. The Cherokee, for example, used the roots for treating menstrual cramps, difficult deliveries, rheumatism, tumors, backache, respiratory disorders, constipation, fatigue, hives, and insomnia. This herb was also of much value to settlers who also used it for snakebite, bronchitis, and dropsy.

WILD QUININE
Parthenium integrifolium var. *integrifolium*
Aster Family (Asteraceae)

Description: The sometimes branched stems are smooth in the lower portion and rough with a few hairs in the upper portion and up to 3' tall. The leaves at the base of the stem are up to 8" long and 4" wide and taper into long stalks; the stem leaves are alternate, smaller, lacking stalks, hairy, and toothed along the margin. The flowers are numerous in flat-topped or slightly rounded clusters. Each individual flower head is ⅓" wide, with 5 tiny petal-like ray flowers with stamens that surround a thick head of sterile disk flowers.

May—August

Habitat/Range: Dry woodlands, prairies, glades; common throughout the state except for the Delta Region.

Remarks: This plant is also known as American Feverfew. The flowering tops of wild quinine were once used for intermittent fevers like malaria. This plant served as a substitute when the tropical supply of quinine from the bark of the cinchona tree was cut off during World War I. The roots were used as a diuretic for kidney and bladder ailments. One study suggests that wild quinine may stimulate the immune system. The plant may cause dermatitis or allergies in some people. Another variety, *Parthenium integrifolium* var. *hispidum*, has shorter stems with noticeable spreading rough hairs, and long hairs on the lower surfaces of the leaves. Occurs on dry open woods, prairies; scattered across the state.

MARBLESEED
Onosmodium molle
Borage Family (Boraginaceae)

Description: A hairy-stemmed perennial from 1 to 4' tall, with numerous leaves along the stem. The leaves are alternate, hairy, narrow, and 1 to 3" long. The flowers are densely coiled at the ends of the upper branches. The tube-like flowers are dull white to greenish white, with 5 lobes and about ½" long.

May—July

Habitat/Range: Rocky woods, rocky prairies, glades, old fields, roadsides; primarily Ozark Region, central Ouachitas, western Gulf Coastal Plains Region.

Remarks: Marbleseed is named for the hard, white nutlet or seed. Another common name, False Gromwell, the latter meaning gritty meal, refers to its resemblance to nutlets of the genus *Lithospermum*. There are 3 varieties of marbleseed in Arkansas.

WHITE AVENS
Geum canadense
Rose Family (Rosaceae)

Description: Often several slender stems emerge from the base to form spreading branches to 2½' tall. The leaves at the base are on long stalks with the leaf margins sometimes cut into 3–5 deep lobes. The stem leaves have 3 leaflets held by a very short stalk or are stalkless. The leaf margins are toothed and the tip pointed. The basal leaves are green all winter. The flowers are few, on velvety stalks. The 5 white petals are interspersed with 5 green sepals. Stamens are from 10 to many. The fruit has numerous hooked ends that attach to clothing and fur, which aids in the plant's dispersal.

May—August

Habitat/Range: Moist or rocky woods on hillsides, in valleys along streams, and in ravines; common throughout the state.

Remarks: The leaves are browsed by white-tailed deer, and wild turkeys eat the seeds in fall and winter.

INDIAN PHYSIC
Gillenia stipulata
Rose Family (Rosaceae)

Description: A leafy, branching plant with thin soft-hairy stems to 3' tall. The basal leaves are divided several times into small leaflets and appear fernlike. The leaves along the stem appear to be divided into 5 leaflets, but the bottom 2 are actually large, leaf-like stipules. The leaflets are broadest towards the base, sharply toothed, and up to 3" long. The flowers are on long stalks with 5 very narrow, spreading petals and about 20 stamens.

May—July

Habitat/Range: Dry woods; statewide.

Remarks: Formerly known as *Porteranthus stipulatus*. Another common name is American Ipecac. Both common names refer to Native American Indian use of this plant for internal cleansing, a widespread ceremonial custom. An "ipecac" is an emetic (an agent that causes vomiting), in this case derived from certain dried roots. The roots are potentially toxic. The foliage is attractive in fall, varying from yellow to red.

FOXGLOVE BEARDTONGUE
Penstemon digitalis
Snapdragon Family (Scrophulariaceae)

Description: A sturdy plant with unbranched stems to a height of 4' tall. The basal leaves are on long stalks and arranged in a rosette. The stem leaves are up to 4" long, opposite, without stalks, with their edges curved inward and toothed. The flowers are on spreading branched stalks at the top of the stem. The white tubular flowers are ¾–1¼" long with 2 upper lobes and 3 lower lobes. There are purple lines running down the white throat of the flower.

May—July

Habitat/Range: Woods, prairies, fields, roadsides; common throughout the state.

Remarks: The common name, Foxglove, and the species name digitalis refers to the similarity of the flower to *Digitalis purpurea*, the foxglove from England used to treat heart ailments.

WHITE WAND BEARDTONGUE
Penstemon tubiflorus
Snapdragon Family (Scrophulariaceae)

Description: A slim, upright plant with unbranched, smooth stems to a height of 30" tall. The basal leaves are about 4" long and about ½" wide, smooth, and tapering to a stalk. The stem leaves are about the same size and clasp the stem. The white flowers are tightly clustered around the stem in tiers. Each flower is ½–¾" long, with the face of the flower appearing flat. The surface of the flowers are covered with gland-tipped hairs.

May—June

Habitat/Range: Prairies, glades and in open woods; Ozark and Ouachita regions and Crowley's Ridge.

Remarks: This plant is also known as Tubed Beardtongue. There are 8 species of penstemons in Arkansas. Penstemon is commonly called Beardtongue because the sterile stamen in the throat of the flower has a tuft of small hairs.

OLD PLAINSMAN
Hymenopappus scabiosaeus
Aster Family (Asteraceae)

Descriptions: A biennial plant with stems up to 5' tall and freely branching near the top. The leaves are finely divided into segments giving them a feathery appearance. Flowers are numerous with globular-shaped flower heads about ¾" across containing several white disk flowers; ray flowers are absent.

May—July

Habitat/Range: Sandy areas, ledges, glades, open ground; northwestern Ozark Region, southwestern Ouachita Region and western Gulf Coastal Plain Region.

Remarks: A similar species, Woolly-White, *Hymenopappus artemisaefolius*, has large, white bracts below the slightly smaller flower heads, and pinkish disk flowers; Gulf Coastal Plain counties of Miller, Nevada, and Ouachita counties.

SPRING LADIES' TRESSES
Spiranthes vernalis
Orchid Family (Orchidaceae)

Description: A downy stem up to 30" tall with a single spiral of up to 50 flowers. The leaves are basal, from 4–5", up to 10" long and often withered at flowering time. The flowers are white, about ⅜" long, somewhat nodding, with a yellowish throat.

May—July

Habitat/Range: Upland prairies, open grassy woodlands, grassy roadsides; scattered statewide but rare in the Delta Region.

Remarks: This is the tallest of the 8 species of ladies' tresses known to occur in Arkansas and the first to bloom. Another spring flowering ladies' tresses, Shining Ladies' Tresses, *Spiranthes lucida*, has glossy, broad leaves, stems to 10" tall, and up to 20 nodding white flowers with bright yellow lips; occurs in seeps and moist ledges along streams; found in 4 north central Ozark Region counties.

MOCK BISHOP'S WEED
Ptilimnium nuttallii
Carrot Family (Apiaceae)

Description: An annual, often growing in dense stands with thin stems up to 2' tall. The leaves have forked, opposite, thread-like segments, up to 4" long. The flowers are tiny, white and tightly grouped in clusters, which in turn form a larger umbrella-shaped cluster about 3" across. There are thread-like bracts below the tiny clusters of ray flowers.

May—August

Habitat/Range: Found in both wet and dry open areas, roadsides, and prairies; statewide.

Remarks: Also known as Ozark Mock Bishop's Weed. A similar species, Atlantic Mock Bishop's Weed, *Ptilimnium capillaceum*, has thread-like leaflets in whorls of 3 along the leaf axis and the flower clusters forming a more spreading, open umbrella-shaped cluster; low, wet areas, swamps, bottomland forests, banks of streams; scattered counties statewide except absent in the Ozark Region.

WHITE PRAIRIE CLOVER
Dalea candida
Pea Family (Fabaceae)

Description: A finely leaved plant having a single or few stems arising from a common base, up to 2' tall. The leaves are smooth, divided into typically 7 narrow leaflets, each up to 1¼" long and less than ¼" wide. The flowers are crowded into cylindrical spikes 1–3" long at the tops of the stems. The small flowers, each about ¼" long, bloom first at the bottom and progress upwards along the column, forming a skirt of white petals.

May—August

Habitat/Range: Prairies, glades, open woodlands; found mostly in the northern two-thirds of the state.

Remarks: Formerly known as *Petalostemon candidum*. White Prairie Clover is sensitive to disturbance, especially grazing; its presence, in addition to other highly selective plants, is an indicator of high-quality habitat. Some Native American Indians used the leaves for tea. The Ponca chewed the root for its pleasant taste. The Pawnee used the tough, elastic stems to make brooms. They also drank root tea to keep away disease.

WHITE WILD INDIGO
Baptisia alba var. *macrophylla*
Pea Family (Fabaceae)

Description: A smooth, shrubby plant to 5' tall, although sometimes taller, often with a thin white coating on the stem and leaves. The branched stems have alternate leaves that are each divided into 3 leaflets, 1–3" long, that are round at the tip and tapering at the base. Stems emerge above the leaves with showy white flowers, each about 1" long, having the structure of other flowers typical of the pea family.

May—August

Habitat/Range: Prairies, glades, streamsides, fields, pastures, roadsides; occasional to common throughout the state.

Remarks: Formerly known as *Baptisia leucantha*. These deep-rooted plants can persist in converted pastures and fields long after native prairie has been destroyed. Plants in the genus *Baptisia* have been used medicinally by Native American Indians and settlers as a tea for internal cleansing and externally for treating skin wounds. White wild indigo has been known to poison cattle if eaten in large quantities.

WATER HEMLOCK
Cicuta maculata
Carrot Family (Apiaceae)

Description: A biennial plant up to 6' tall with several branches holding umbrella-shaped clusters of tiny white flowers. The stem is streaked or spotted with purple and is hollow toward the base. The leaves are alternate on the stem, up to 12" long, and divided into numerous, sharply toothed leaflets. The umbrella-shaped flower heads contain tiny 5-petaled, white flowers, each less than ⅛" wide.

May—September

Habitat/Range: Marshes, wet prairies, low ground along streams, wet ditches; common; statewide.

 Remarks: This plant is highly poisonous. Members of many Native American tribes used the roots to commit suicide. Children have been poisoned by using the hollow stems as peashooters. A walnut-sized piece of the root is enough to kill a cow.

DAISY FLEABANE
Erigeron strigosus
Aster Family (Asteraceae)

Description: An annual or rarely biennial plant with hairy stems to 2½' tall, with small daisy-like flowers. All leaves are narrow, less than 1" wide; the basal leaves are toothed and on stalks, while the stem leaves are alternate, without teeth, and stalkless. The flowers are in spreading clusters at the top of branched stems. The flower heads are about 1" across with over 40 white, threadlike, ray flowers surrounding a yellow center of densely packed disk flowers.

May—September

Habitat/Range: Open woods, dry prairies, fields, pastures, roadsides, disturbed areas; common throughout the state.

Remarks: A related species, Annual Fleabane, *Erigeron annuus*, has spreading, rigid hairs on the stem and wider, sharply toothed leaves; occurring in similar habitats in every county. Annual Fleabane was used by the Lakota to make a tea to treat children with sore mouths and adults who had difficulty urinating.

HAIRY ANGELICA
Angelica venenosa
Carrot Family (Apiaceae)

Description: This tall member of the parsley family is an unexpected find in the woods. The plants can grow to a height of 5' and has fine hairs on the upper portion of the purplish stem, giving it a gray cast. The leaves are on stalks, up to 8" long and are divided into smaller leaflets, with the margins finely toothed. The flower heads are few but they are filled with tiny, white, clustered flowers.

May—June

Habitat/Range: Dry, rocky woodlands, low moist woods along streams, and along roadsides; northern Ozark Region.

Remarks: Hairy Angelica is poisonous when eaten. The Iroquois applied a poultice (held against the skin) of the plant to sprained muscles and twisted joints.

YARROW
Achillea millefolium
Aster Family (Asteraceae)

Description: Strongly-scented, hairy plants up to 2' tall, with alternate fernlike leaves and flat-topped flower clusters. The lower leaves are up to 10" long on stalks, the upper leaves are smaller and without stalks. Numerous flower heads are arranged in a branching, flat-topped flower cluster. Each head is about ¼" across with 4–6 white ray flowers surrounding a central disk of up to 20 yellow disk flowers.

May—August

Habitat/Range: Fields, roadsides, pastures, disturbed sites; native to Eurasia as well as North America; common; in every county.

Remarks: Also called Common Milfoil, fossil records reveal yarrow pollen in Neanderthal burial caves. More recently, yarrow has been used in a wide variety of medicinal treatments by at least 58 Native American Indian tribes as a stimulant, laxative, painkiller, diuretic, wound healer, antiseptic, and tonic, to name a few.

OX-EYE DAISY
Leucanthemum vulgare
Aster Family (Asteraceae)

Description: Plants are often multi-stemmed to 2½' tall, displaying a bouquet-like arrangement of attractive daisies. The basal leaves are round to spoon-shaped, toothed, and on stalks; the stem leaves are narrow, deeply cut, and lack stalks. The flower heads are up to 2" across with about 30 white ray flowers surrounding a central disk of numerous bright yellow tubular disk flowers.

May—August

Habitat/Range: Prairies, fields, pastures, roadsides; native to Europe; most common in the Ozark and Ouachita regions.

Remarks: This flower was formerly known as *Chrysanthemum leucanthemum*. In the lore of ancient Greece, Ox-Eye Daisy was considered a sacred plant to the soldiers of Artemis (the hunter-goddess of the moon and women). The practice of picking the petals (ray flowers) one by one, to find if one is loved or not, dates back to medieval times. The plant has been used for treating gastritis, enteritis, diarrhea, and infections of the upper respiratory tract. It has also been used externally for skin disorders, wounds, and bruises. In Europe, the young leaves are used in salads and soups.

FLOWERING SPURGE
Euphorbia corollata
Spurge Family (Euphorbiaceae)

Description: A smooth, leafy plant, up to 3' tall, usually single stemmed, with milky sap and widely branching flower clusters. The narrow, smooth-edged leaves are alternate on the lower stem but opposite or whorled near the flower clusters. The flower heads are numerous, each about ⅓" across, with 5 chalky white false petals surrounding a cup of tiny yellow male flowers and a single female flower. The fruit is a 3-parted ball on a tiny stalk.

May—October

Habitat/Range: Open woods, prairies, fields, pastures, and roadsides; common; in every county.

Remarks: Native American Indians used a leaf or root tea to treat chronic constipation, rheumatism, and diabetes. The root was mashed and applied to the skin to treat snakebites. The flowers, fruits, and leaves are eaten by wild turkey and white-tailed deer. The seeds are eaten by bobwhite quail and mourning doves.

LEAFCUP
Polymnia canadensis
Aster Family (Asteraceae)

Description: A tall, very hairy, branching plant to 5' in height, with large, soft leaves that are aromatic when crushed. The leaves are opposite, 3–5 lobed, with small teeth scattered along the margin. The base of the leaf tapers onto the upper part of the leaf stalk. The flower heads are few, small, with 5 white ray flowers, usually 3-lobed, that surround the yellow disk flowers.

May—October

Habitat/Range: Moist woods on slopes; Ozark Region and a few counties in the Ouachita Region.

Remarks: A related species, Bear's Foot, *Smallanthus uvedalius*, formerly *Polymnia uvedalia*, has yellow ray flowers, leaf tissue that extends down the length of the leaf stalk, and leaves that are 3-lobed. Blooms from July to September; found in moist woods; statewide. *July—September*

CLEAVERS
Galium aparine
Madder Family

Description: A spreading, sprawling annual plant with a 4-sided stem. The leaves occur along the stem in whorls of 6–8, each about 2" long and very narrow. The stem and leaves have recurved hairs that cling ("cleave") to animal hair as well as the clothing of hikers, hence the name. The small white flowers have 4 petals and are attached on long stalks arising from leaf axils.

May—July

Habitat/Range: Moist woods, shaded disturbed areas; common throughout the state.

Remarks: The other common name, Bedstraw, refers to settlers' use of the aromatic plants as "hay" to fill bedding. There are 14 species in the genus *Galium* in Arkansas, all of which have in common the whorls of leaves along the stem and small, 4-petaled flowers.

PURPLE MEADOW RUE
Thalictrum dasycarpum
Buttercup Family (Ranunculaceae)

Description: A stout-stemmed plant to 6' tall, stem sometimes purplish, with leaves divided into numerous leaflets, each up to 2" long with 3 pointed lobes at the tip. The flowers are in branching clusters with male and female flowers on separate plants. There are no petals, and the sepals drop early. The male flowers have many showy threadlike stamens; the female flowers have a bur-like head of pistils.

May—June

Habitat/Range: Moist wooded ravines, stream banks; a few scattered counties across the northern part of the state.

Remarks: The Dakota broke off fruits when they were approaching maturity and stored them away for their pleasant odor, later rubbing and scattering them over their clothing. The hollow stems were used by small boys to make toy flutes. The Pawnees used this plant as a stimulant for horses, by mixing plant material with a certain white clay and applying it as a snuff on the muzzle of the horse. This was done when making forced marches of three or more days' duration in order to escape enemies. A related species, Waxy Meadow Rue, *Thalictrum revolutum*, occurs in similar habitats. The leaves have a bad odor when crushed and have gland-tipped hairs on their undersides. Another, Early Meadow Rue, *Thalictrum dioicum*, also occurring in similar habitats, has middle and upper leaves on stalks; leaflets with 3–12 lobes, and their margins with rounded teeth.

INDIAN HEMP
Apocynum cannabinum
Dogbane Family (Apocynaceae)

Description: The shrub-like plants are up to 4' tall with reddish stems, milky sap, and upright leaves with white to red veins. The leaves are opposite, stalked, widest at the middle, pointed at the tip, with smooth margins, and up to 6" long and 3" wide. The flower clusters are usually overtopped by the side branches. The flowers are small, less than ¼" wide, and bell-shaped with five tiny lobes. The seedpods are in pairs, slender, long-pointed at the tip, and up to 6" long, with seeds that have silky hairs attached at one end.

May—August

Habitat/Range: Open woods, prairies, fields pastures, and roadsides; common but less so in the southern counties.

Remarks: Indian hemp fibers have been found in fabric from the early Archaic period, from 3,000–5,000 years ago. The fibers were also used for rope and nets. Root tea was used to treat colds, dropsy, fevers, headaches, and sore throats. The Blackfeet used the tea as a laxative and as a wash to prevent hair loss. The Kiowas made chewing gum from the milky latex of the sap by letting it harden. Another species, Spreading Dogbane, *Apocynum androsaemifolium*, has pink or pink-tinged flowers, rarely white; found in woods, prairies; scattered in a few western counties.

NORTHERN SPIDERLILY
Hymenocalis occidentalis
Amaryllis Family (Amaryllidaceae)

Description: Leafless flower stalks, up to 30" tall, produce large, showy white flowers. The smooth, somewhat flattened stalks arise from a whorl of basal leaves, each up to 2' long, 1¾" wide, and somewhat folded. There are 2 to 6 flowers at the tip of each stem. The flowers are from 2 to 4" long with 6 narrow, spreading lobes that give it a distinctive spider-like appearance. The 6 stamens extend well past the lobes.

May—August

Habitat/Range: Wet woodlands, low marshy areas, and low areas that have been cutover; central counties and the Grand Prairie.

Remarks: These showy flowers have a strong fragrance and the plants are sometimes cultivated as an ornamental. A similar species, Western Marsh Spiderlily, *Hymenocalis liriosome*, has narrower leaves that are up to 1¼" wide and with somewhat smaller flowers that have an earlier, shorter blooming period. Found in the Gulf Coastal Plain Region and the Grand Prairie.

HEDGE PARSLEY
Torilis arvensis
Carrot Family (Apiaceae)

Description: A hairy, much-branched plant up to 2½' tall. The leaves are finely dissected and resemble parsley. The small flowers occur in flat-topped clusters on long stalks that extend well above the leaves. The fruit is densely covered with bristles that attach to clothes and fur.

May—August

Habitat/Range: Disturbed sites and fields, and along roadsides and railroads; native to Europe; common; throughout the state.

Remarks: A similar species, Japanese Hedge Parsley, *Torilis japonica*, has several leaf-like structures below each flower cluster while hedge parsley has none or one; also the fruit on the former has small prickles with hooks while the latter has straight prickles. Japanese hedge parsley also occupies disturbed sites; native to Europe; found in surrounding states and likely to occur in Arkansas.

BUNCHFLOWER
Melanthium virginicum
Lily Family (Liliaceae)

Description: Erect, stout plants up to 5' tall, with long grass-like leaves at the base, which alternate up the stem. The leaves are up to 20" inches long and up to 1" wide, with upper leaves being much shorter. The flowers occur along short branches at the top up to 18" tall. Individual stalked flowers are ½–1" across, with 6 creamy white petals.

May—July

Habitat/Range: Open or wooded moist sites; found in eight scattered counties.

Remarks: Formerly known as *Veratrum virginicum*. The towering plumes of white flowers are very conspicuous in open areas making their identification from a distance very easy. The roots and stems are poisonous to livestock, and the root has been used to kill intestinal parasites. The flower turns black with age.

fruit

GINSENG
Panax quinquefolius
Ginseng Family (Araliaceae)

Description: Plants up to 1 1/2' tall with a whorl of 3–4 leaves each divided into 5 stalked toothed leaflets. A leafless stem arises from the ground supporting a cluster of small, greenish white flowers. Bright red berries develop in late summer.

June—July

Habitat/Range: Moist woods; Ozark and a few Ouachita counties, also Crowley's Ridge

Remarks: The roots of ginseng have long been known to have medicinal properties that aid in mental efficiency and physical performance. However, large doses are said to raise blood pressure. Over-collecting of the roots has decreased populations over many areas which have led to harvest regulations and quotas nationwide.

PRAIRIE INDIAN PLANTAIN
Arnoglossum plantagineum
Aster Family (Asteraceae)

Description: This plant has large distinctive leaves at the base and a flowering stalk up to 5' tall but usually less. The single stem is smooth and angled and grooved along the surface. The leaves along the stem are few, alternate, small, and lack teeth along the margins. The basal leaves are large with parallel veins and long leaf stalks. The flower heads are numerous in open branches forming a flat-topped cluster. Each head is up to 1" tall, containing 5 white tubular flowers.

June—August

Habitat/Range: Prairies, glades, old fields; not common; widely scattered in the state.

Remarks: This species was formerly known as *Cacalia tuberosa* and *Cacalia plantaginea*. Native American Indians applied mashed leaves to the skin to treat cancers, cuts, and bruises, and to draw out blood or poisonous substances.

PALE INDIAN PLANTAIN
Arnoglossum atriplicifolium
Aster Family (Asteraceae)

Description: A plant with a smooth whitish cast and widely spaced leaves, growing to a height of 4–6' tall but sometimes to 8'. The leaves are alternate on the stem and have a whitish coating on the underside. The lower leaves are large and broadly triangular. Numerous flower heads form a somewhat flattened top with the flowers in the center of the cluster opening first.

June—October

Habitat/Range: Moist woods, dry open woods, prairies; Ozark Mountain and Crowley's Ridge.

Remarks: Formerly known as *Cacalia atriplicifolia*. A closely related species, Great Indian Plantain, *Arnoglossum reniforme* (formerly *Cacalia muhlenbergii*), differs by having the stem and leaves green (lacking a whitish coating) and having the lower leaves semicircular or lima-bean-shaped. Found in moist woods; not common; scattered in a few northern counties.

ILLINOIS BUNDLEFLOWER
Desmanthus illinoiensis
Pea Family (Fabaceae)

Description: Smooth, bushy plants to 4' tall. The angled stem supports alternate, highly dissected leaves with numerous paired leaflets that appear fernlike. At the axils of the leaves, slender stalks emerge that support small, round flower clusters about ½" across. The fine, long stamens projecting from each flower give the cluster a fuzzy appearance. The fruit is a round cluster up to 1½" across with twisted or curved pods with 2–6 smooth seeds in each pod.

June—August

Habitat/Range: Prairies, moist soil, roadsides, pastures; statewide.

Remarks: The children of some tribes used the dried seed pods as rattles. The boiled leaves were used by the Pawnee as a wash to relieve itching. The leaves and seeds are considered an important source of protein for wildlife and livestock.

HELIOTROPE
Heliotropium tenellum
Borage Family (Boraginaceae)

Description: Slender, wiry, much-branched annual plant, up to 10" tall with stems and leaves covered with dense, white hairs. The leaves are alternate, very narrow, up to 1" long and ⅛" wide, with their margins often rolled, and lacking stalks. The flowers are small, white, and solitary to numerous on short, small branches.

June—September

Habitat/Range: Open areas, glades; northern Ozark and Gulf Coastal Plain regions.

Remarks: Heliotrope endures harsh living conditions in the Ozarks. It seems quite suited to the thin soils over dolomite bedrock, where it can reach over 110 degrees F in the summer months.

STARRY CAMPION
Silene stellata
Pink Family (Caryophyllaceae)

Description: Several stiff, slender stems emerge from the base to 3' tall. The leaves are in whorls of 4 along the stem with pointed tips and up to 3" long. Showy bell-shaped flowers with fringed margins open to ¾" across.

June—August

Habitat/Range: Open woods, slopes, and along streams; found throughout most of the state except for the Gulf Coastal Plain Region.

Remarks: The lacy fringe of the petals produces the "starry" appearance from which the common name is derived. The Potawatomi and Mesquakie tribes used the roots as a poultice (plant material mashed and applied warm) to dry up infected sores. Starry Campion is related to the carnations and pinks familiar to flower gardeners.

HORSEWEED
Conyza canadensis
Aster Family (Asteraceae)

Description: A tall annual with a single stem to a height of 7' tall. The slender leaves, up to 3" long and ⅜" wide, are alternate along the stem and hairy. The flower heads are small and numerous.

June—November

Habitat/Range: Disturbed soil, fields, roadsides; very common; in every county.

Remarks: This plant was formerly known as *Erigeron canadensis*. Native American Indians and settlers boiled the leaves and drank the liquid to treat dysentery. An oil obtained by distilling the plant has been used to treat diarrhea, hemorrhoids, and pulmonary problems. The pollen is an irritant to some hay fever sufferers, and the plant can cause skin irritation. A related species, Dwarf Fleabane, *Conyza ramosissima*, has stems thickly branched from near the base; purplish rays; less than 10" tall; occurs in disturbed soil; a few counties across the state.

CULVER'S ROOT
Veronicastrum virginicum
Figwort Family (Scrophulariaceae)

Description: A tall, graceful plant growing to a height of 6', with branching flower stems that resemble a candelabra. The leaves are in whorls of 3–8 and up to 6" long and 1" wide. The leaf margins are finely toothed. The flowers are in dense clusters on spikes 3–9" long. The stamens have noticeable yellow to brownish red tips.

June—September

Habitat/Range: Moist prairies, open woods; mostly the northern half of the state.

Remarks: The Cherokee drank a root tea for treating backaches, fever, hepatitis, and typhus. The Seneca made a root tea to use as a mild laxative. For the Menomini, Culver's root served as a strong physic, a reviver, and as a means of purification when they had been defiled by the touch of a bereaved person. Early doctors used the root to treat a variety of ailments including liver disorders, pleurisy, and venereal diseases.

WOOLLY CROTON
Croton capitatus
Spurge Family (Euphorbiaceae)

Description: Small, annual plants, up to 18" tall, with a dense woolly layer of tiny star-shaped hairs on the stems and leaves. The leaves are alternate, stalked, up to 4" long and 1" wide, smooth along the margins, and with rounded bases. The flowers are in short compact clusters near the ends of branches. Tiny male and female flowers are in each cluster. The female flowers lack petals, while the male flowers have 5 tiny white petals.

June—September

Habitat/Range: Sandy soil, glades, pastures, idle fields, and other disturbed areas; statewide.

Remarks: Also called Hogwort, the oil is toxic, and cattle have been poisoned from eating hay containing the plants. A smaller species, Prairie Tea, *Croton monanthogynus*, has smaller leaves and flower clusters, and occurs in similar habitats, but it is less weedy; statewide.

BIENNIAL GAURA
Gaura longiflora
Evening Primrose Family (Onagraceae)

Description: A tall annual or biennial plant reaching up to 7', branching toward the top. The leaves are alternate on the stem, up to 6" long and ⅜" wide, with widely spaced teeth along the margin. The flowers are scattered along the stem; each flower with 4 white petals ¼–½" long, opening near sunset, turning pinkish with age. The petals point up in a semicircular or fan shape with 8 downward pointing stamens.

June—September

Habitat/Range: Open woods, old fields, roadsides, other disturbed sites; statewide.

Remarks: A similar species, Demaree's Gaura, *Gaura demareei*, has larger flowers, opening near sunrise, about 1" across; occurs in fields, roadsides, edge of woods; found in the southwestern part of the state.

DODDER
Cuscuta spp. *(several species)*
Dodder Family (Cuscutaceae)

Description: Leafless plants, with stringy orange stems that twine around and over other plants. Since dodder lacks green chlorophyll, which is needed to produce food from sunlight, these parasitic plants attach to a host plant with special roots that penetrate the host plant's stem and absorb its nutrients. The flowers appear in dense clusters scattered along the stems. Each flower is small, about ¼" across, with 5 spreading white lobes.

June—October

Habitat/Range: Edges of streams, prairies, fields, thickets, and open ground; occasional to common depending on the species; some are found throughout the state.

Remarks: There are 9 species of Dodder that occur in Arkansas. All are difficult to identify. Most dodder species have specific host plants such as members of the aster family like goldenrods, asters, sunflowers, ragweeds, and fleabanes; also milkweeds, penstemon, alders, buttonbush, water willow, smartweed, and others.

SLENDER MOUNTAIN MINT
Pycnanthemum tenuifolium
Mint Family (Lamiaceae)

Description: Aromatic plants with smooth, square stems growing to a height of 3'. The stem, with numerous pairs of leaves, branches toward the top. The narrow, pointed leaves are up to 2" long and ¼" wide. Flower heads are densely packed with small, 2-lipped flowers often with small purple spots.

June—August

Habitat/Range: Open woods, prairies, old fields, pastures, roadsides; statewide.

Remarks: Native American Indians used mountain mint, with its alluring scent, to bait mink traps; also as a tea for treating a rundown condition. The tea has been used as a seasoning in cooking. Hairy Mountain Mint, *Pycnanthemum pilosum*, has hairy stems and leaves; found in dry woods, prairies; occurs in the northern counties.

WOOD NETTLE
Laportea canadensis
Nettle Family (Urticaceae)

Description: An upright branched or unbranched plant with a somewhat zigzagged stem up to 3' tall. The stem and leaves have numerous stinging hairs. The alternate leaves are broad, up to 6" long, with coarse teeth along the margins. The tiny flowers are crowded into branched clusters; the male and female flowers are separate but on the same plant.

June—September

Habitat/Range: Wet or moist low woodlands, in valleys, and along streams; found throughout the state except for the Gulf Coastal Plain Region.

Remarks: Also called Stinging Nettle. The stinging hairs contain formic acid, like that felt in the bite of an ant. One preventive measure when hiking in lowland woods is to wear thick material like fairly new blue jeans, which prevents the needlelike hairs from reaching the skin. Once stung, the juice from the soft stem of Spotted Touch-Me-Not or Pale Touch-Me-Not, when applied to the skin, can reduce the sting.

ROUND-HEADED BUSH CLOVER
Lespedeza capitata
Pea Family (Fabaceae)

RATTLESNAKE MASTER
Eryngium yuccifolium
Carrot Family (Apiaceae)

Description: This stout-stemmed plant can grow to a height of 5', with bluish-green leaves at the base that resemble a yucca. The leaves are up to 2' long, 1⅜" wide, with pointed tips, and small, soft, needlelike bristles scattered along the margin. The tiny flowers are tightly packed in round balls up to 1" across. Whitish bracts stick out sharply from the flowers, which gives the flower head a rough, prickly feel and appearance.

June—August

Habitat/Range: Open woods, prairies; statewide.

Remarks: The Mesquakies used the leaves and fruit in their rattlesnake medicine song and dance. They also used the root for bladder problems and for treating poisons including rattlesnake bites. They also mashed the roots in cold water to make a drink for relieving muscular pains.

Description: A slender, unbranched legume that grows to 5' high and is covered with fine, silvery hairs. The leaves are alternate along the stem and divided into 3 narrow leaflets. The flowers occur in dense rounded heads up to 1½" in diameter. The flowers are creamy white with a reddish to purplish spot at the base. Each flower has an upper petal, 2 side petals, and a lower lip.

July—October

Habitat/Range: Prairies, woodlands; found primarily in some northwestern and southeastern counties.

Remarks: The Comanche used the leaves to make a tea. The Omahas and Poncas moistened one end of a short piece of the stem so it would stick to the skin, then lit the other end and allowed it to burn down to the skin. This was used to treat the sharp pain associated with nerves and rheumatism. The seeds are eaten by songbirds, gamebirds, and other wildlife. This plant provides nutritious, high-protein forage for livestock.

WHITE TURTLEHEAD
Chelone glabra
Snapdragon Family (Scrophulariaceae)

Description: An upright, usually unbranched plant, up to 3' tall, with angled stems. The leaves are opposite along the stem, broadest at the middle, toothed along the margin, and up to 6" long and 1½" wide. The white flowers are clustered at the top, each about 1" long. The upper lip of the flower has two lobes, which extend over the 3-lobed lower lip.

July—October

Habitat/Range: Low areas in wet soil, marshes, wet woods; known from a few locations in the northeast part of the state.

Remarks: The common name is very fitting especially when viewing the profile of the flower. A leaf tea was said to stimulate appetite, also a folk remedy for worms, fevers, jaundice, and as a laxative. Another species, Rose Turtlehead, *Chelone obliqua* var. *speciosa*, has reddish-purple flowers; occurs in marshes, wet woods, low areas; Greene County.

leaves

RATTLESNAKE PLANTAIN
Goodyera pubescens
Orchid Family (Orchidaceae)

Description: An orchid with a finely hairy, slender stalk, up to 12" tall, with an attractive rosette of bluish-green basal leaves that overwinter. The 5–7 basal leaves are from 1½–2" long and about 1" wide, with a prominent network of silvery white veins. The flowers appear in an alternate, spiral-like pattern towards the top of the stem. Each white flower is ⅜" long, with 3, petal-like sepals; 2 slightly smaller petals; and a pointed, saclike lower lip.

July – September

Habitat/Range: Moist woods; found in a few Ozark and Ouachita Region counties.

Remarks: The genus name is in honor of John Goodyear, a 17th century English botanist. The common name, Rattlesnake, is for the similarity of the leaf shape and venation pattern to the head of a snake, while another source states that the name is derived from the early belief that the leaves, when chewed and applied to a rattlesnake bite, would provide antidotal relief. The name "plantain" is for the similarity of the leaves to that of the common plantain.

FALSE BONESET
Brickellia eupatorioides
Aster Family (Asteraceae)

Description: One or more often reddish stems emerge from the base of this whitish or cream-colored plant to a height of 3'. The somewhat hairy leaves are alternate, up to 4" long and 1⅜" wide, with prominent raised veins on the underside. The small, numerous, white or yellowish flowers occur in clusters at the tips of branches. The styles extend beyond the flowers, giving them a fringed look.

July–October

Habitat/Range: Prairies, dry, open woods; found mostly in the western half of the state.

Remarks: Formerly known as *Eupatorium eupatorioides*. Great Plains Indians used false boneset to reduce swelling. Its bitter taste restricted its use as a medicine or food plant. The dried seed head has been used in winter flower arrangements. False boneset is sometimes confused with Tall Boneset, *Eupatorium altissimum*; false boneset has alternate leaves with one central vein, while tall boneset has opposite leaves with 3 veins.

COMMON BONESET
Eupatorium perfoliatum
Aster Family (Asteraceae)

Description: A plant up to 4' tall with noticeable spreading hairs on the stem and leaves. The leaves are up to 8" long and opposite, with their bases joining and circling the stem. The leaves taper toward the end and the margins are toothed. The dome-shaped flower clusters have flower heads that contain 9–23 small disk flowers but no ray flowers.

July–October

Habitat/Range: Moist to wet ground, low open woods, prairies, and along streams; statewide except for some Delta Region counties.

Remarks: The settlers called boneset Indian Sage because it was widely used by Native American Indians, who considered it a panacea for all ills, aches, and pains. The settler's use of the name "boneset" is confusing because it refers to its use in the treatment of flu, rather than for treating bones–a flu that caused severe body aches was called a "breakbone fever."

SERICEA LESPEDEZA
Lespedeza cuneata
Pea Family (Fabaceae)

Description: A single-stemmed plant, up to 6' tall, with many erect, leafy branches which are green to ashy in color. The stem has appressed hairs along its length. The leaves are divided into 3 leaflets, each from ¼–1" long. The 2 lower leaves have stalks, with the end leaflet stalkless or nearly so. The flowers are in clusters of 2–3 in the upper leaf axils. The flowers are about ¼" long and are a pale creamy color with conspicuous purple or pink markings.

July—October

Habitat/Range: Woodlands, prairies, fields, disturbed open ground, gravel bars in streams, borders of ponds, and along roadsides; statewide, a native of eastern Asia.

Remarks: Sericea Lespedeza was first introduced into the United States in the earlier part of the last Century. The intent was to aid in soil cover for erosion control, soil improvement, and food and cover for wildlife. Unfortunately, this plant has become a major nuisance and has been found to be very difficult to eradicate. It has now been declared a state noxious weed in many states. There are many native plants that can be used in the place of Sericea Lespedeza for erosion control, soil improvement, and wildlife purposes.

WHITE SNAKEROOT
Ageratina altissima
Aster Family (Asteraceae)

Description: A plant growing to 4' tall, with branching stems toward the top. The leaves are up to 6" long, opposite, long-stalked, and somewhat heart-shaped, with large teeth along the margins. The network of veins is conspicuous, giving the leaf a slightly crinkled appearance. The flower heads are arranged in branching, flat-topped clusters 2–3" across. Each flower head has small white flowers with extended styles that give them a tufted look.

July—October

Habitat/Range: Moist woodlands, along streams, and disturbed sites; statewide.

Remarks: Also known as *Eupatorium rugosum*. Native American Indians used a root tea for treating diarrhea, painful urination, fevers, and kidney stones, and as an application for snakebites. White snakeroot was responsible for "milk sickness," a deadly disease encountered during early settlement by Europeans. Cows that eat the plant secret a poison into their milk. The cattle themselves develop a disease called "trembles" for its chief symptom. In 1818, Abraham Lincoln's mother, Nancy Hanks Lincoln, died from a brief, agonizing bout of milk sickness. Research has shown that the active ingredient eupatorin in white snakeroot may have anticancer properties.

CLIMBING FALSE BUCKWHEAT
Fallopia scandens
Smartweed Family (Polygonaceae)

Description: A climbing, twining, annual plant often forming curtain-like masses of flowers and leaves. The red stems support round to heart-shaped leaves up to 6" long. Numerous, small flowers on long stalks form showy clusters.

July—October

Habitat/Range: Moist, open or shaded bottomlands, floodplains, and thickets; statewide.

Remarks: Formerly known as *Polygonum scandens*, the black, shiny seeds look and taste like buckwheat.

COWBANE
Oxypolis rigidior
Carrot Family (Apiaceae)

Description: A slender plant, up to 5' tall, with alternate palm-like leaves that are divided into 5–9 leaflets. These leaflets are smooth and up to 5" long and 1⅜" wide on the lower part of the stem and smaller towards the top. The flowers are in flat, dome-shaped clusters up to 6" wide. Each tiny white flower has 5 petals.

July—September

Habitat/Range: Moist woodlands and in wet soils along streams; primarily in northern Ozark and northern Ouachita Region counties.

Remarks: The roots and leaves of cowbane are poisonous and have been known to poison cattle as the name implies. Skin contact with the plant can cause dermatitis among some individuals.

SWEET EVERLASTING
Pseudognaphalium obtusifolium
Aster Family (Asteraceae)

Description: A biennial plant, up to 2½' tall, with felt-like hairs on the stems and undersides of leaves that give it a whitish cast. The leaves are alternate, narrow, up to 4" long and ½" wide, green on the top, white below, and lacking teeth along the margins. Numerous small flower heads occur on branches near the top. Each flower head is about ¼" tall, with white bracts surrounding a narrow tubular head of yellowish-white disk flowers.

July—October

Habitat/Range: Open woods, prairies, fields, pastures; statewide.

Remarks: Formerly known as *Gnaphalium obtusifolium*. Dried plants have a maple or balsam fragrance, hence the other name, Old Field Balsam. Pillows filled with dried flowers were used to quiet coughing. Plants laid in drawers and wardrobes kept away moths. The Mesquakies burned sweet everlasting as a smudge to restore consciousness or to treat insanity. Other tribes used it for colds, fever, and other infirmities. When chewed, it increases saliva flow. Because of this quality, it was given to cattle that had lost the ability to ruminate (produce cud); this is supposedly why it is also called Cudweed.

FIREWEED
Erechtites hieracifolia
Aster Family (Asteraceae)

Description: An annual plant up to 8' tall with a grooved, often hairy stem. The leaves are alternate, somewhat lance-shaped, with ragged to deeply cut teeth along the margins, and stalkless, with the midvein of the leaf sometimes whitish. The flower heads are surrounded by cylindrical green bracts that enclose numerous small disk flowers that are barely visible.

July—November

Habitat/Range: Moist woods, eroding slopes, disturbed ground, recently burned areas; statewide.

Remarks: The common name, Fireweed, refers to the plant's tendency to grow in recently burned over areas. Seeds often lie dormant for many years until overlying debris is burned off or cleared away, which stimulates the seeds to germinate.

TALL WHITE LETTUCE
Prenanthes altissima
Aster Family (Asteraceae)

Description: A slender plant with milky sap, up to 6' tall, with the upper branches supporting hanging cream-colored flowers. The thin leaves are alternate, smooth, on stalks, and variable in shape. The long, slender flower heads each contain 5–6 flowers.

July—September

Habitat/Range: Moist woods and ravines; primarily in the Ozark and Ouachita regions.

Remarks: Also known as Rattlesnake Root, because Native American Indians used the leaves and roots for treating snakebites, as well as bites from dogs. A tea was drunk for dysentery. There are 5 species of white lettuce in Arkansas.

NODDING POGONIA
Triphora trianthophora
Orchid Family (Orchidaceae)

Description: A short, delicate orchid with a smooth stem, from 3–8" tall. The stem leaves are alternate, about ½" long, broadest at the base, and clasping the stem. There are from 1–6 white to pinkish flowers, upright or nodding, each lasting but a day. The flowers are about ½" long, with a 3-lobed lip.

July—September

Habitat/Range: Moist woods; scattered counties in the western half of the state.

Remarks: Also called Three-Birds Orchid, for its tendency to produce 3 flowers. This small, slender orchid is easily overlooked on the forest floor.

CAROLINA ELEPHANT'S FOOT
Elephantopus carolinianus
Aster Family (Asteraceae)

Description: A branching plant, up to 3' tall, with large basal leaves in proportion to the size of the plant. The leaves are alternate, up to 8" long and 4" wide, with rounded teeth along the margins, and a leaf base that abruptly ends to a long leaf stalk. The large basal leaves are often absent at the time of flowering. The upper leaves are smaller and lack stalks. Below the flower cluster are 1–3 leaf-like bracts. Each cluster has 2–5 small flowers that are white to violet to lavender.

July—October

Habitat/Range: Woodlands, wooded lowlands in valleys, ravines, along streams; statewide.

Remarks: *Elephantopus* is Greek for "elephant foot," which may describe the basal leaves of these mainly tropical plants. A related species, Devil's Grandmother, *Elephantopus tomentosus*, differs by having large basal leaves lying flat on the ground and present during flowering, flowers usually darker in color and less spreading; occurs in the southern half of the state.

FALSE ASTER
Boltonia asteroides
Aster Family (Asteraceae)

Description: A much-branched plant, up to 6' tall, with alternate leaves broadly linear to broadest below the middle. Leaves are up to 6" long and ¾" wide, reduced in size upward along the stem. The flower heads are numerous, about ½" across, with 25–35 white petal-like ray flowers and yellow disk flowers.

July—September

Habitat/Range: Moist ground; scattered counties throughout the state.

Remarks: The genus name is in honor of James Bolton, an 18th century English botanist. A related species, Doll's Daisy, *Boltonia diffusa*, differs by having narrower leaves, less than ½", with many diffuse, scattered smaller flower heads; moist woods and other low areas; nearly statewide except for the Ozark Region.

PALE GENTIAN
Gentiana alba
Gentian Family (Gentianaceae)

LATE ALUMROOT
Heuchera parviflora
Saxifrage Family (Saxifragaceae)

Description: Small, sparse-looking plants with flower stalks extending to a height of not more than 16". The leaf and flower stalks are covered with gland-tipped hairs. The rounded leaves with rounded lobes emerge from the base of the plant on long stalks. Large, coarse teeth line the leaf margins. The underside of the leaf is usually red. The small flowers appear on spreading branches and have 5 white petals that curl back, revealing yellow stamens.

August—October

Habitat/Range: Shaded sandstone cliffs; scattered Ozark Region counties; also Dallas County.

Remarks: Native American Indians and early settlers used a powder made from the roots of various species of alumroots as an astringent to close wounds. A similar species, Arkansas Alumroot, *Heuchera villosa* var. *arkansana*, is only found in Arkansas; leaves have triangular lobes and flowers in a tighter cluster; scattered Ozark Region counties.

Description: Stems are erect to somewhat reclining, unbranched, and up to 2' tall. Leaves are smooth, opposite, attached to the stem without a stalk, up to 4" long, and about 1" wide at the base. The flowers are greenish-white or yellowish-white, bottle-shaped, closed to slightly open at the tip, and up to 1½" long.

August—October

Habitat/Range: Moist wooded slopes; scattered in a few northern Ozark Region counties; also Logan and Yell counties.

Remarks: Formerly known as *Gentiana flavida*. The bitter-tasting root of several species of gentian was used to increase the flow of gastric juice, promoting the appetite and aiding digestion. The bumblebee is one of the few insects strong enough to open the bottle-shaped flower and achieve pollination.

BEECHDROPS
Epifagus virginiana
Broomrape Family (Orobanchaceae)

Description: A parasitic plant on the roots of American beech trees, the wiry brown stems with several branches are up to 20" tall. Minute leaf scales are alternate along the stem. The white flowers have purplish-brown stripes, about ⅜" long, with 4 lobes at the tip. The lower flowers along the stem are fertile (produce fruit).

August—October

Habitat/Range: Parasitic on American beech roots in moist woods; scattered counties across the western half of the state, also Crowley's Ridge.

Remarks: The plants lack green chlorophyll necessary for food production so they attach to the roots of American beech trees in order to obtain nutrients. The highly bitter tea was once used for diarrhea, dysentery, mouth sores, and cold sores.

HAIRY ASTER
Symphyotrichum pilosum
Aster Family (Asteraceae)

Description: A widely branched, spreading aster to a length of 4'. The leaves at the base are up to 4" long and usually die back before the flowers emerge. The stem leaves are alternate, thin, and needlelike. The flowers are numerous, about ½" wide, each with 15–30 white, petal-like ray flowers and a central yellow disk with 20 or more disk flowers.

August—December

Habitat/Range: Old fields, pastures, roadsides, cleared woods; common throughout the state.

Remarks: Formerly known as *Aster pilosus*. Several tribes thought the smoke from burning aster plants was helpful in reviving a person who had fainted. Some tribes brewed a tea of the aster plant for headaches. The green basal leaves are eaten by white-tailed deer in the spring while the stem and flower heads are eaten during summer and early autumn. Songbirds, especially various sparrows, eat the seeds.

ARROW-LEAVED ASTER
Symphyotrichum urophyllum
Aster Family (Asteraceae)

Description: A widely branching aster, up to 5' tall. The leaves are alternate, lacking hairs, shallowly toothed, arrow-shaped, with a heart-shaped base, a long and winged stalk, and small teeth along the margins. Leaves on the upper part of the stem are narrow and taper at the base. The flower heads are numerous and are typically white, but shades of pale blue or lilac are also possible. There are 8–20 petal-like ray flowers surrounding the yellow disk flowers.

August—October

Habitat/Range: Dry and moist woods, prairies; common throughout the state.

Remarks: Formerly known as *Aster sagittifolius* and *Aster cordifolius*. There are 27 species in the genus *Symphyotrichum*, formerly *Aster*, in Arkansas.

FROSTWEED
Verbesina virginica
Aster Family (Asteraceae)

Description: Stout plants with leafy wings along the stem and up to 7' tall. The leaves are alternate and lance-shaped to 7" long, with widely spaced, small teeth. The flower heads are about 1–1½" across and clustered at the end of the stem on branches. Each flower head has 3–5 white petal-like ray flowers that surround each white disk.

August—October

Habitat/Range: Open woods, valleys, and streamsides; nearly statewide except for some southeast counties.

Remarks: In late fall, during hard freezes, frostweed produces "frost flowers." These are ribbons of ice oozing out of cracks at the base of the stem. Sap from still-active roots freezes as it emerges from the dead stem, growing like a white ribbon as more fluid is pumped out. Another name for this plant is White Crownbeard.

NODDING LADIES' TRESSES
Spiranthes cernua
Orchid Family (Orchidaceae)

Description: A slender orchid, up to 10" tall, with fine hairs on the stem and flowers. The 3–4 basal leaves are grass-like, up to 9" long, and often die back at the time of flowering. The upper stem leaves are reduced to scales. The flowers are up to ½" long, slightly nodding, with the sepals and petals forming a tube around the lip. The mouth of the flower is sometimes light yellow. The creamy flowers have a light vanilla-like scent.

August—October

Habitat/Range: Dry or moist woods, prairies, old fields; nearly statewide except for a few eastern Delta Region counties.

Remarks: A closely related species, Great Plains Ladies' Tresses, *Spiranthes magnicamporum*, differs by having a strong vanilla-like scent, the sepals on either side of the lip spreading, and a yellow center on the lip. Found in dry prairies; scattered throughout the state except the southernmost counties.

SLENDER LADIES' TRESSES
Spiranthes lacera
Orchid Family (Orchidaceae)

Description: This slender, delicate orchid has a single stalk that grows to 1' tall. There are 2–3 round basal leaves, with the stem leaves reduced to scales. The upper part of the stalk twists with a graceful spiral of evenly spaced flowers along the spike. The flowers are about ¼" long and white, with green on the center of the lip. The sepals and petals form a tube surrounding the ragged-edged lip.

August—October

Habitat/Range: Dry upland woods; primarily in the northwest quarter of the state.

Remarks: A similar species, Little Ladies' Tresses, *Spiranthes tuberosa*, differs by being less than 10" tall and having a more irregular spiral of flowers and a lower lip lacking a green spot. Found in dry, open woods; in scattered counties across the state.

TALL BONESET
Eupatorium altissimum
Aster Family (Asteraceae)

Description: Hairy plants, 3–6' tall, with a single stem that branches towards the top. The opposite leaves are either attached to the stem or sometimes on short stalks. They are up to 5" long and 1½" wide, with 3 prominent veins along the length of the blade and a few widely spaced small teeth on the upper half of the leaf. Narrow, flattish clusters of flower heads branch at the top of the stem. Each flower head has 3–7 tubular flowers.

August—October

Habitat/Range: Open woodlands, prairies, pastures, old fields; Ozark and Ouachita regions.

Remarks: A closely related species, Late Boneset, *Eupatorium serotinum*, has leaves with long stalks, 1 prominent vein running the length of the blade, coarse teeth along the leaf margins, and 12–15 flowers in each flower head. Found in moist open woods, pastures, disturbed areas; common throughout the state.

INDIAN PIPE
Monotropa uniflora
Indian Pipe Family (Monotropaceae)

Description: Small with single to multiple stems up to 8" tall, each stem with a single flower. The fleshy stem has rudimentary, scale-like leaves. The flowers droop to form the "pipe," then become erect as the fruit forms. The flowers are about 1" long, with 4–6 whitish petals that slightly flare at the end.

September—October

Habitat/Range: Moist woods, ravines, on slopes of ridges, usually in dense leaf mulch; scattered counties across the state.

Remarks: The plants are white and lack green chlorophyll needed to produce their own food. They feed on fungi that in turn feed on decaying organic material in the soil. Native American Indians and early settlers used the juice of Indian pipe for treating sore eyes. One Indian legend tells that this plant always appeared on the exact spot where some Indian had knocked the white ashes of his pipe on the forest floor.

SNOW-ON-THE-PRAIRIE
Euphorbia bicolor
Spurge Family (Euphorbiaceae)

Description: Plants from 1 to 4' tall, with slender upper leaves, 2 to 4" long that are green and edged with a narrow band of white. The lower leaves are solid green, grow close to the stem and are 1–1¼" long. The flower heads are numerous, with several chalky white false petals (bracts) surrounding a cup of tiny yellow male and female flower.

September—November

Habitat/Range: Edges of woods, prairies, open areas, and pastures; western Gulf Coastal Plain Region and Polk County.

Remarks: When the stem is broken, it exudes a white milky sap that can be irritating to the skin of some people. This spurge can spread across large areas, often seeming to blanket the fields with what appears to be snow, hence the origin of the common name.

Yellow Flowers

This section includes yellow, golden, and yellowish orange to pale, creamy yellow flowers. Also, multiple-colored flowers that are predominantly yellow are included in this section.

Lance-Leaved Coreopsis, page 94

HARVEY'S BUTTERCUP
Ranunculus harveyi
Buttercup Family
(Ranunculaceae)

Description: A slender, branched plant up to 1' tall. The leaves at the base of the stem are kidney-shaped with shallow lobes along the margin. The stem leaves lack stalks and are divided into narrow segments. The flowers are on long stalks, with 4–8 yellow petals and many stamens.

March—May

Habitat/Range: Rocky wooded slopes, ledges of bluffs and outcrops, and upland ridges; Ozark Region and a few scattered counties elsewhere.

Remarks: There are 18 species of buttercups in the genus *Ranunculus* in Arkansas. Beggars in the Middle Ages rubbed the leaves of a buttercup on their arms and legs to produce blisters and ulcers in order to look more pitiful and thus collect more money.

BRISTLY BUTTERCUP
Ranunculus hispidus
Buttercup Family
(Ranunculaceae)

Description: Sparse to densely hairy plant up to 1' tall. The basal leaves are on long stalks and divided into 3 leaflets. The stem leaves lack stalks and are usually divided into 3 narrow, irregular lobes. The stems just below the flowers usually lack hairs. Each flower has 5 waxy yellow petals and many stamens.

March—June

Habitat/Range: Dry, open woods; nearly statewide except for the Delta Region.

Remarks: Illinois-Miami Indians used crushed roots of buttercups to treat gunshot or arrow wounds. Cherokees used the juice from the leaves as a sedative or in a tea for treating sore throats. Modern medical opinion is that these plants are poisonous if taken internally.

YELLOW DOGTOOTH VIOLET
Erythronium rostratum
Lily Family (Liliaceae)

Description: A pair of soft, hairless leaves flank a single stem with one flower at the top. The basal leaves are about 6" long, with green and brown blotches on the surface. Two leaves are always produced on flowering plants, but most plants in the colony have only single leaves. A single flower is produced on a stalk up to 8" long. The flowers tilt slightly up, displaying 6 yellow spreading petals.

March—May

Habitat/Range: Moist woods on lower slopes and in valleys; Ozark and Ouachita regions.

Remarks: This plant is also called Yellow Trout Lily because the mottled leaves resemble the sides of a brown or brook trout. Dogtooth is so named for the shape of the corm, a type of root.

YELLOW VIOLET
Viola pubescens
Violet Family (Violaceae)

Description: Small plants with smooth to slightly hairy stems up to 10" tall. The basal leaves plus 2–4 on the upper stem are heart-shaped, up to 2" across, on long stalks, with rounded teeth along the margins. The flowers are on long stalks, with 5 bright yellow petals with brown-purple veins near the base.

March—May

Habitat/Range: Moist woods; nearly statewide except for some of the eastern and southern counties.

Remarks: Formerly known as *Viola pensylvanica*. There are 14 species of violets in the genus *Viola* in Arkansas.

GROUND PLUM
Astragalus crassicarpus var. *trichocalyx*
Pea Family (Fabaceae)

Description: Several sparsely hairy branches emerge from the base and trail or sprawl to 20" long (but often 12" or less). The leaves are alternate, with 15–23 leaflets usually with flattened hairs on both sides. The creamy white flowers are in small clusters at the end of stalks; each flower is about 1" long and drooping. The fruit is round and about ¾" across.

March—May

Habitat/Range: Rocky open woods and glades; Ozark Region, western Ouachita Region, and Ouachita County.

Remarks: Formerly known as *Astragalus mexicanus*. The unripe green fruits, which resemble small plums, have been eaten either raw or cooked.

BLACK MEDIC
Medicago lupulina
Pea Family (Fabaceae)

Description: A sprawling annual plant that sometimes grows to 20" long. The branching stem has soft hairs with alternate leaves divided into 3 leaflets. The leaflets are up to ¾" long with very shallow teeth along the margins. The flowers are crowded together in dense heads up to ¾" long with the heads attached to a long stalk that emerges from the leaf axil. The flowers are small, with 5 yellow petals in an arrangement typical of the pea family.

March—October

Habitat/Range: Disturbed ground, lawns, fields, along roadsides; native to Eurasia and Africa; nearly statewide.

Remarks: Black Medic was introduced into the United States for livestock forage but generally has a low yield. The seeds can be parched and eaten out of hand or ground into flour. There are 5 species of black medic in the genus *Medicago* in the state. None are native to the United States.

PALE CORYDALIS
Corydalis flavula
Fumitory Family (Fumariaceae)

Description: A delicate, low-growing plant, much branched, up to 10" tall. The leaves are green, fernlike, alternate, the lowermost on long stalks, the uppermost on short or no stalks. There are several pale yellow flowers clustered at the end of a stalk, with each flower less than ½" long. There are 4 petals, one of them protruding at the base into a spur, the outer petal has a toothed crest down its back.

March—May

Habitat/Range: Moist woods; nearly statewide except for the southeastern part of the state.

Remarks: Another species, Small-Flowered Corydalis, *Corydalis micrantha*, has bright yellow flowers, the outer petal lacks a toothed crest down its back; it occurs in rocky soil; nearly statewide except for the Delta Region.

YELLOW STAR GRASS
Hypoxis hirsuta
Lily Family (Liliaceae)

Description: Small, hairy plants producing yellow star-like flowers with grassy leaves, hence the common name. When flowering begins the plants are about 5" tall; as they mature, they may reach up to 1' in height. The long grass-like leaves are about 8" long and ¼" wide. The flower stalks are shorter than the leaves with 2–7 flowers appearing in succession. The flowers are about ½" wide, with 6 yellow petals and 6 yellow stamens.

April—June

Habitat/Range: Prairies, dry woods, sandstone outcroppings, and fields; nearly statewide except for a few Delta and Gulf Coastal Plain Region counties.

Remarks: The seeds are eaten by bobwhite quail.

WOOD BETONY
Pedicularis canadensis
Figwort Family (Scrophulariaceae)

Description: Several hairy stems emerge from a clump of fernlike basal leaves. The stems are about 6–10" tall when in flower and grow to about 18" tall as they mature. The basal leaves are narrow, deeply divided, and about 6" long. In the spring, they start out as a beautiful wine color before they turn green. Leaves along the stem are scattered and alternate. The snapdragon-like flowers are nearly 1" long and densely clustered at the top of the stem. There are two lips: The yellow or purple upper lip is flattened and curves in a long arch to form a hood. The lower lip is yellow and has 3 rounded lobes.

April—May

Habitat/Range: Prairies, dry open woods, along streams; nearly statewide but less frequent in the Delta Region.

Remarks: Also called Lousewort, from the belief that cattle and sheep grazing in pastures with this plant were once expected to become infested with lice. The Mesquakie and Potawatomi boiled the whole plant to make a tea for reducing internal swelling, tumors, and some types of external swelling. The Ojibwa used the plant as a love charm. The chopped-up root was put into food that was cooking, without the knowledge of the couple who were to eat it. If they had been quarrelsome, then they would again become lovers. Another species, Swamp Wood Betony, *Pedicularis lanceolata*, has stem leaves opposite; occurs in fens; found in Fulton County.

SELENIA
Selenia aurea
Mustard Family (Brassicaceae)

Description: A showy winter annual that produces a flower stalk up to 1' tall. The fernlike leaves form a basal rosette, with each leaf up to 3" long. The stem leaves are also deeply cut and alternate. The flowers are about ¾" wide with 4 bright yellow to golden petals.

April — June

Habitat/Range: Sandstone glades, rocky prairies, and sandy fields; scattered in the Ozark and Ouachita regions.

Remarks: This showy wildflower is known from Texas and Oklahoma to Arkansas, Kansas, and southwestern Missouri.

LARGE-FLOWERED BELLWORT
Uvularia grandiflora
Lily Family (Liliaceae)

Description: A graceful plant, with several smooth stems and a whitish coating, emerging from a common base up to 18" tall. The stem is usually branched at the top. The leaves are alternate, without teeth, smooth, up to 4" long, with the base of the leaf surrounding the stem. The flowers are solitary, drooping, up to 1½" long, with 6 long petals.

April — May

Habitat/Range: Moist woods; Ozark and Ouachita regions and Crowley's Ridge.

Remarks: Early settlers cooked the upper stem and leaves as greens. The upper stems served as a substitute for asparagus. Canker sores in the mouth were treated with a concoction made from the roots. Another species, Small Bellwort, *Uvularia sessilifolia*, has the base of the leaf not encircling the stem and has smaller leaves and flowers; well-drained to moist woods; nearly statewide but less common in the Delta Region.

YELLOW SEDUM
Sedum nuttallianum
Stonecrop Family
(Crassulaceae)

Description: Small, winter annuals, with fleshy stems from ¾–4½" tall that are green and become tinged with red or pink at maturity. The leaves are also fleshy, alternate along the stem and less than ¼" long. Several leafy branches arise at the tip of the stem with yellow flowers attached along the upper side of each branch. The flowers have 5 petals, each about ⅛" long, with pointed tips.

April—June

Habitat/Range: Sandstone glades, bluffs, and ledges; found in a few Ozark Region counties and Montgomery and Pike counties in the Ouachita Region.

Remarks: Also known as Nuttall's Sedum. This sedum has a limited range from southwestern Missouri to southeastern Kansas, then south to Louisiana and Texas.

CELANDINE POPPY
Stylophorum diphyllum
Poppy Family
(Papaveraceae)

Description: More or less upright plant to 12" long, hairy, with yellow sap and showy yellow flowers. Leaves at the base of the plant and along the stem are divided into 5–7 segments, with large, irregular teeth along each segment. The flowers are arranged in clusters of 1–4 at the end of stems; each flower is up to 2" across with hairy stalks. The 4 petals are bright yellow with rounded at the tips.

April—May

Habitat/Range: Moist wooded slopes and ravines; reported from Carroll, Marion, Newton, Stone, and Searcy counties in the Ozark Region.

Remarks: A yellow dye was made from the root. This is a showy wildflower that adapts well to shaded gardens.

FIELD MUSTARD
Brassica rapa
Mustard Family (Brassicaceae)

Description: An annual that germinates in the fall and overwinters, growing to 3' tall in the spring. The upper leaves are stalkless, toothed and clasp the stem; the lower leaves have deep lobes along the margins and are on stalks. The yellow flowers are clustered at the tips of branches, with each flower about ½" across and containing 4 petals.

April—September

Habitat/Range: Disturbed areas; native to Europe; nearly statewide except for the northern counties.

Remarks: A similar species, Black Mustard, *Brassica nigra*, differs by having leaves with stalks on the upper and lower parts of the stem; also native to Europe; found in disturbed sites; less commonly encountered than field mustard.

YELLOW ROCKET
Barbarea vulgaris
Mustard Family (Brassicaceae)

Description: A biennial plant, branched, smooth, and up to 2' tall. The basal leaves are up to 5" long, featherlike, with the end leaflet larger than the rest, and on long stalks. The upper leaves are alternate, toothed, and usually without a stalk. The flowers are crowded together at the end of a stem with each flower up to ⅜" across with 4 bright yellow petals. The fruit has elongated pods up to 1½" long.

April—June

Habitat/Range: Idle and cultivated fields, pastures, wet ground near streams, and along roadsides; native to Europe; scattered across the state.

Remarks: Yellow Rocket was introduced into the United States early. Cherokees ate the greens as a "blood purifier." Leaf tea was used to treat coughs and scurvy and to stimulate appetite. Studies indicate this plant may cause kidney malfunctions, so internal use should be avoided.

HAIRY BUTTERCUP
Ranunculus sardous
Buttercup Family (Ranunculaceae)

Description: A hairy annual plant, up to 2' tall that typically carpets disturbed areas in a mass of yellow. Leaves arising from the base have 3 broad lobes; those along the stem have 3 narrow lobes. Flowers are yellow, about 1" across with 5 petals.

April—June

Habitat/Range: Moist fields, along roadsides, other disturbed sites; statewide; introduced from Europe.

Remarks: This plant contains an irritant oil called *protoanemonin* that is present in several species of buttercups. If ingested, it can cause abdominal pain, severe diarrhea, convulsions, and death. Buttercup poisoning occasionally occurs in cattle when other food is in short supply.

YELLOW WILD INDIGO
Baptisia sphaerocarpa
Pea Family (Fabaceae)

Description: A smooth, branched, shrub-like plant, up to 4' tall. The leaves are alternate, divided into 3 leaflets, each less than 2" long. The flowers are on stalks well above the leaves. Each bright yellow flower is about ½" long, with an upper petal, 2 smaller side petals, and a middle keep-shaped lip. The seed pods are inflated to ¾" and turn tan to brown when ripe.

April—June

Habitat/Range: Prairies, pinelands, sandy soils, roadsides; western Ozark counties and Ouachita Region.

Remarks: Similar to Blue False Indigo in appearance, Yellow Wild Indigo is a sturdy, drought resistant plant that does well in a backyard garden setting.

KENTUCKY LADY'S-SLIPPER ORCHID
Cypripedium kentuckiense
Orchid Family (Orchidaceae)

Description: Stout, unbranched stem up to 2' tall with 1 to 2 showy flowers at the top. Stem leaves are from 6–8" long and forms a sheath at the base which joins to the stem. Flowers have 2 twisted narrow petals on either side of an inflated petal called a "slipper," which is 2–3" long and pale yellow; above and below the slipper are 2 broad sepals. The sepals and lateral petals are yellowish-green to purplish-brown.

April—May

Habitat/Range: Moist low woods, ravines; a few western Ozark counties, and the Ouachita Region.

Remarks: There are two other yellow lady's-slippers in the state. The Large Yellow Lady's-Slipper, *Cypripedium parviflorum* var. *pubescens* has a slipper about 2" long; occurs on moist lower wooded slopes; found in 4 Ozark counties. The Small Yellow Lady's-Slipper, *Cypripedium parviflorum* var. *parviflorum*, has a smaller slipper, about 1" long; occurs on moist lower wooded slopes; found in 3 Ozark counties, also Pulaski County.

PRAIRIE PARSLEY
Polytaenia nuttallii
Carrot Family (Apiaceae)

Description: A stout plant, to 3' tall, with thick, long-stalked, alternate, highly dissected leaves. The leaf stalks have wide, flat bases that clasp the stem. The flowers are clustered in numerous branches that form a flat-topped head. Each cluster has 15–25 pale yellow flowers, each about $\frac{1}{8}$" wide, with 5 tiny petals.

April—June

Habitat/Range: Prairies, glades, and rocky, open woods; nearly statewide but less common in the northeast and southwest part of the state.

Remarks: Prairie Parsley is the tallest wildflower blooming in prairies in early spring, towering over Indian paintbrush, yellow star grass, orange puccoon, shooting star, and others.

MEADOW PARSNIP
Thaspium trifoliatum
Carrot Family (Apiaceae)

Description: A much-branched plant, up to 2½' tall and lacking hairs. The basal leaves are simple, heart-shaped or sometimes divided into 3 leaflets. The leaves along the stem are on long stalks and divided into 3 leaflets, with a rounded base and small teeth along the margins. The flower heads are on stalks forming an umbrella-shaped cluster, with numerous, very small flowers that are yellow but sometimes dark purple. The flowers are all on short stalks.

April—June

Habitat/Range: Rocky open woods; scattered throughout the state.

Remarks: Another species, Hairy Meadow Parsnip, *Thaspium barbinode*, has a fringe of hairs at the nodes (the point at which the leaf emerges from the stem); found in moist woods, usually near streams; Ozark and Ouachita Mountain regions. Meadow Parsnip can sometimes be confused with Golden Alexanders, *Zizia aurea*, but differs most noticeably by the latter having the central flower in a flower head without a stalk so that the flower is slightly recessed.

GOLDEN ALEXANDERS
Zizia aurea
Carrot Family (Apiaceae)

Description: A smooth, branched plant up to 3' tall, with alternate leaves divided into 3 leaflets. The leaflets can sometimes be divided again into 1–3 leaflets. The lance-shaped leaflets are up to 3" long and 1" wide, with teeth along the margins. The flower heads are flat-topped and have several branches arising from a common point on the stem. The central flower within each cluster lacks a stalk causing the central flower to be slightly depressed.

April—June

Habitat/Range: Moist woods, prairies, and along streams; nearly statewide, less common in the Delta Region.

Remarks: The Mesquakie used the root to reduce fever. Early settlers considered the plant useful for treating syphilis and for healing wounds. Another species, Heart-Leaved Meadow Parsnip, *Zizia aptera*, has leaves at the base of the stem not divided into leaflets and the leaf bases are heart-shaped; reported from Craighead County.

ROUND-LEAVED GROUNDSEL
Packera obovata
Aster Family (Asteraceae)

Description: Unbranched stems to 2' tall, with creeping roots that form colonies. The basal leaves are roundish and blunt with teeth along the margins and tapering at the base to continue as leafy tissue along the hairless stalks. The leaves along the stem are alternate, narrow, with teeth along the margins, and lack stalks. The flower heads are clustered into an umbrella shape with bright yellow flowers. There are 10–15 ray flowers that surround the central disk flowers.

April—June

Habitat/Range: Moist or rocky woods; nearly statewide, less common in the Delta and Gulf Coastal Plain regions.

Remarks: Formerly known as *Senecio obovatus*. Another species, Woolly Ragwort, *Packera tomentosa*, formerly *Senecio tomentosa*, has dense hairs along the stem; mid-stem leaves toothed or with a few deep lobes near the base; nearly statewide except for some northern and eastern counties. Another species, Prairie Ragwort, *Packera plattensis*, formerly *Senecio plattensis*, has a densely hairy stem only at the base; mid-stem leaves deeply lobed almost to the base; northern and eastern part of the state.

DWARF DANDELION
Krigia biflora
Aster Family (Asteraceae)

Description: A dandelion-like plant with milky sap and a branching smooth bluish-green stem to 2' tall. The leaves at the base of the plant are spoon-shaped on a long stalk. The 1–3 stem leaves are much smaller and clasp the stem. There are 2–7 orange-yellow flower heads on each stem with each head about 1½" across.

April—June

Habitat/Range: Open woods, prairies, and along streams; Ozark and Ouachita regions.

Remarks: Also called Two-Flowered Cynthia. A similar species, Potato Dandelion, *Krigia dandelion*, is named for its tuberous root; it has no leaves on the flowering stem, which is about 12–15" tall, with only 1 flower per stem; open woods, prairies, glades, pinelands, lawns, fields; statewide. Another Dwarf Dandelion, *Krigia virginica*, has a hairy flowering stem only up to 8" tall and also lacks leaves on the stem; rocky or sandy open woods, glades, sandy fields; nearly statewide but absent in the Delta Region.

GOLDEN RAGWORT
Packera aurea
Aster Family (Asteraceae)

Description: A smooth, branching plant, up to 2½' tall, with a reddish-brown stem. The leaves are mostly basal, long stalked, heart-shaped, with coarse teeth along the margins. The stem leaves are fewer and smaller, with deeply cut lobes. The flower heads are in a somewhat flat-topped cluster. Each flower head has 8–12 golden yellow ray flowers surrounding a central yellow disk.

April—June

Habitat/Range: Wet ground along spring branches, streams, and in moist low woods and wooded ravine slopes; Ozark and Ouachita regions

Remarks: Formerly known as *Senecio aureus*. Native American Indians, settlers, and herbalists used root and leaf tea to treat delayed and irregular menstruation and childbirth complications; it was also used for lung ailments, dysentery, and difficult urination. Like many ragworts, this plant is now considered highly toxic.

BUTTERWEED
Packera glabella
Aster Family (Asteraceae)

Description: An annual from slender roots, with a smooth, unbranched stem, up to 3' tall. The leaves at the base of the stem are deeply divided with lobes and teeth, up to 8" long and 3" wide. The stem leaves are similar and gradually reduced in size upward. The flowers are in a terminal cluster with numerous flower heads. The flower heads are ¾–1" across, with 12–20 yellow petal-like ray flowers surrounding a yellow disk.

April—July

Habitat/Range: Low, wet woods, fields, roadsides; statewide.

Remarks: Formerly known as *Senecio glabellus*. The genus *Senecio* is from the Latin *senex*, an old man; an allusion to the gray-haired tufts of filaments attached to the seeds. Butterweed is in reference to the color of the flowers.

ORANGE PUCCOON
Lithospermum canescens
Borage Family (Boraginaceae)

Description: Single stems, with several emerging from the base of older plants, grows 6–18" tall, with dense soft hairs that give the plant a gray-green color. The leaves are alternate, stalkless, about 2½" long, less than ½" wide, lack teeth and are rounded at the tip. The deep golden flowers are in a flattened cluster at the top of the plant. Each flower is about ½" wide, about ½" long, with 5 spreading, rounded lobes.

April—June

Habitat/Range: Dry to moist prairies, glades, open woodlands; mostly in the Ozark and Ouachita regions.

Remarks: North American Indians used leaf tea (as a wash) for fevers accompanied by spasms and also as a wash rubbed on persons thought to be near convulsions. To the Menomini, the white, ripened seed of this plant was a type of sacred bead used in special ceremonies. A red dye was extracted from the roots. A similar species, Carolina Puccoon, *Lithospermum caroliniense*, is densely hairy, has narrower leaves with pointed tips, and yellow flowers; found in the southwestern part of the state, also Saline and Pulaski counties.

LANCE-LEAVED COREOPSIS
Coreopsis lanceolata
Aster Family (Asteraceae)

Description: Branching plants with several smooth stems, up to 2' tall, all emerging from a clump. Leaves mainly near the base, up to 8" long and 1" wide, lacking teeth along the margins. The showy flower heads, up to 2" across, are on long stalks. Each head has 8–10 fan-shaped ray flowers with jagged teeth at the tip and numerous central disk flowers.

April—June

Habitat/Range: Prairies, glades, sandy or rocky soil; nearly statewide but uncommon in the Delta Region.

Remarks: This showy, long-blooming perennial is easily grown from seed. Another species, Large-Flowered Coreopsis, *Coreopsis grandiflora*, has opposite, threadlike leaves along the lower stem, a smaller flower disk, and 8 fan-shaped ray flowers with fringelike teeth at the tip; the range and flowering period are same as the above. Another species, Star Tickseed, *Coreopsis pubescens*, is hairy throughout and has broad leaves scattered along the stem; occurs in dry woods; found in the Ozark and Ouachita Mountain regions.

COMMON CINQUEFOIL
Potentilla simplex
Rose Family
(Rosaceae)

Description: A trailing plant often rooting at the nodes, with a stiff hairy stem up to 3' long. The leaves are alternate along the stem, with long stalks. The leaflets are arranged like 5 fingers on a palm, each up to 3" long, with teeth along the upper ½ of the leaflets. The flowers are on long stalks emerging at the axil of the stem and leaf. Each flower is about ½" across, with 5 rounded petals and about 20 stamens.

May—July

Habitat/Range: Prairies, dry open woods, fields; statewide.

Remarks: The root was boiled in water and the liquid was taken to treat dysentery. Also, the root was eaten by ballplayers for stamina. In folklore, the plant was particularly used as a magic herb in love potions.

ROUGH-FRUITED CINQUEFOIL
Potentilla recta
Rose Family (Rosaceae)

Description: A stout, hairy, much-branched plant up to 2' tall. The leaves are alternate, with 5–7 fingerlike leaflets. The leaflets are rounded at the tip, tapering at the base, with teeth along the margins, hairy, and up to 3" long. The flowers are bright sulfur yellow, up to ¾" across, and attached to hairy stalks. The 5 petals are free from each other and shallowly notched at the tip. The fruits have a wrinkled surface, which explains the common name.

May—August

Habitat/Range: Fields, pastures, roadsides, disturbed ground; native to Europe; nearly statewide, less common in the Delta Region.

Remarks: In folk medicine, a tea made from various species of cinquefoil was used to treat a variety of inflammations, for throat and stomach ulcers, and for fever and diarrhea. As a mouthwash and gargle, the tea was used to treat sore throat, tonsil, and gum inflammations.

YELLOW WOOD SORREL
Oxalis dillenii
Wood Sorrel Family (Oxalidaceae)

Description: Small hairs lying flat along the stem give the plant a grayish appearance. The stems grow 6–12" tall. The leaves have 3 leaflets on long stalks. Individual flowers are on long stalks and arranged in a loose cluster at the tips of branches. Each flower is about ½" across with 5 yellow petals. The fruits are upright, hairy, and attached to stalks that are at right angles to the stem.

April—October

Habitat/Range: Prairies, open woods, fields, roadsides; statewide.

Remarks: The leaves and flowers were eaten by Native American Indians of various tribes. The powdered leaves were boiled in water and used to expel intestinal worms, reduce fevers, and to increase the flow of urine. The distinctive sour taste, which comes from oxalic acid, has been used to flavor salads. A similar Yellow Wood Sorrel, *Oxalis stricta*, has the fruit stalk upright and hairs that are spreading and not with a grayish cast; similar habitat; statewide. Creeping Lady's Sorrel, *Oxalis corniculata*, has a creeping stem that roots at the nodes; greenhouses, gardens; native to South America; statewide.

YELLOW PIMPERNEL
Taenidia integerrima
Carrot Family (Apiaceae)

Description: Slender, delicate plants with a whitish powdered appearance up to 3' tall. The leaves are alternate and divided into 2–3 segments with 3–5 leaflets per segment. The leaflets are almost rounded, ½–1" long, and lack teeth along the margins. The flower heads form a loose umbrella-shaped cluster up to 3" across. The cluster contains 10–20 stalks, each tipped with its own small head of flowers. Each tiny flower has 5 yellow petals that curve inward at their tips.

May—July

Habitat/Range: Prairies, dry, often rocky open woods; mostly in the Ozark and Ouachita regions.

Remarks: Both Native American Indians and settlers mixed the root of yellow pimpernel with other medicines to impart a pleasant aroma. The Mesquakie used it as a seasoning agent for some of their foods. In early folk medicine, a root tea was given for lung ailments. Yellow Pimpernel is similar in appearance to Golden Alexanders, *Zizia aurea*, but the latter has teeth along the leaf margins.

fruit

GOAT'S BEARD
Tragopogon dubius
Aster Family (Asteraceae)

Description: A biennial plant, with milky sap, growing to a height of 2'. The stem is smooth and noticeably thickened just below the flower head. The leaves are alternate, long, and narrow, with the base of the leaves clasping the stem. The flower head opens up to 3" across with pointed green bracts that extend beyond the yellow ray flowers. The flowers close just around midday. The fruit is similar to that of a dandelion but much larger.

May—July

Habitat/Range: Fields, pastures, roadsides, disturbed soil; native to Europe; primarily Ozark Region.

Remarks: The young, tender leaves at the base of the stem can be eaten raw in salads or cooked as greens. The roots, harvested in autumn or winter, are boiled or roasted and eaten. The taste varies from parsnip-like to oyster-like. Another Goat's Beard, *Tragopogon pratensis*, has pointed green bracts that do not extend beyond the yellow ray flowers; also native to Europe; found in disturbed sites.

MOTH MULLEIN
Verbascum blattaria
Snapdragon Family (Scrophulariaceae)

Description: A biennial plant with a slender form up to 5' tall. The stem is either single or branched, and is smooth on the lower part with round gland-tipped hairs above. The leaves at the base are large, tapering to the base, and toothed along the margins. The leaves along the stem are smaller, alternate, and somewhat clasping or simply lacking a stalk. The flowers, about 1" across, are loosely spaced along the branch. The 5 petals are either yellow or white with 5 stamens displaying woolly filaments that are violet to reddish-brown.

May—September

Habitat/Range: Pastures, fields, roadsides and other disturbed sites; native to Europe; scattered throughout the state.

Remarks: Both White and Yellow-Flowering Moth Mulleins appear equally as common. Looking at the flower, with some imagination, one may see a moth, hence the common name; others say it is because the flowers attract moths.

FALSE DANDELION
Pyrrhopappus carolinianus
Aster Family (Asteraceae)

Description: A winter annual or biennial plant, branched, smooth, up to 3' tall with milky sap. The leaves at the base of the stem are lobed, the leaves along the stem are barely toothed or without teeth, narrow, and up to 6" long. The flower heads are up to 1½" across with numerous sulphur yellow ray flowers and 5 teeth along the tip of the petals. The fruit is similar to that of a dandelion.

May—October

Habitat/Range: Dry open woods, prairies, roadsides, disturbed ground; statewide.

Remarks: The flowers are open during the morning hours.

WILD PARSNIP
Pastinaca sativa
Carrot Family (Apiaceae)

Description: A stout, smooth-stemmed, biennial plant to 5' tall with grooves along the stem. The leaves are alternate and divided into leaflets up to 3" long that are round and deeply lobed, with teeth along the margins. The flower heads are large, up to 5" across, on long stalks, and shaped like an umbrella. Numerous yellow flowers, each with 5 petals and 5 stamens, are borne on slender stalks.

May—October

Habitat/Range: Roadsides, fields, disturbed ground; native to Europe and Asia; few reports in the state but this plant has the potential to spread rapidly.

Remarks: The sap from this plant reacts with sunlight to form a toxin and can cause a skin rash similar to that of poison ivy on some individuals, with the affected area remaining reddened for several months. The fleshy taproots from the first year reportedly can be excellent when eaten raw or as a cooked vegetable.

PRAIRIE SUNDROPS
Oenothera pilosella
Evening Primrose Family (Onagraceae)

Description: Unbranched alternate-leaved plants, up to 2½' tall, with soft hairy stems and leaves. The leaves are widest at the middle, up to 4" long and 1" wide. The yellow flowers arise singly at the axils of the leaves. Flowers are about 2" across, with 4 broadly rounded petals with irregular edges.

May–July

Habitat/Range: Moist prairies, open woodland, low wet areas; primarily Delta and Gulf Coastal Plain regions.

Remarks: Prairie Sundrops flowers bloom once during the day, unlike most others in the primrose family, which are one-time night bloomers.

MISSOURI PRIMROSE
Oenothera macrocarpa
Evening Primrose Family (Onagraceae)

Description: A low, sprawling to erect plant, up to 15" long. The alternate narrow leaves are several on a stem and up to 5" long. The leaves are long-pointed at the tip with a tapering base and small silky hairs. The base of the leaves and the stem are often red. The showy flowers emerge from leaf axils on the upper part of the stem. They are up to 5" across with 4 large petals that turn orange when fading. The fruit is a brown papery capsule 3–4" long, with 4 broad wings.

May–August

Habitat/Range: Dolomite glades, bluffs, and roadsides; northern tier of Ozark Region counties.

Remarks: Formerly known as *Oenothera missouriensis*. The flowers open late in the evening and close the next day by midmorning. The flowers are pollinated by night-flying sphinx moths.

OX-EYE SUNFLOWER
Heliopsis helianthoides
Aster Family (Asteraceae)

Description: A spreading, branched plant to 5' tall. The leaves are opposite, on stalks, shaped like arrowheads, and up to 6" long and 3" wide. The margins have coarse teeth. The flower head is 2–4" across and on a long stalk. There are up to 20 pale to golden yellow ray flowers surrounding a conical yellow disk.

May–October

Habitat/Range: Open woods, prairies; nearly statewide but absent in some Delta and Gulf Coastal Plain counties.

Remarks: Ox-Eye Sunflower blooms over a long period, making this plant a good candidate for a wildflower garden; however, it can be aggressive.

YELLOW SWEET CLOVER
Melilotus officinalis
Pea Family (Fabaceae)

Description: This legume, depending on conditions, grows as an annual or biennial. The branching, smooth stems may reach 7' tall. The leaves are alternate, divided into 3 leaflets, with each leaflet about 1" long, oval, rounded at the top, and finely toothed. The flowers are clustered on 4" stalks, with each flower about ¾" long and fragrant.

May–November

Habitat/Range: Roadsides, fields, waste ground, invasive in dry and moist prairies; native to Asia; common in every county.

Remarks: This plant is similar in all respects to White Sweet Clover except for the flower color and the fact that yellow sweet clover blooms two weeks earlier than white sweet clover. The two species have been combined under *Melilotus officinalis*. (See p. 37.) This weedy plant is highly drought resistant and has spread from its intended use as hay, pasture, and green manure. It is also a popular honey plant by beekeepers. The leaves have a sweet vanilla-like odor when crushed.

CREAM WILD INDIGO
Baptisia bracteata var. *leucophaea*
Pea Family (Fabaceae)

Description: A coarse, hairy, bush-like plant with spreading branches up to 2' tall. The leaves are alternate on the stem and divided into 3 leaflets, each up to 3½" long. The bracts at the base of the leaflets are large and give the appearance of 5 leaflets instead of 3. The flower spike, up to 1' long, droops with numerous pale yellow flowers, each about 1" long and having the arrangement typical of members of the pea family. The seed pods are black, pointed at the tip, and up to 2" long.

May—July

Habitat/Range: Prairies, glades, and open woods; nearly statewide, less common in the Delta Region.

Remarks: Formerly known as *Baptisia leucophaea* and also called Long-Bracted Wild Indigo. Native American Indians used the plant to treat cuts and certain fevers. The Pawnee pulverized the seeds, mixed the powder with buffalo fat, and rubbed it on the stomach as a treatment for colic. Indian boys often used seedpods as rattles when they imitated their elders doing a ceremonial dance. A similar species, Nuttall's Wild Indigo, *Baptisia nuttalliana*, has flowers scattered over the entire plant; found in the southern third of the state.

COMMON PRICKLY PEAR
Opuntia humifusa
Cactus Family (Cactaceae)

Description: A low-growing cactus with enlarged fleshy, spiny, green stems that often grow in colonies. The stem segments or pads are up to 5" long and 3" wide. The upper third of the pad may have 1–2 needle-like spines, spreading, which emerge from clusters of small bristles. These clusters or tufts are scattered across the surface of the pad. The showy flowers are up to 4" across and open from single buds along the edge of the pad (new pads also emerge along the edge). The 8–12 bright yellow petals have a waxy surface, often with a reddish center. Numerous yellow stamens surround a stout central style. The fruit is cylindrical, up to 2" long, and red when ripe.

May—July

Habitat/Range: Dry sandy soil, sandstone glades, ledges; nearly statewide, less common in the Delta Region.

Remarks: Formerly known as *Opuntia compressa*. The common name refers to the red, bristly, pearlike fruit. The spines and bristles are covered with microscopic reflexed barbs at their tips, making them difficult to extract. Native American Indians ate the ripe fruit, pads, buds, and flowers raw, cooked, or dried. Another species, Plains Prickly Pear, *Opuntia macrorhiza*, has 2–3 spines per cluster that are turned back (reflexed) against the pad, and the spines are found along the upper ⅔ of the pad; dry sandy soil, sandstone glades, ledges; scattered counties statewide except absent from the Delta Region.

LOOSESTRIFE
Lysimachia lanceolata
Primrose Family (Primulaceae)

Description: A single-stemmed plant, up to 2' tall, with very short side branches. The stem sends out stolons (runners) at the base to produce more plants. The leaves are opposite, closely spaced, and vary in shape from rounded and stalked on the lower stem to narrow and tapering on the middle and upper parts. The stem leaves are up to 6" long, less than ¾" wide, pointed at the tip, and tapering at the base. The flowers dangle on long individual stalks, with each flower about ¾" across. The 5 yellow petals have ragged lobes and finely pointed tips.

May—August

Habitat/Range: Moist woods, prairies, borders of streams, moist areas along roadsides; statewide.

Remarks: Another species, Fringed Loosestrife, *Lysimachia ciliata*, has leaves over 1" wide and a fringe of short hairs along the leaf stalk; moist woods, bottomlands; Ozark Mountain Region.

NARROW-LEAVED LOOSESTRIFE
Lysimachia quadriflora
Primrose Family

Description: Slender plants up to 2' tall, with very narrow stalkless leaves that are opposite on the stem. The leaves are 3" long, less than ¼" wide, with smooth edges that are slightly turned down. The flowers are on long slender stalks that bend, causing the flowers to droop. There are 5 broad yellow petals that are somewhat ragged along the outer edges.

June—August

Habitat/Range: Moist prairies, wet soil along springs and streams; northeast Ozark Region.

Remarks: Native American Indians made tea from loosestrife plants for kidney trouble, bowel complains, and other problems. Tea from the root was used to induce vomiting. There are 6 loosestrife species in the genus *Lysimachia* in Arkansas.

MONEYWORT
Lysimachia nummularia
Primrose Family (Primulaceae)

Description: Creeping stems spread low over the ground, with small almost round, opposite, semi-evergreen leaves, up to 1" long and wide. Flowers are yellow on slender stalks emerging from the leaf axils, about 1" across with 5 petals.

May—August

Habitat/Range: Moist, partially shaded areas mainly bordering streams, sometimes forming dense mats; native to Europe; reported from a few northern counties.

Remarks: The species Latin name *nummularia* means coin-shaped in reference to the leaves.

HAIRY HAWKWEED
Hieracium gronovii
Aster Family (Asteraceae)

Description: Slender stems up to 4' tall, with conspicuous spreading hairs, up to ¼" long, near the base. The leaves at the base and lower part of the stem are up to 8" long and up to 2" wide, bristly hairy on the upper surface with star-shaped hairs on the lower surface. The flower heads are branched along the upper stem with gland-tipped hairs along the flower stalks. Each flower head has 15–30 yellow ray flowers.

May—October

Habitat/Range: Dry open woods and fields; nearly statewide, uncommon in the Delta Region.

Remarks: Another species, Long-Bearded Hawkweed, *Hieracium longipilum*, has long, dense hairs on the lower stem leaves over ½" long, a narrower cluster of flower heads, and 40–60 ray flowers on each head; open woods, prairies, fields; *June—September*; Ozark Mountain Region.

YELLOW PASSION FLOWER
Passiflora lutea
Passion Flower Family (Passifloraceae)

Description: A vine, up to 15' long, that climbs or sprawls with the help of tendrils. The leaves are alternate, with 3 broad, rounded lobes, usually smooth, and up to 4" across. The unusual flowers are single, arising on stalks from the axils of leaves. Individual flowers are small, about 1" across, with several greenish yellow petals and a greenish yellow fringe. There are 5 drooping stamens around the pistil, which has 3–4 curved stigmas. The fruit is oval, smooth, black when ripe, up to ½" long, and contains dark brown seeds with gelatinous coverings.

May—August

Habitat/Range: Moist or rocky woods, thickets; statewide.

Remarks: The young shoots and tendrils of the plant are eaten by wild turkey.

PENCIL FLOWER
Stylosanthes biflora
Pea Family (Fabaceae)

Description: Small, wiry-stemmed, often branched at the base, hairy, up to 8" tall. The leaves are alternate, divided into 3 leaflets, each up to 2" long and ½" wide. There are widely scattered bristles along the leaf margins. The flowers are nested in leafy clusters at the tops of branches and are arranged in the style typical of the pea family. The orange-yellow flowers are about ¼" long.

May—September

Habitat/Range: Dry open woods, fields; statewide.

Remarks: The beanlike seeds are eaten by wild turkey and bobwhite quail.

BLACK-EYED SUSAN
Rudbeckia hirta
Aster Family (Asteraceae)

Description: This short-lived perennial grows 1–3' tall with rough and hairy leaves and stems. The basal leaves are up to 5" long and 1" wide. Along the stem, the leaves are alternate, spreading, up to 4" long, widest in the middle, and tapering towards the tip. Flower heads are single at the top of each stem branch with showy heads about 2–3" across. There are 10–20 bright yellow ray flowers that surround a dark brown to purple-brown, dome-shaped disk.

May—October

Habitat/Range: Prairies, open woods, pastures, old fields, and along roadsides; statewide.

Remarks: The Potawatomi prepared a root tea for curing colds. Early settlers used the plant as a stimulant and a diuretic. A yellow dye is made from this plant. Another species, Large Coneflower, *Rudbeckia grandiflora*, has upright leaves, ray flowers up to 3" long and drooping; *July—August;* open, dry areas, prairies; nearly statewide except for the far eastern counties.

BROWN-EYED SUSAN
Rudbeckia triloba
Aster Family (Asteraceae)

Description: A bushy plant with several often reddish-colored branches, up to 5' tall, with spreading hairs on the stems. The leaves are alternate, hairy, with the lower ones 3-lobed and often shed at the time of flowering. The upper stem leaves are narrow, stalkless, about 4" long, and with toothed edges. The flower heads are numerous, with each head up to 1¾" across. Each head has 6–12 yellow petal-like ray flowers surrounding a dome-shaped brown disk.

June—October

Habitat/Range: Woods, fields, moist thickets, stream banks; nearly statewide, less common in the Delta and Gulf Coastal Plain regions.

Remarks: The flower heads of Brown-Eyed Susan are smaller and much more numerous than those of Black-Eyed Susan. The plants are also taller and widely branched, which also helps to differentiate them from Black-Eyed Susan.

WOOLLY MULLEIN
Verbascum thapsus
Figwort Family (Scrophulariaceae)

Description: This stocky biennial can reach a height of 6' with large woolly leaves and a spike of densely packed yellow flowers. The first year's leaves form a basal rosette with each leaf up to 1' long, with soft, woolly hairs. The second year, a flower stalk emerges with alternate leaves scattered along the stem. The leaf bases extend down the stem forming wings. The short, tubular flower opens to about 1" across, with 5 yellow lobes.

May—September

Habitat/Range: Dry fields, pastures, disturbed ground, and along roadsides; native to Europe; statewide.

Remarks: In ancient Greece, the leaves were rolled, dried, and made into wicks for oil lamps and candles. Dioscorides used mullein to treat lung diseases, diarrhea, insomnia, and to relieve pain. In the Middle Ages, carrying a twig of *mullein* was said to protect a person from witchcraft and wild beasts. Arriving early with settlers in the United States, the plant was used by Native American Indians as a leaf tea for treating coughs. Settlers used the large leaves for baby diapers, and early pioneers and even today's campers have used the woolly leaves in place of toilet paper.

YELLOW CONEFLOWER
Echinacea paradoxa
Aster Family (Asteraceae)

Description: Attractive, smooth, yellow-green plants with stout stems, up to 3' tall. The leaves lack hair and are smooth to the touch, up to 10" long and 1½" wide, tapering at each end with several parallel veins running along the length of the leaf. The basal leaves are on long stalks, while the stem leaves are few. The flower heads are single on long stalks, with several drooping bright yellow rays each up to 3½" long surrounding a broad, purplish-brown, conical central disk. The stamens are yellow.

May—June

Habitat/Range: Dolomite glades; Baxter, Boone, and Stone counties.

Remarks: Native American Indians used the plant as a pain killer especially for toothaches, sour gums, snakebites, bee stings, and to treat burns.

WINGSTEM
Verbesina helianthoides
Aster Family (Asteraceae)

Description: Flaps of leaf tissue or "wings" run down the length of the hairy stem, which can reach a height of 3½'. The leaves are alternate, up to 6" long, with coarse hairs on the upper surface, soft-hairy on the lower surface, with teeth along the margins. The flower heads are large, with 8–15 yellow petal-like ray flowers surrounding a yellow disk.

May – July

Habitat/Range: Prairies, open woods, along streams; nearly statewide but uncommon in the Delta Region.

Remarks: This plant is also known as Yellow Crownbeard. Bobwhite quail, songbirds, and small mammals eat the seeds.

SEEDBOX
Ludwigia alternifolia
Evening Primrose Family (Onagraceae)

Description: A widely branching plant, up to 4' tall. The leaves are alternate, up to 4" long and less than 1" wide, broadest at the middle and tapering to the tip and base. The flowers are single, on short stalks, and arising at the junction of the leaf and stem. Each flower is about ¾" wide, with 4 yellow petals, which fall shortly after flowering, and 4 stamens. The seed capsules are distinctly square, up to ¼" across, angled or narrowly winged, and containing numerous small seeds.

May – August

Habitat/Range: Wet ground in prairies and meadows; along streams, shores of ponds and lakes; and in moist idle fields and roadside ditches; statewide.

Remarks: There are 16 species of seedbox in the genus *Ludwigia* in Arkansas. This seedbox is the only one in the state with sharply angled square fruits; the others have tubular to slightly squarish fruits.

PURPLE-HEADED SNEEZEWEED
Helenium flexuosum
Aster Family (Asteraceae)

Description: A single-stemmed plant, up to 3' tall, with branching toward the top. The stem has leafy wings that originate at the base of the leaf and continue down the stem. The leaves are alternate, lacking stalks, up to 3" long, and less than 1" wide. The distinctive flower head has a round, brownish-purple, central disk surrounded by 8–14 fan-shaped, yellow, petal-like ray flowers, each with 3 lobes. Each flower head is about 1" across.

May—July

Habitat/Range: Moist areas along streams, pastures, and old fields; statewide.

Remarks: Sneezeweeds are considered poisonous to cattle if eaten in sufficient quantity. This is unlikely to happen, however, because of the plant's bitter taste. The plant is also poisonous to fishes and worms as well as to insects. Research by the National Cancer Institute has demonstrated significant antitumor activity in this plant's chemistry.

BITTERWEED
Helenium amarum
Aster Family (Asteraceae)

Description: A very leafy, much-branched annual plant to 1' tall. The leaves are threadlike, alternate but sometimes whorled on the stem, up to 1½" long. The flower heads are fan-shaped, up to 1" across, with yellow, petal-like ray flowers that have notches on the ends, and a central dome-shaped yellow disk.

June—October

Habitat/Range: Fields, pastures, disturbed soil, and along roadsides; statewide.

Remarks: This plant has a strong bitter smell. Cattle often avoid it, and those that graze on the plant give milk with a bitter flavor, hence the common name. There are cases of sheep, cattle, horses, and mules having been poisoned from eating this plant.

GRAY-HEAD CONEFLOWER
Ratibida pinnata
Aster Family (Asteraceae)

Description: A slender, hairy-stemmed plant, up to 5' tall, often branching toward the top. The leaves are divided into 3–7 slender leaflets with a few teeth or small side lobes along the margins. The leaves at the base of the stem are on long stalks with the leaf blade up to 7" long. The leaves on the stem are alternate and smaller. Each flower head has its own long stalk. The 5–10 yellow ray flowers droop downward, each about 2" long and less than ½" wide. They surround a conical disk about ¾" tall. Prior to opening, the small disk flowers are ashy-gray, hence the common name, but they turn brown as the flowers open. The crushed seed heads have a distinct anise scent.

June—September

Habitat/Range: Prairies, edges of woods, along roadsides; northern part of Ozark Region, also Clark and Hempstead counties.

Remarks: Native American Indians made a tea from the flower cones and leaves. The Mesquakie used the root to cure toothaches.

BIRD'S FOOT TREFOIL
Lotus corniculatus
Pea Family (Fabaceae)

Description: A sprawling plant, up to 2' long, with the branching stems upright toward the tips. The leaves are divided into 5 leaflets, each up to ¾" long, with the 2 lower leaflets some distance below the 3 upper leaflets. The flowers are clustered on a long stalk that arises from a leaf axil. The flowers are golden yellow, about ¾" long, and arranged in the pattern typical of members of the pea family. The seeds form in slender, upright pods.

June—September

Habitat/Range: Fields, roadsides, and disturbed sites; native to Europe; northern counties.

Remarks: Bird's Foot Trefoil is low growing and has been planted along roadsides to reduce mowing. It has also been cultivated for its pasture value. Because it can be weedy and spreads into habitat occupied by native vegetation, its use should be discouraged.

YELLOW-PUFF
Neptunia lutea
Pea Family (Fabaceae)

Description: Plants with hairy, creeping stems that can grow up to 4' long, with bright yellow flower heads. The leaves are compound and divided into numerous small leaflets that look like tiny fern fronds. The flowers have 5 petals and numerous yellow stamens that form a cylindrical head about 1" in diameter.

June—September

Habitat/Range: Prairie, pinelands, and roadsides; Arkansas River Valley and Gulf Coastal Plain Region.

Remarks: The leaves close upon touch, as well as at night and during periods of cloudy weather.

PALE TOUCH-ME-NOT
Impatiens pallida
Jewelweed Family (Balsiminaceae)

Description: Annual plants growing to 4' tall, with branched stems that are weak and watery. The stems are pale green and translucent with leaves alternate, oval, thin, and bluish-green. The leaves are up to 3½" long with long stalks and widely spaced teeth along the margins. Flowers are shaped like a cornucopia up to 1¼" long and hang on a slender stalk. The smaller end of the flower is a curved spur that holds the nectar. The fruit is a slender capsule about 1" long, which splits and propels the seed when touched.

June—October

Habitat/Range: Moist to wet woodlands and banks of streams; Ozark Region, also Lonoke and Pulaski counties.

Remarks: The Potawatomi and settlers applied the juice of Touch-Me-Not to relieve the itch of poison ivy. The juice is also used to relieve the burning sensation of Stinging Nettle, which is often found occupying the same habitat as Touch-Me-Nots. Livestock have been poisoned by eating large amounts of the fresh green plants.

WILD FLAX
Linum sulcatum
Flax Family (Linaceae)

Description: A pale green annual plant, up to 2½' tall, with a stiff stem that branches near the top. The branches have conspicuous grooves or ridges. The leaves are alternate on the stem, about 1" long and only ⅛" wide, pointed at the tip, and stalkless. Two tiny round glands are found where the leaf attaches to the stem. The flowers are scattered among the branches on short flower stalks. The flowers are about ¾" across, with 5 pale yellow petals that drop off shortly after flowering.

June—September

Habitat/Range: Sandy soil, hill prairies; northern counties, also Pulaski and Sebastian counties.

Remarks: A related species, Small Yellow Flax, *Linum medium* var. *texanum*, is a perennial, lacks the small round glands at the base of the leaf, and lacks the grooves or furrows on the branches. Found in dry soil, open areas; statewide. Various species of flax have been cultivated since before recorded history for the fibers in their stems, used to make linen, and the oil in their seeds, linseed oil. The seeds were also used for a variety of medicinal remedies.

SPOTTED ST. JOHN'S WORT
Hypericum punctatum
St. John's Wort Family (Clusiaceae)

Description: The sturdy stem of this plant is somewhat branched at the top and up to 3' tall. The undersides of the leaves, sepals, and petals are covered with numerous tiny black dots. The leaves are opposite, lacking stalks, up to 2½" long, ¼" wide, and thick and leathery in texture. The flowers are clustered at the top of the stem and in short side branches. Each flower is about ½" across with 5 yellow petals and numerous stamens surrounding a flask-shaped central ovary.

June—August

Habitat/Range: Woods, along streams; fields, and roadsides; nearly statewide.

Remarks: The Menomini treated tuberculosis with a type of St. John's wort; they also mixed it with raspberry root for treating kidney troubles. A similar species, Common St. John's Wort, *Hypericum perforatum*, has black dots along the margins of the petals, sepals, and stems, with stems much branched; native to Europe and has been popularized recently by its ability to treat depression; disturbed areas; scattered counties across the state.

MULLEIN FOXGLOVE
Dasistoma macrophylla
Figwort Family (Scrophulariaceae)

Description: A stout, biennial plant with branching stems to 7' tall. The basal leaves are large, up to 10" long, and deeply cut. The expanding basal leaves in early spring are an attractive reddish-purple before turning green. The stem leaves are progressively smaller toward the top of the plant, lance-shaped, and smooth along the margins. The flowers lack stalks and emerge directly from the axil of the leaves and stem. The flower is a short tube, woolly inside, less than ¾" long, with 5 yellow petals and 4 stamens.

June—September

Habitat/Range: Moist to dry woods, rocky slopes; northern counties in the Ozark Range, also Woodruff, Sevier and Clark counties.

Remarks: Formerly known as *Seymeria macrophylla*. The plant, although rarely seen in large numbers, is a preferred food of white-tailed deer.

PRAIRIE COREOPSIS
Coreopsis palmata
Aster Family (Asteraceae)

Description: Narrow, rigid-stemmed plants, usually 1–2½' tall. The leaves are opposite on the stem, with each leaf divided into 3 long, narrow segments. The middle segment can sometimes be divided again for another 1–2 segments. The flower heads are on individual stalks, with each head having 8 yellow, petal-like ray flowers that surround a yellow central disk. The ends of the ray flowers are notched or toothed.

June—August

Habitat/Range: Prairies, dry open woods; primarily Ozark Region.

Remarks: The Mesquakie boiled the seeds and drank the brew. Some tribes applied the boiled seeds to painful areas of the body to relieve ailments such as rheumatism.

PLAINS COREOPSIS
Coreopsis tinctoria
Aster Family (Asteraceae)

Description: A multi-branched, annual plant 2–4' tall, with smooth stems and opposite leaves. The leaves are up to 4" long and divided into very narrow leaflets. The flower heads are about 1" across, numerous, on long stalks, and very showy. The 7–9 petal-like ray flowers are yellow with a prominent reddish spot at the base and are toothed at the tip. The central disk is reddish-brown.

June — September

Habitat/Range: Idle land, disturbed soil, fields, ditches, roadsides; statewide.

Remarks: Also called Golden Coreopsis, this plant is a popular ornamental in gardens and in restoration sites where quick color is desired. The Lakotas boiled the flowers in water, which turned red, and used it as a beverage. The plant tops were used in a tea to strengthen the blood. The Mesquakies boiled the plant to make a drink to treat internal pains and bleeding.

TALL COREOPSIS
Coreopsis tripteris
Aster Family (Asteraceae)

Description: Tall, stout stems, sometimes with a whitish coating, up to a height of 8' but typically shorter. The leaves are opposite, with stalks, and divided into 3 (sometimes 5), narrow leaflets. The flower heads are on several slender stalks at the top of the plant. Each head is about 1½" across, with 6–10 yellow, petal-like ray flowers surrounding a brown central disk. The flower heads have an anise scent.

June — October

Habitat/Range: Prairies, dry open woods; statewide.

Remarks: Also called Tall Tickseed. The Mesquakies boiled the plant to make a drink to treat internal pains and bleeding.

PINEWEED
Hypericum gentianoides
St. John's Wort Family (Clusiaceae)

Description: Looking like a pine seedling (hence the common name), this annual plant has a multi-branched, wiry stem, with a powdery blue-green to reddish color, and grows up to 12" tall. The scale-like leaves are extremely small, opposite, and hug the stem. The flowers are stalkless, singly attached at the stem nodes, with 5 tiny yellow petals that open on bright, sunny days.

June–October

Habitat/Range: Sandy soil in woods and prairies, sandstone glades, on bluffs; nearly statewide but absent in the Delta Region.

Remarks: Adapted to living in sandy soil, often over bedrock, Pineweed minimizes water loss by having scale-like leaves. Pineweed is one of the smallest of 14 species in the genus *Hypericum* in Arkansas.

LONGLEAF GROUNDCHERRY
Physalis longifolia
Nightshade Family (Solanaceae)

Description: An upright, branching plant, up to 1' tall, with sparsely hairy to smooth stems and leaves. The leaves are alternate along the stem, up to 2" long and about 1" across. The flowers dangle from slender stalks that arise from the base of the leaf stalks and the stem. The yellow, bell-shaped flowers are about ½–¾" across with purple blotches inside. The papery, lantern-shaped fruit is from 1–1½" long.

June–August

Habitat/Range: Disturbed woods, fields, pastures; in scattered counties throughout the state.

Remarks: There are 12 species of groundcherry in Arkansas, with 2 not being native to the state. The potentially toxic groundcherries have been useful for treating difficult urination, fevers, and inflammation, and are being researched for antitumor activity.

PARTRIDGE PEA
Chamaechrista fasciculata
Pea Family (Fabaceae)

Description: An annual plant, up to 2' tall, with alternate leaves, each divided into about 20 pairs of leaflets. The leaflets are narrow, less than 1" long, and rounded at both ends, with a small bristle-like tip. Near the middle of each leaf stalk there is a small, saucer-shaped gland. There are 1–6 flowers, up to 1½" across, on slender stalks that emerge at the axil of the leaf and stem. There are 5 yellow petals, with 3 slightly smaller than the other 2. There is a tinge of red at the base of each petal. There are 10 yellow to dark red stamens.

June—October

Habitat/Range: Prairies, savannas, roadsides, fields, disturbed ground; statewide.

Remarks: Partridge Pea was formerly known as *Cassia fasciculata*. Cherokees and settlers used the root for treating fevers, cramps, heart ailments, and constipation. A closely related species, Sensitive Partridge Pea, *Chamaecrista (Cassia) nictitans*, has smaller flowers (less than ¾" wide), 5 stamens, and a short stalk below the saucer-shaped gland on the leaf stalk. Occurs in edge of woods, fields, roadsides; statewide.

GOLDEN ASTER
Chrysopsis pilosa
Aster Family (Asteraceae)

Description: A branched annual plant with densely spreading hairs along the leaves and stems. The leaves are numerous, narrow, less than 3" long and ½" wide, toothed to mostly smooth along the margins, and without a stalk. The bright golden yellow flower heads are several, hairy and less than 1" across.

June—September

Habitat/Range: Sandy disturbed areas, glades, idle fields; nearly statewide, less common in the Delta Region.

Remarks: Formerly known as *Bradburnia pilosa* and *Heterotheca pilosa*.

WILD SENNA
Senna marilandica
Pea Family (Fabaceae)

Description: A perennial plant, often with a single stem up to 6' tall, with large, alternate leaves. The leaves are divided into 8–12 pairs of leaflets, each about 2" long and 1" wide, with small, bristle-like points at the tips. The flowers vary from being numerous on branched clusters to only 1–4 on stalks emerging from the junction of a leaf and stem. Each flower is about 1" across, with 5 narrow yellow petals that are often curled and 10 brownish-red stamens.

July—August

Habitat/Range: Moist areas along streams, bottomland woods along streams, edges of woods, open fields, and thickets; nearly statewide, less common in the Delta and Gulf Coastal Plain Region.

Remarks: Wild Senna was formerly called *Cassia marilandica*. The Mesquakies ate the seeds, softened by soaking, as a mucilaginous medicine for sore throat. The Cherokees used the bruised root moistened with water for dressing sores. They also used the root in a tea to cure fevers and as a laxative.

EVENING PRIMROSE
Oenothera biennis
Primrose Family (Onagraceae)

Description: A biennial with a stout, sometimes hairy stem tinged with red, as are parts of the older leaves, up to 7' tall. The leaves are alternate, lance-shaped, pointed at the tip, hairy on both sides, toothed along the margin, and up to 6" long. The flowers are numerous along a long column, with yellow petals that open to 2½" across. The 4 yellow petals have a shallow notch at the end. There are 8 yellow stamens.

June—September

Habitat/Range: Prairies, fields, pastures, roadsides, disturbed ground; statewide.

Remarks: The flowers open in the evening and close by midmorning on sunny days. The flowers emit a creosote smell that attracts night-flying sphinx moths. Native American Indians ate the seeds and the first-year roots (the second-year roots are too woody). After this plant was introduced to Europe from North America in the early 1600s, Europeans ate its roots and put the young shoots into salads. The entire plant was prepared and used to treat whooping cough, hiccups, and asthma.

DOTTED MONARDA
Monarda punctata
Mint Family (Lamiaceae)

Description: The pinkish-purple bracts obscure the dull yellow flowers of this plant, which reaches a height to 3', with a finely hairy stem and toothed, opposite leaves on short stalks. The leaves are about 3½" long and up to 1" wide. The flowers are arranged in whorls; with 2–5 whorls stacked one above the other, separated by a whorl of pinkish purple bracts. Each yellow, tubular flower is about 1" long and peppered with dark spots. The lower lip has 3 lobes.

June—September

Habitat/Range: Sandy fields and woods, roadsides; known from the southern, north central and northwestern parts of the state.

Remarks: Also known as Horsemint. Native American Indians used leaf tea for colds, fevers, flu, stomach cramps, coughs, and bowel ailments. Historically, doctors used this mint as a stimulant and diuretic.

YELLOW FRINGED ORCHID
Platanthera ciliaris
Orchid Family (Orchidaceae)

Description: A plant from 1½–3' tall with a column of showy orange flowers. The leaves are alternate, with 2–5 leaves up to 12" long that are reduced in size progressively upward along the stem. The flowers are clustered at the top of the stem with 30 to 60 bright orange flowers. The lower lip is narrow and deeply fringed along the margin. There is a slender spur that protrudes from the base of the flower.

July—August

Habitat/Range: Moist or dry sites in sandy soil, near springs, low pineland areas; scattered counties across the state but absent in the Delta Region and the northern counties except for Clay County.

Remarks: The flowers are typically orange and not yellow as the common name implies. The Cherokee made a tea of the plant parts for treating headaches. The Seminole used the root for treating snakebites.

WOODLAND GOLDENROD
Solidago petiolaris
Aster Family (Asteraceae)

Description: Erect plants to 3' tall, with stems smooth below and hairy on the upper part. The stem leaves are thick, firm, lance-shaped to nearly oval, ¼–1" wide, somewhat toothed and hairy along the margins, with the upper surface hairy. The showy flower heads are clustered in the upper leaf axils to form a long, narrow column. The heads have 5–6 yellow, petal-like ray flowers.

July–October

Habitat/Range: Dry, rocky, open woods; nearly statewide, uncommon in the Delta Region.

Remarks: The larger flower heads and long ray flowers of woodland goldenrod are quite showy. A similar goldenrod, Buckley's Goldenrod, *Solidago buckleyi*, has thin, not thick, leaves, 1–2" wide, with the margins sharply toothed.

OLD FIELD GOLDENROD
Solidago nemoralis
Aster Family (Asteraceae)

Description: The stems vary from arching to upright, growing up to 2½' tall. Dense, short, gray hairs on the stems and leaves give the plant a gray-green appearance. The basal leaves are large and present at the time of flowering. The stem leaves are progressively smaller towards the top of the stem. The flower heads are densely packed on the tops of short branches. Each head is less than ¼" across with 5–9 yellow, petal-like ray flowers.

July–November

Habitat/Range: Prairies, dry open woods, pastures, old fields, and along roadsides; nearly statewide, less common in the Gulf Coastal Plain Region.

Remarks: Also called Gray Goldenrod. The upright form is easy to identify at a distance by its slightly bent tip. There are 34 species of goldenrods in Arkansas.

GOLDENGLOW
Rudbeckia laciniata
Aster Family (Asteraceae)

Description: A large plant, up to 9' tall, with a smooth whitish stem that branches near the top. The leaves are alternate, on long stalks, large, up to 10" long and 6" wide, deeply divided into 3–7 segments, and often have teeth along the margins. The flower heads have 6–10 narrow, golden yellow, petal-like ray flowers that angle downward. The rays surround a green central disk.

July—September

Habitat/Range: Low, wet woodlands and along streams; Ozark Region and a few Ouachita Region counties.

Remarks: Native American Indians used root tea for indigestion, and a mixture of flowers from goldenglow, blue cohosh, and blue giant hyssop applied to burns. They also cooked and ate spring greens for "good health."

SWEET CONEFLOWER
Rudbeckia subtomentosa
Aster Family (Asteraceae)

Description: Plants up to 6' tall, branched near the top, often with dense short hairs along the upper stem. The stem leaves are alternate with short stalks or stalkless, have large teeth along the margins, and are often covered with soft, dense hairs. The leaves, at least on the lower part of the stem, are divided into 3 deep lobes. The flower heads are on long, individual stalks, with each head up to 3" wide. The heads have 6–20, yellow, petal-like ray flowers surrounding a dome-shaped, brown central disk.

July—September

Habitat/Remarks: Open woods, prairies, thickets, banks of streams; occasional throughout the state except for the Delta Region.

Remarks: The common name comes from the flower's anise scent. Other common names are Fragrant Coneflower and Sweet Black-Eyed Susan.

CUP PLANT
Silphium perfoliatum
Aster Family (Asteraceae)

Description: Large plants, branching near the top to 8' tall with stout, square stems. The large upper leaves are cupped around the stem tight enough to hold rainwater. The leaves have wavy margins, large teeth, and are rough to the touch on both sides. The flower heads are at the tops of branches, numerous, and up to 3" across. Each head has 20–30 yellow, petal-like ray flowers surrounding a yellow central disk.

July—September

Habitat/Range: Moist areas along borders of streams, floodplains, roadsides; scattered counties in the northern half of the state.

Remarks: The Omahas and Poncas used the root as a smoke treatment, inhaling the fumes for head colds, nerve pains, and rheumatism. Also, the resinous sap that exudes from the stem was chewed as a gum to help prevent vomiting. This plant is also known as Carpenter's Weed because of its straight, square stem.

PRAIRIE DOCK
Silphium terebinthinaceum
Aster Family (Asteraceae)

Description: A tall, wand-like stem rises up to 10' above a cluster of large, spade-shaped basal leaves. The leaves are up to 16" long, very rough in texture, with a heart-shaped base and coarse teeth along the margins. The flower heads occur at the top of a smooth, shiny, nearly leafless stalk. The heads are 2–3" across with 12–20, yellow, petal-like ray flowers surrounding a yellow central disk.

July—September

Habitat/Range: Prairies, glades, roadsides; northern Ozark Region.

Remarks: Native American Indians used a root tea as a general tonic for feebleness and to expel intestinal worms. Leaf tea was used for coughs, lung ailments, and asthma.

COMPASS PLANT
Silphium laciniatum
Aster Family (Asteraceae)

Description: A tall, stout plant, up to 8' in height, with very large basal leaves sometimes over 1' long. The deeply cut basal leaves are commonly oriented in a north-south direction, hence, the common name. The stem leaves are smaller, alternate, and clasping at the base. The flower heads are along the upper part of a single, long, hairy stalk. Each head is up to 4½" across with 20–30, yellow, petal-like ray flowers surrounding a yellow central disk.

July—September

Habitat/Range: Prairies, open areas; nearly statewide, absent from eastern counties in the Delta Region.

Remarks: The Omaha and Ponca avoided camping wherever compass plants grew abundantly because they believed the plants attracted lightning. They sometimes burned the dried root during an electrical storm to act as a charm against a lightning strike. The root was used by Native American Indians and early settlers to alleviate head colds or pains. The dried leaves were used for treating dry, obstinate coughs and intermittent fevers.

ROSINWEED
Silphium integrifolium
Aster Family (Asteraceae)

Description: Often occurring in colonies, these stout, mostly smooth plants grow up to 6' tall. The leaves are opposite but may be slightly alternate or even whorled. The leaves lack stalks, have a rough, sandpapery texture, and vary in shape from narrow and long to broad and round; teeth may be present along the margins. The flower heads are about 3" wide, with 15–35, yellow, petal-like ray flowers surrounding a yellow central disk.

July—August

Habitat/Range: Prairies, dry open woods, glades; nearly statewide.

Remarks: Like others in the genus *Silphium*, rosinweed has a fragrant resin while in flower, which was chewed as gum by Native American Indian children. A similar species, Starry Rosinweed, *Silphium astericus*, has alternate leaves and stems with coarse spreading hairs; the flowering period and habitat is similar to rosinweed; nearly statewide but absent from the Delta Region.

BRISTLY SUNFLOWER
Helianthus hirsutus
Aster Family (Asteraceae)

Description: Often in colonies, this plant grows up to 4' tall, with stiff hairs along the stem and leaves. The upper leaves are mostly opposite, short-stalked, with a sandpapery texture and small, widely spaced teeth along the margin. The leaves have 1 central vein and 2 side veins. The flower heads are up to 3" across with 8–15, yellow, petal-like ray flowers surrounding a yellow central disk.

July—September

Habitat/Range: Open woods, thickets, roadsides; statewide.

Remarks: The heads and upper stems are often nipped by white-tailed deer in mid-to late summer. A similar species, Woodland Sunflower, *Helianthus divaricatus*, has leaves and stalks lacking hairs, the leaves lack stalks or nearly so; open woods, fields; common throughout the state.

DOWNY SUNFLOWER
Helianthus mollis
Aster Family (Asteraceae)

Description: Usually growing in colonies, these grayish-green plants reach a height of 4'. The stem and leaves have dense gray hairs that can be rubbed off. The leaves are opposite, stiff, up to 6" long and 3" wide, with rounded to notched, stalkless bases. The flower heads are on long stalks, with each head 2½–4" across. There are up to 30, yellow, petal-like ray flowers surrounding a yellow central disk.

July—September

Habitat/Range: Woodlands, prairies; nearly statewide, less common in the Delta and Gulf Coastal Plain regions.

Remarks: Also called Ashy Sunflower for the gray-colored leaves that are similar in appearance to ash-covered leaves after a fire. Downy Sunflower is sometimes mistaken for Rosinweed, but the latter has leaves with a rough, sandpapery surface and lacks the dense gray hairs.

SAWTOOTH SUNFLOWER
Helianthus grosseserratus
Aster Family (Asteraceae)

Description: A tall, many-branched, colony-forming sunflower, up to 12' in height, often with several smooth stems emerging from a single base. The leaves are alternate, large, about 8" long and 2" wide, tapering at each end, with hairs on the underside. The margins have teeth, hence the common name. The flower heads are numerous, up to 3½" across, with 10–20, yellow, petal-like ray flowers surrounding a yellow disk.

July – October

Habitat/Range: Prairies, edge of woods, roadsides; in scattered counties across the state.

Remarks: The Mesquakies mashed the flowers and applied them to burns. In the Southwest, Zuni medicine men cured rattlesnake bites by chewing the fresh or dried root and then sucking the snakebite wound. A similar species, Maximilian Sunflower, *Helianthus maximilianii*, has white, densely hairy stems and leaves curved and folded along the middle; naturalized in old fields and along roadsides; native to the western United States; reported from a few counties in Arkansas.

COMMON SUNFLOWER
Helianthus annuus
Aster Family (Asteraceae)

Description: A robust annual, with branching stems often up to 9' tall. The stems are stout and coarsely hairy. The leaves are alternate, on long stalks, large, up to 10" long, heart-shaped, with sandpapery surfaces and coarse teeth along the margins. The flower heads are large, 4–10" across, with 20 or more yellow, petal-like ray flowers surrounding a purplish-brown central disk 1" or more in diameter.

July – October

Habitat/Range: Disturbed ground, pastures, roadsides; native to western United States; occasional throughout the state.

Remarks: Originally cultivated by North American Indians, the sunflower seeds were used as food and a source for oil. They used the oil as hair grease and as a warm rub for rheumatic joints. The roots were baked or used in a tea for respiratory ailments, rheumatism, bruises, contusions, snakebites, and malaria. Today, cultivated varieties with larger seed heads and seeds are used to produce oil, food, and birdseed.

JERUSALEM ARTICHOKE
Helianthus tuberosus
Aster Family (Asteraceae)

Description: This stout, reddish-stemmed sunflower is up to 7' tall and covered with rough hairs. The leaves are opposite on the lower stem and usually alternate on the upper part. Rough sandpapery hairs are also on the leaves, which are up to 10" long, lance-shaped, and stalked. The flower heads are on individual stalks at the tops of branches, with each head up to 4" across. There are 10–20, yellow, petal-like ray flowers surrounding a yellow central disk.

August—October

Habitat/Range: Moist ground bordering woods, thickets, and prairie draws, and along streams and roadsides; occasional in the northern two-thirds of the state.

Remarks: When the roots of this plant grow in good soil, they form edible tubers that have been grown and marketed commercially for centuries. The tubers are cooked as potatoes, sliced and added to salads, and even pickled.

SWAMP AGRIMONY
Agrimonia parviflora
Rose Family (Rosaceae)

Description: Stout, hairy stems with wand-like branches, up to 6' tall. The leaves are alternate, stalked, and divided into 11–17 leaflets. The leaflets are hairy, with many teeth along the margins. The flowers are arranged alternately along the stem, small, about ¼" across, with 5 yellow petals. The flowers develop into bur-like fruits with hooked bristles that easily cling to clothes and hair.

August—September

Habitat/Range: Wet ground in prairies, woods, marshes, thickets, and along streams; scattered counties, absent from the Gulf Coastal Plain Region

Remarks: An herbal tea made from the whole plant has been used to stop internal bleeding; also used for diarrhea, inflammation of the gall bladder, jaundice, and gout. Another species, Beaked Agrimony, *Agrimonia rostellata*, has leaves divided into 5–9 leaflets; scattered counties throughout the state.

WILD LETTUCE
Lactuca canadensis
Aster Family (Asteraceae)

Description: Often multi-branched at the tips, this smooth-stemmed biennial grows to 8' tall and has milky orange to tan sap. The leaves are alternate, stalkless, and up to 12" long and 6" wide (but usually smaller). The leaves vary from deeply lobed to rounded. The numerous flower heads are small and occur in large branching clusters. Each head is less than ½" across with 15–22 yellow or dull orange, petal-like ray flowers surrounding a yellow central disk. The flower and seed heads resemble miniature dandelions.

July—September

Habitat/Range: Dry open woods, pastures, disturbed soil; statewide.

Remarks: Native American Indians used a root tea for treating diarrhea, heart and lung ailments, hemorrhaging, and nausea, and to relieve pain. The milky sap from the stems was used for treating skin eruptions. The bruised leaves were applied directly to insect stings. Both Native American Indians and settlers used a leaf tea to hasten milk flow after childbirth. Another species, Prickly Lettuce, *Lactuca serriola*, (formerly *L. scariola*), has margins of the leaves with deep lobes and prickly teeth. Native to Europe, it occurs in disturbed soil; scattered across the state.

YELLOW FALSE FOXGLOVE
Aureolaria grandiflora
Figwort Family (Scrophulariaceae)

Description: A shrubby plant, with dense short hairs on the branches, up to 3' tall. The leaves are opposite, short-stalked, with the lower leaves deeply cut; the upper leaves are much reduced with small teeth or rounded along the margins. The flowers are large, up to 3" long, yellow, with a long tube and 5 lobes, and emerge from the leaf axils.

July—September

Habitat/Range: Dry woodland; scattered counties across the state.

Remarks: A closely related species, Smooth False Foxglove, *Aureolaria flava*, lacks hairs on the stems, leaves, and flowers; has smaller flowers about 1½" long; found in rocky woods; northern half of the state and southcentral counties. Another species, Fern-leaved False Foxglove, *Aureolaria pectinata* (formerly *A. pedicularia*), has finely cut fernlike leaves and gland-tipped hairs on the 1½" long flower tube; an annual; found in sandy woods; scattered counties in the Ozark and Ouachita Mountain regions.

BLUE-STEM GOLDENROD
Solidago caesia
Aster Family (Asteraceae)

Description: A graceful, arching, wand-like plant, up to 3' long, with often bluish-gray stems with a whitish coating. The leaves are alternate, smooth, stalkless, lance-shaped, 2–5" long, up to 1" wide, and slightly hairy above. The flower heads are small and appear in tufts along the stem, emerging from the leaf axils. The heads have 3–5, yellow, petal-like ray flowers.

August—October

Habitat/Range: Moist or rocky woods; nearly statewide, less common in the Delta Region, except for Crowley's Ridge.

Remarks: The graceful arching yellow wands of Blue-Stem Goldenrod are a welcome sight when walking through the woods. The Latin species name, *caesia*, means "bluish gray," hence, the common name.

ELM-LEAVED GOLDENROD
Solidago ulmifolia
Aster Family (Asteraceae)

Description: A single-stemmed, smooth plant to 4' tall, with widely spreading branches and leaves similar in appearance to elm leaves, hence, the common name. The leaves are alternate, coarsely toothed along the margins, thin, hairy underneath, with broad stalks on the lower leaves, which fall away by flowering time. The lower leaves are up to 5" long and 2" wide, with the upper leaves much reduced in size. The flower heads are on long, arching branches, with crowded heads. Each head has 3–5 yellow, petal-like ray flowers.

August—October

Habitat/Range: Dry open woods; scattered across the state.

Remarks: Goldenrods, in general, have been unfairly blamed for the allergic reaction of hay fever. It is the wind-blown pollen of the ragweeds that is the primary cause for late-summer hay fever. The pollen of goldenrods is distributed by bees, fall wasps, and beetles and is not wind-blown.

TALL GOLDENROD
Solidago altissima
Aster Family (Asteraceae)

Description: A large, hairy-stemmed goldenrod, up to 7' tall, with many alternate leaves, the largest of which occur along the middle part of the stem. The leaves are up to 6" long and 1¼" wide, with some teeth along the margins, especially toward the tip. The upper side of the leaf is rough, while the underside is hairy, with 3 prominent veins. The flower heads are arranged in a pyramidal cluster with the heads all occurring on the upper side of branches. Each head is about ¼" across, with 10–15 yellow, petal-like ray flowers. The circle of bracts below each flower head is more than ⅛" high.

August—October

Habitat/Range: Disturbed soil in prairies, fields, pastures, roadsides; common throughout the state.

Remarks: Native American Indians made a tea from this plant to treat kidney problems; they also chewed crushed flowers for sore throats. Of the goldenrods, this species is the most commonly infected by the goldenrod gall. This round swelling along the stem is caused by certain moths and flies that lay an egg in the stem. The larva hatches and secretes a chemical that causes the plant tissue to swell around it; the larva then eats the tissue and overwinters in its protected home, emerging in the spring as an adult. A similar species, Canada Goldenrod, *Solidago canadensis*, begins flowering one month earlier, has 3–7, yellow, petal-like ray flowers, and its circle of bracts below each flower head less than ⅛" high. It occupies similar habitats and range as tall goldenrod.

DRUMMOND'S GOLDENROD
Solidago drummondii
Aster Family (Asteraceae)

Description: Usually arching over cliffs, the soft-haired stems grow 1½–3' long. The basal and lowermost stem leaves are typically absent at flowering time. The upper stem leaves are broadest in the middle, 1½–3½" long and 1–3" wide, short-stalked, with 3 veins along the leaf, and fine, dense hairs beneath. The flower heads are at the end of the arching stem on short branches. Each head has 3–7, yellow, petal-like ray flowers.

September—October

Habitat/Range: Ledges and cliffs along rivers; scattered across the state.

Remarks: This is the only goldenrod that is typically found growing on the face of cliffs; it is also called Cliff Goldenrod.

YELLOW IRONWEED
Verbesina alternifolia
Aster Family (Asteraceae)

Description: A tall, coarse, branching plant, up to 7' tall, with narrow wings of leafy tissue extending down the stems from the leaf bases. The leaves are alternate, rough, lance-shaped to broadest in the middle, up to 10" long, with toothed edges. The flower heads have 2–8, yellow, drooping, petal-like ray flowers that often vary in size, surrounding a yellow rounded disk.

August—October

Habitat/Range: Low, moist ground in wooded valleys along streams; nearly statewide although less common in the Delta and Gulf Coastal Plain regions.

Remarks: In September, Yellow Ironweed often forms large, dense patches of yellow in bottomland forests.

TICKSEED SUNFLOWER
Bidens aristosa
Aster Family (Asteraceae)

Description: A smooth, much-branched, annual, growing to 3' tall but sometimes to a height of 6' on rich soils. The leaves are opposite, stalked, and divided into 5–11 narrow, coarsely toothed leaflets. The flower heads are on individual stalks, with each head about 1½–2½" across with 8 golden yellow, petal-like ray flowers surrounding a yellow central disk. The seeds resemble ticks and have 2 barbed, needle-like teeth that attach to clothing and hair.

August—November

Habitat/Range: Wet ground in prairies, low cultivated and idle fields, ditches, and along roadsides; statewide.

Remarks: Also called Swamp Marigold and Beggar's Ticks. The Cherokees used a similar species of *Bidens* in leaf tea to expel worms. The leaves were chewed for sore throats. Seeds of *Bidens* species are eaten by ducks, bobwhite quail, and some songbirds; the plants are eaten by cottontail rabbits. There are 9 species of *Bidens* in Arkansas.

GUM PLANT
Grindelia lanceolata
Aster Family (Asteraceae)

Description: This multi-branched, reddish-stemmed plant grows to 3' tall, with sticky or gummy bracts resembling round burs below the flower heads. The leaves are upturned, alternate, smooth, up to 4" long and 1" wide, with the tip ending abruptly to a point, and scattered bristle-like teeth along the margins. The flower heads are about 1½" across with 20–30 yellow, slender, petal-like ray flowers that are upturned, forming a cup. The yellow disk at the center of the flower head is flat.

August—October

Habitat/Range: Glades, open land, pastures, and along roadsides; mostly Ozark Region and some southwestern counties.

Remarks: Native American Indians, made a root tea for treating liver ailments. Crushed and soaked plants were applied to relieve the pain and swelling of rheumatic joints. An extraction has been used as a wash to relieve the skin rash of poison ivy.

SNEEZEWEED
Helenium autumnale
Aster Family (Asteraceae)

Description: A very leafy-stemmed plant to 5' tall, with branching near the top. The stem has narrow wings of leafy tissue extending downward along the stem from the leaf bases. The leaves are alternate, up to 6" long and 1½" wide, broadest near the middle, and tapering at both ends. There are a few small, widely spaced teeth along the margins. The flower heads have 10–20 drooping, yellow, petal-like ray flowers surrounding a rounded yellow central disk. The ray flowers have 3 lobes along their edges.

August—November

Habitat/Range: Wet to moist ground in prairies, marshes, fens, along streams, and openings in low woods; mostly in the northern ¼ of the state and a few southern counties.

Remarks: The Mesquakies dried the flower heads and used them as an inhalant to treat head colds. To reduce fever, the Comanches soaked sneezeweed stems in water and bathed the patient's body. The dried flower heads were reportedly used as snuff by early settlers. Sheep, cattle, and horses have been poisoned by eating large amounts of the plant, especially the seed heads.

Red/Orange Flowers

This section includes red and orange flowers.
Since red flowers grade into both pink flowers and purple flowers,
those sections should also be checked.

Indian Pink, page 137

INDIAN PAINTBRUSH
Castilleja coccinea
Figwort Family (Scrophulariaceae)

Description: A biennial plant, with single, hairy stems typically about 12" tall. The leaves are alternate, stalkless, yellowish-green, hairy, and divided into 3 narrow lobes. The flowers are concentrated in a dense cluster at the top of the stem that elongates as the flowers open. The brilliant red color does not come from the flower but from leafy bracts just under each flower. The inconspicuous flower is greenish-yellow, tubular, and up to 1½" long. Although typically red, Indian Paintbrush is sometimes yellow.

April—June

Habitat/Range: Prairies, glades; primarily found in the Ozarks and a few Gulf Coastal Plain counties.

Remarks: Typical of many members of this family, Indian Paintbrush is a partial parasite, sometimes attaching to roots of other plants to obtain nourishment. Native American Indians used weak flower tea for rheumatism and as a contraceptive; also as a secret love charm in food, and as a poison "to destroy your enemies."

COLUMBINE
Aquilegia canadensis
Buttercup Family (Ranunculaceae)

Description: A smooth to slightly hairy plant with openly branching stems, up to 2' tall. The few basal leaves and lower stem leaves have long stalks, with clusters of 3 leaflets, with each leaflet having several lobes. The upper stem leaves have 3 leaflets on short stalks with lobed margins. The distinctive flowers are up to 2" long, nodding, and on slender curved stalks. The 5 triangular sepals are red, and the 5 petals have yellow blades that transcend into hollow red spurs that contain the nectar. Numerous stamens extend from the flower.

April—June

Habitat/Range: Moist rocky woods, ledges; primarily in the Ozarks, also a few Ouachita counties.

Remarks: The flower is pollinated by hummingbirds, moths, and butterflies, which all have long tongues in order to reach the nectar. Omaha and Ponca men rubbed pulverized seeds on their palms as a love potion before shaking hands with a loved one. This practice also was supposed to make them more persuasive when speaking to a council. The root was chewed or taken as a weak tea for diarrhea, stomach troubles, as a diuretic, and to stop uterine bleeding.

FIRE PINK
Silene virginica
Pink Family (Caryophyllaceae)

Description: A plant up to 2' tall, with several spreading, hairy, sticky stems. The basal leaves are long, narrow, 1½–4" long and ¼–¾" wide, and stalked, while the stem leaves are opposite, narrow, stalkless, and up to 3" long. The flowers, up to 1½" across, are on long stems that arise above the upper leaves. The brilliant red flowers have 5 narrow petals, with a notch at each tip.

April–June

Habitat/Range: Dry, open, rocky woods; Ozarks, Ouachitas, and Crowley's Ridge.

Remarks: A common name for the genus *Silene* is Catchfly, which refers to the sticky, insect-trapping hairs on the stem and the cylindrical tube below the petals called the calyx.

CRIMSON CLOVER
Trifolium incarnatum
Pea Family (Fabaceae)

Description: A showy annual, from 1–4" tall with hairs flattened against the stem. The leaves are alternate, 3-parted, and downy, with leaflets from ½–1½" wide. The flowers are in an elongated cluster, 1–2" long. The flowers are crimson or scarlet and about ½" long.

April–June

Habitat/Range: Fields, open areas, roadsides; native to Eurasia; statewide.

Remarks: Crimson Clover, also known as Italian Clover, is native to most of Europe. It has been used as a ground cover planting to help stabilize and rebuild soil.

INDIAN PINK
Spigelia marilandica
Logania Family (Loganiaceae)

Description: Plants with smooth, square stems, up to 2' tall, with opposite leaves. The leaves are stalkless, broadest towards the base, with pointed tips, up to 4" long, and lack teeth along the margins. The flowers are showy, bright red with yellow inside and about 1½" long, tubular, with 5 sharp lobes that flare out.

April—June

Habitat/Range: Moist woods and wooded banks along streams; nearly statewide.

Remarks: Native American Indians used root tea to expel intestinal worms. The plant was also once used by physicians to treat worms, especially in children. Side effects include increased heart action, vertigo, convulsions, and possibly death.

FIREWHEEL
Gaillardia pulchella
Aster Family (Asteraceae)

Description: An annual or short-lived perennial up to 24" tall with freely branching, hairy stems. The leaves are alternate, 1–4" long, ¼–1" wide, either lacking teeth along the margins, or toothed, or lobed. The showy flower heads are 1–2" across with the ray flowers red or reddish-purple and yellow-tipped and the disk flowers purple.

April—November

Habitat/Range: Prairies, sandy soils, fields; Baxter, Columbia, Hempstead, Jefferson, Pulaski, and Sebastian counties.

Remarks: Also known as Indian Blanket, this showy wildflower is often planted as an ornamental in gardens. A similar species, Blanketflower, *Gaillardia aestivalis*, has yellow ray and disk flowers with the rays narrow at the base; the leaves are smaller; Gulf Coastal Plain and Delta regions; *July—October*

ORANGE DAY LILY
Hemerocallis fulva
Lily Family (Liliaceae)

Description: The leafless flower stalks are up to 5' tall and produce flowers that each last but a day. The leaves are at the base, narrow, up to 2' long, ½" wide, and pointed at the tip. The flowers are clustered at the top, orange with yellow centers, and up to 4" across. There are 3 slightly smaller sepals along with 3 petals, each with a yellow strip down the center. The 6 stamens are long and curve upward.

May—August

Habitat/Range: Along roadsides, homesites, waste ground; native to Europe and Asia; scattered across the state.

Remarks: The plants have been eaten in salads, as a cooked vegetable (sometimes as a substitute for asparagus), in fritters, and as a seasoning. In China, a root tea is used as a diuretic; also to treat jaundice, nosebleeds, and uterine bleeding. Recent Chinese reports warn that the roots and young leaf shoots are considered potentially toxic because the toxin accumulates in the body and adversely affects the eyes, even causing blindness in some cases. Their studies also warn that the roots contain colchicine, a carcinogen.

BUTTERFLY WEED
Asclepias tuberosa
Milkweed Family (Asclepiadaceae)

Description: Several stems may arise from a common base, giving the plant a bushy appearance, up to 2½' tall. The stems are covered with coarse spreading hairs and lack the milky latex sap that is typical of the milkweed family. The mostly alternate leaves are stalkless, about 4" long and 1" wide, widest in the middle and tapering at both ends, very hairy, and dark green. The flowers are in clusters at the tops of stems. The flowers vary from deep red to brilliant orange and pale yellow, with each flower less than ¾" long, with 5 reflexed petals below 5 erect hoods. The seedpods are about 6" long and ¾" thick, with fine hairs.

May—September

Habitat/Range: Prairies, dry open woods, old fields, roadsides; statewide.

Remarks: Also called Pleurisy Root because it was considered to be a cure for pleurisy, an inflammation of the covering of the lungs. Several tribes revered this plant as a healer. They used the leaves to induce vomiting, and the roots for treating dysentery, diarrhea, constipation, lung inflammations, rheumatism, fever, and pneumonia. The roots were also mashed and applied externally to bruises, swellings, and wounds. Butterfly Weed is appropriately named for its popularity with butterflies, especially the monarch butterfly. The larvae consume the leaves, while the adults feed on the nectar.

SPOTTED TOUCH-ME-NOT
Impatiens capensis
Jewelweed Family (Balsaminaceae)

Description: Annual plants growing to 5' tall, with branched stems that are somewhat weak and watery. The stems are pale green and translucent with leaves alternate, oval, thin, and bluish-green. The leaves are up to 3½" long, with long stalks and widely spaced teeth along the margins. The orange flowers are shaped like a cornucopia, up to 1¼" long, hanging on a slender stalk. The smaller end of the flower is a curved spur, which holds the nectar. The fruit is a slender capsule about 1" long, which splits and propels the seed when touched.

May—October

Habitat/Range: Moist to wet woodlands and banks of streams; statewide.

Remarks: Also called Jewel-Weed. The Potawatomi and settlers applied the juice of Touch-Me-Not to relieve the itch of poison ivy. Even today, the juice is used to relieve the burning sensation of Stinging Nettle, which often grows not far from Touch-Me-Not. The juice is also thought to neutralize the sap of poison ivy after contact. Livestock have been poisoned by eating large amounts of the fresh green plants.

LONG-HEADED CONEFLOWER
Ratibida columnifera
Aster Family (Asteraceae)

Description: Plants with single stems but more often in clusters, up to 2' tall. The leaves are up to 6" long and divided into narrow leaflets. There are from 4–11 drooping ray flowers that are red to reddish-brown with varying amounts of yellow towards the tip. Some petals can be all yellow. The flower column is cylindrical and contains numerous disk flowers that vary from yellow to red to purple.

June—October

Habitat/Range: Prairies, pinelands, open areas, roadsides; scattered widely across the state.

Remarks: Also known as Mexican Hat. Formerly called *Ratibida columnaris*. The Cheyenne made a tea from the leaves and stems and rubbed it on a rattlesnake bite to relieve the pain; also for treating areas affected by poison ivy rash.

BLACKBERRY LILY
Belamcanda chinensis
Iris Family (Iridaceae)

Description: A stout flower stalk, up to 3' tall, supports attractive orange flowers which each last but a day. The leaves are alternate, up to 12" long and 1" wide, clasping at the base, with parallel veins along the length of the blade. The flowers are clustered at the top of the stem. Each lily-like flower is up to 2" across, with the 3 sepals and 3 petals similar in shape and color. The fruit capsule splits open to reveal shiny black fleshy seeds resembling a blackberry.

June—August

Habitat/Range: Roadsides, rocky open woods, edges of cliffs, old homesites; native to Asia that was introduced as a garden plant and has escaped; northern part of the state.

Remarks: Although the flowers resemble lilies, the leaves along the stem are typical of irises. The orange rhizome distinguishes this iris from other irises.

TURK'S CAP LILY
Lilium michiganense
Lily Family (Liliaceae)

Description: A stately plant with a smooth, stout stem to 6' tall. The lower leaves are in whorls around the stem, and the upper leaves are alternate. The leaves are waxy and thick, up to 5" long, and tapering at both ends with margins and veins roughened. The flowers hang down from long stalks at the top of the stem. There are 1–12 flowers, depending upon the age of the plant and the growing conditions. Each flower is up to 3" wide, with 3 sepals and 3 petals similar in shape and color that strongly curve back. The orange petals sometimes fade to yellow on the underside and have many dark purple spots. The 6 stamens and the stigma show prominently. The anther is about ½" long.

June—July

Habitat/Range: Moist prairies and low woods; less than 15 counties scattered across the state.

Remarks: Also called Michigan Lily. Some tribes of Native American Indians used the roots to thicken soups, and others used a tea made from the bulbs to treat snakebites. When chewed to a paste, the flower was a treatment for spider bites. Another Turk's Cap Lily, *Lilium superbum*, has smooth leaf margins and veins, and anthers ¾—1" long; occurs in Arkansas, Logan, Pope, and Stone counties.

ROYAL CATCHFLY
Silene regia
Pink Family (Carophyllaceae)

Description: Slender plants, up to 5' tall, with generally smooth stems on the lower part but with sticky hairs near the top. The leaves are opposite, stalkless, with 10–20 pairs along the stem, each leaf is about 5" long, 3" wide, and slightly pointed at the tip. The flowers are crimson, with sticky hairs along the calyx, which is the cylindrical tube below the 5 narrow petals. There are 10 stamens extending beyond the petals.

July—August

Habitat/Range: Dry, open, rocky woods; a few northern Ozark counties and Hot Spring County.

Remarks: A very showy plant that is rare due to loss of habitat. The bright, tubular flowers attract humingbirds.

CARDINAL FLOWER
Lobelia cardinalis
Bellflower Family (Campanulaceae)

Description: The leafy stem is usually unbranched, up to 4' tall, with milky sap. The basal leaves have short stalks and are up to 6" long and about 2" wide. The stem leaves are alternate, stalkless, narrow, and less than 2" long. The leaves are widest in the middle and taper at both ends, with fine teeth along the margins. The crimson flowers are alternately arranged on individual stalks along a dense spike at the top of the plant. Each flower is about 1½" long with 2 lips; the upper lip has 2 small, narrow deeply cut lobes, and the lower lip has 3 deeply cut lobes. The 5 stamens and style are in a red central column.

August—October

Habitat/Range: Wet ground along borders of streams, spring branches, low wet woods, and ditches; statewide.

Remarks: The crimson, tubular flowers are a favorite with hummingbirds. The Mesquakie crushed and dried the plant and threw it to the winds to ward off approaching storms. It was also scattered over a grave as the final ceremonial rite. Other tribes used a root tea for stomachaches, intestinal worms, and as an ingredient in a love potion. Leaf tea was used for colds, nosebleeds, fevers, headaches, and rheumatism.

Pink Flowers

This section includes flowers ranging from pale pinkish white to vivid electric pink to pinkish magenta.
Since pink flowers grade into purple flowers or white flowers, those sections should also be checked.

Rose Pink, page 159

ROSE VERBENA
Glandularia canadensis
Vervain Family (Verbenaceae)

Description: A low spreading plant with hairy stems up to 2' long, often with several stems arising from the base and rooting at the lower nodes. The leaves are hairy, stalked, opposite, up to 4" long, and usually divided into 3 or more lobes with teeth along the margins. The flowers are arranged in a flat-topped cluster, with each flower about ½" wide and shaped like a narrow tube with 5 spreading lobes. The flowers vary from pink to rose-purple to magenta.

March—September

Habitat/Range: Sandy or rocky soils, open woods, edges of fields, pastures; nearly statewide, uncommon in the Delta Region.

Remarks: Also called Rose Vervain and formerly known as *Verbena canadensis*. The long flowering period is due to the plant's tendency to flower in the spring and then again in the fall if there is sufficient rain.

HENBIT
Lamium amplexicaule
Mint Family (Lamiaceae)

Description: A winter annual, with soft, square stems branching from the base, up to 10" tall. The leaves are opposite, roundish, bluntly toothed, and hairy above. The lower leaves have stalks; the upper leaves are up to 1" wide, lack stalks, and clasp the stem. The flowers are about ½" long, hairy, arising from clusters in the axils of the leaves, with long tubes that open to two lips (typical of the mint family), with the lips having red spots.

February—May; occasional in the fall

Habitat/Range: Disturbed soil in fields, lawns, and along roadsides; native to Europe, Asia, and Africa; statewide.

Remarks: Cropfields in spring are often carpeted with a dazzling pink from millions of henbit flowers. In the Old World, the seeds are eaten by chickens, hence the common name. The first flowers in late winter do not open, fertilizing themselves inside the closed tube of the flower.

PURPLE DEAD NETTLE
Lamium purpureum
Mint Family (Lamiaceae)

Description: A winter annual with soft, square stems branching from the base, up to 10" tall. The leaves are opposite, overlapping near the top, about 1" long, stalked, triangular-shaped, bluntly toothed, hairy above, and often purplish. The flowers are slightly paler than Henbit but are otherwise similar: about ½" long, hairy, arising from clusters in the axils of the leaves, with long tubes that open to two lips (typical of the mint family), with the lips having red spots.

March—May; occasional in the fall

Habitat/Range: Disturbed soil in fields, lawns, and along roadsides; native to Europe, Asia, and Africa; statewide.

Remarks: Although the flowers are identical to those of Henbit, the triangular, overlapping leaves of dead nettle tend to hide some of the flower color. The overall display is certainly not as showy as its close relative. The nettle-like leaves lack a "sting," hence the common name.

WILD GERANIUM
Geranium maculatum
Geranium Family (Geraniaceae)

Description: The stems are hairy and sometimes branched, up to 1½' tall. The basal leaves are on long stalks, hairy, about 5" across and divided into 5–7 lobes with prominent teeth along the margins. The stem leaves are few, usually 1 opposite pair, hairy, with short stalks and smaller than the basal leaves. The flowers are in clusters at the top of stems, up to 1½" across, with 5 pink to rose-lavender petals with fine veins.

April—May

Habitat/Range: Moist woods, streamsides, roadbanks; nearly statewide, less common in the Delta and Coastal Plain regions.

Remarks: Wild Geranium is considered an astringent—a substance that causes contraction of the tissues and stops bleeding. The Chippewas dried and powdered the roots to provide a treatment for mouth sores, especially in children. Both Chippewa and Ottawa tribes made a tea of the plant for treating diarrhea. The Mesquakie brewed a root tea for toothache and painful nerves, and mashed the roots for treating hemorrhoids.

SHOOTING STAR
Dodecatheon meadia
Primrose Family (Primulaceae)

Description: The leaves spread out from the base of the plant, which sends a flower stalk up to 2' tall. The basal leaves are smooth, up to 8" long and 3" wide, gradually tapering to a stalk. The flowers are clustered at the top of a smooth stem on numerous arching stalks, each ending in a single drooping flower. Each flower has 5 petals that bend back, resembling a fanciful tail of a shooting star. The petals vary in color from white to dark pink to lavender. The 5 stamens, with their dark brown bases, are held together to form a beaklike cone. The flower stalks become upright as fruits develop. The fruit capsules are dark reddish-brown, with thick, woody walls.

April—June

Habitat/Range: Woods, prairies, shaded ledges of bluffs; Ozarks, Ouachitas, and the Grand Prairie of the Delta region.

Remarks: Flowers of Shooting Star have a fragrance similar to the odor of grape juice. Pollination is by bumblebees, which are strong enough to pry open the beaklike cone. Another, French's Shooting Star, *Dodecatheon frenchii*, has leaves broadest below the middle and abruptly ending at a distinct stalk; found at the base of sandstone cliffs; Cleburne and Newton counties.

VIOLET WOOD SORREL
Oxalis violaceae
Wood Sorrel Family (Oxalidaceae)

Description: Small plants up to 6" tall with numerous 3-parted leaves arising from the base on stalks. The leaflets are slightly to deeply folded with small notches at the tip, often with spots or blotches of purple on the upper surface, and often solid purple underneath. The flower stems extend past the leaves, with several individually stalked flowers at the top. Each flower is about ½" across, with 5 pink petals.

April—June; also September—November

Habitat/Range: Dry, rocky woods, prairies, glades, idle fields, along roadsides; statewide.

Remarks: The plant parts contain a sour watery juice from which the name "sorrel" is derived, which is Old German for "sour." Native American Indians used powdered leaves boiled in water to expel intestinal worms. The plant was also used to reduce fevers and to increase urine flow.

DOWNY PHLOX
Phlox pilosa
Phlox Family (Polemoniaceae)

Description: Hairy, usually single-stemmed to 2' tall, with widely spaced pairs of opposite, stalkless leaves. The leaves are hairy, up to 3" long and ½" wide, broadest at the base, and gradually tapering to pointed tips. The pink-to-purple flowers are grouped into loosely branched clusters. Each flower is about ¾" across, with a long tube and 5 rounded lobes.

April—July

Habitat/Range: Dry, open, rocky woods, glades, prairies; nearly statewide, less common in the Delta Region.

Remarks: Sometimes Downy Phlox is found with white flowers and pink centers. The Mesquakie made a tea of the leaves and used it as a wash for treating eczema. They also used the root mixed with several unspecified plants as part of a love potion.

GOAT'S RUE
Tephrosia virginiana
Pea Family (Fabaceae)

Description: A small plant, up to 2' tall, with one to several hairy stems emerging from the base. The leaves are alternate, hairy, and divided into as many as 15 pairs of leaflets, with a single leaflet at the tip. Each leaflet is up to 1¼" long and ⅜" wide, with a small bristle at the tip. The dense hairs give the plant a gray cast. The flowers are in dense clusters at the tops of stems, with each flower about ¾" long and consisting of a spreading pale yellow upper petal and 2 pink side petals that flank a keel-like lip. The fruits are narrow, whitish, hairy, and about 2" long.

April—June

Habitat/Range: Dry woods, open areas; Statewide.

Remarks: Native American Indians and early settlers made a tea from the roots to treat intestinal parasites. Cherokee women washed their hair in it, believing the toughness of the roots would transfer to their hair and prevent it from falling out. Several tribes used the root, which contains rotenone, to stun fish. The plant was fed to goats by settlers in an effort to increase milk production. Some early ball players rubbed their hands, arms, and legs with goat's rue to toughen them.

WILD GARLIC

Allium canadense var. *canadense*
Lily Family (Liliaceae)

Description: A plant up to 2' tall, arising from a bulb. The leaves, which emerge mostly from the base of the plant, are long, narrow, flat, and about ⅛" across. A single, long stem contains a rounded cluster of flowers at the top of individual stalks. Each flower has 6 petals and 6 stamens. All or some of the flowers are replaced by small, hard, stalkless bulbs (bulblets) that fall to the ground to produce new plants.

May—July

Habitat/Range: Dry to moist woods, prairies, disturbed ground, roadsides; statewide.

Remarks: Also called Wild Onion, the plant has strong antiseptic properties. Native American Indians and settlers often applied the plant juices to wounds and burns. The Dakota and Winnebago used the plant to treat bee stings and snakebites. Settlers used Wild Garlic for fevers, blood disorders, lung troubles, internal parasites, skin problems, hemorrhoids, earaches, rheumatism, and arthritis. When Father Marquette made his famous journey from Green Bay to the present site of Chicago, in 1673, Wild Garlic was an important part of his food supply.

WILD ONION

Allium canadense var. *mobilense*
Lily Family (Liliaceae)

Description: A plant up to 1½' tall, arising from a bulb. The leaves emerge at the base, with long, narrow, flat leaves, about ⅛" across. A single, long stem contains a rounded cluster of flowers at the top of individual stalks. Each pink flower has 6 petals and 6 stamens that do not extend beyond the petals.

April—June

Habitat/Range: Dry woodlands, glades, prairies; nearly statewide, less common in the Delta Region.

Remarks: Formerly known as *Allium mutabile*. Wild Onion is similar to Wild Garlic but the former lacks bulblets that replace all or some of the flowers.

WIDOW'S CROSS
Sedum pulchellum
Stonecrop Family (Crassulaceae)

Description: Small, winter annuals, up to 8" tall, with fleshy stems and leaves. The leaves are alternate, crowded along the stem, narrow, round in diameter, and up to ¾" long; lower leaves wither at flowering time. The flowers are densely packed along 3–5 horizontal branches at the top of the stem. Each flower is small, about ⅜" across, with 5 narrow white to pink petals and 5 red-tipped stamens. The stem and leaves often turn red with age and exposure to sun.

May—July

Habitat/Range: Shallow acid soils derived from sandstone, sandstone glades; northern Ozarks, uncommon in the Ouachitas.

Remarks: The genus name, *Sedum*, is from the Latin, *sedo*, to sit, referring to the manner in which some species attach themselves to stones and walls. The species name *pulchellum* is Latin for beautiful.

OKLAHOMA GRASS PINK ORCHID
Calopogon oklahomensis
Orchid Family (Orchidaceae)

Description: A slender, smooth, single-stemmed plant less than 2' tall, with a single grass-like leaf that emerges from the base and somewhat exceeds the height of the stem. Up to 8 pale pink, fragrant, flowers occur at the top of the stem. Each flower has 1 upright petal containing dense yellow hairs, 2 narrow petals and 3 broad sepals. Unlike other Arkansas orchid flowers the lip is at the top rather than at the bottom.

May—July

Habitat/Range: Prairie, open wet areas; Grand Prairie and a few northwestern counties.

Remarks: A similar species, Grass Pink Orchid, *Calopogon tuberosus*, formerly known as *Calopogon pulchellus*, has a single grass-like leaf that does not exceed the height of the flower stem and with bright pink flowers that are not fragrant; occurs in wet pine woodlands; Saline County.

SELF-HEAL
Prunella vulgaris ssp. *lanceolata*
Mint Family (Lamiaceae)

Description: The stems are hairy and slightly creeping but mostly erect to 12" long. The leaves are opposite, hairy, narrow, and up to 4" long and 1½" wide, with some small teeth along the margins. The lower leaves have stalks. The flowers are in elongated clusters at the tops of stems. Each flower is about ½" long, with the upper lip forming a hood that is darker in color. The lower lip has 3 lobes, with the center lobe rounded and fringed at the tip.

May—August

Habitat/Range: Low woodlands, banks of streams, pastures, old fields, and along roadsides; statewide.

Remarks: Many Native American tribes used the aromatic Self-Heal, also called Heal-all, for treating sore throats, hemorrhages, diarrhea, stomach troubles, fevers, boils, urinary disorders, liver ailments, gas, colic, and gynecological problems. A closely related species, *Prunella vulgaris* ssp. *vulgaris*, was introduced into the United States from Europe by early settlers. It differs by having the upper leaves rounded at their bases and about ½ as broad as long. The native Self-Heal has leaves that taper at their base and narrower leaves, about ⅓ as broad as long. The nonnative Heal-All is found mostly in more disturbed sites.

DEPTFORD PINK
Dianthus armeria
Pink Family (Caryophyllaceae)

Description: A slender, but stiff-stemmed annual, sparsely branched, with fine hairs, up to 1½' tall. The leaves are opposite, narrow, up to 3" long and ¼" wide, pointed at the tip, and hairy on the surface and margins. The flowers are in clusters at the ends of stems. At the base of each cluster are long, narrow, pointed bracts. Each flower is up to ½" wide, with bright pink to rose petals having white speckles and toothed margins.

May—August

Habitat/Range: Old fields, pastures, along roadsides; native to Europe; Ozarks and Ouachitas, less common in the Delta and Coastal Plain regions.

Remarks: The beauty of these flowers is only revealed upon close-up examination. The common name refers to Deptford, England, which is now a part of London.

WILD FOUR-O'CLOCK
Mirabilis nyctaginea
Four-O'clock Family (Nyctaginaceae)

Description: The stems are nearly square, somewhat hairy, branching, to 4' tall, with widely spaced opposite leaves. The leaves are short-stalked, with smooth margins, up to 4" long, and heart-shaped with pointed tips. The flowers are in open-branched clusters at the tops of stems. As many as 5 flowers are seated upon a shallow, green, cup-shaped platform, which is 5-lobed and ¾" across. Each flower is ½" across with no petals and 5 pink to red sepal-like bracts, which form a spreading bell with 5 shallow notches and 3–5 yellow-tipped stamens. The flowers open in late afternoon.

May—October

Habitat/Range: Disturbed open ground, pastures, old fields, roadsides, and railroads; northern two-thirds of the state, also extreme southwestern part of the state.

Remarks: The Poncas chewed the root and spit it into wounds to heal them. The Pawnee ground the dried root and applied it as a remedy for sore mouth in teething babies. Some tribes pounded the root and used it to treat swellings, sprains, and burns. The plant is considered poisonous. Another species, White Four-O'clock, *Mirabilis albida*, has narrower leaves without stalks and white-lilac to pinkish flowers; *May—August*, woodlands; western half of the state.

PINKWEED
Persicaria pensylvanica
Buckwheat Family (Polygonaceae)

Description: A hairy, slender-stemmed, widely branching plant, up to 5' tall. The leaves are alternate, short-stalked, up to 6" long and 1½" wide, widest at the base and tapering to a pointed tip. The pink to white flowers are packed in a dense cylindrical cluster, to about 1½" long. The flower stalks have hairs that are sometimes tipped with round glands.

May–October

Habitat/Range: Wet ground bordering streams, gravel bars, disturbed sites, and along roadsides; nearly statewide but less common in the Gulf Coastal Region.

Remarks: Formerly known as *Polygonum pensylvanicum*. Smartweed seeds were a prehistoric food source and are frequently found in archaeological sites such as a Hopewellian village near Kansas City that was occupied in 635–870 A.D. Smartweeds have long been eaten as cooked greens, but some species have a too bitter or peppery taste; this is what gave rise to the family name of "smartweed." The seeds of various smartweeds are eaten by a variety of songbirds, bobwhite quail, woodcock, mourning dove, waterfowl, and small mammals. The plants are eaten by white-tailed deer.

CROWN VETCH
Securigera varia
Pea Family (Fabaceae)

Description: Densely spreading plants, up to 12" tall, with branched, smooth stems. The leaves are alternate and divided into 15–25 leaflets. Each leaflet is up to ¾" long, narrow, abruptly pointed at the tip, lacking hairs, and smooth along the margins. The flowers are in dense clusters (like a crown), on long stalks arising from the axils of the leaves. Each flower is about ½" long, with 5 pink and white petals arranged to form a flower typical of the pea family.

May – September

Habitat/Range: Roadsides, disturbed sites; native to Europe, Asia, and Africa; often planted and escapes; Ozarks but can be expected elsewhere in the state.

Remarks: Formerly known as *Coronilla varia*. This plant has been commonly planted along roadsides to control soil erosion. Unfortunately, like soybeans and some other legumes, crown vetch provides no cover in contact with the ground, so the soil remains bare even though there is dense foliage above it. This leaves the soil exposed to surface erosion.

FALSE DRAGONHEAD
Physostegia virginiana
Mint Family (Lamiaceae)

Description: Single or sparingly branched stems, up to 4' tall. The leaves are opposite, stalkless, narrow, up to 5" long and 1½" wide, with teeth along the margins. The flowers are tightly clustered in long spikes at the tops of stems. Each pink tubular flower is about 1" long, with 2 lips, the upper lip resembling a hood, the lower lip divided into 3 lobes.

May – August

Habitat/Range: Moist to dry prairies, streambanks, roadsides, moist open areas; scattered across the state but rare in the Coastal Plain.

Remarks: Also called Obedient Plant because the flowers, when moved to the side, remain in that position. The closely related Narrow-Leaved False Dragonhead, *Physostegia angustifolia*, has leaves that are narrower (less than ½" wide) and flowers more loosely spaced along the spike. Found in moist soil, moist prairies; central and northwestern counties.

SENSITIVE BRIER
Mimosa nuttallii
Pea Family (Fabaceae)

Description: A trailing or sprawling plant, up to 4' long, with angled stems and abundant hooked prickles. The leaves are alternate, stalked, and divided twice, with the numerous individual leaflets less than ½" long. The flowers are densely packed in round clusters on individual stalks arising from the leaf axils. The overall pink color and shape comes from the 8–10 stamens in each flower. The fruit is a very prickly pod up to 3½" long.

May—September

Habitat/Range: Prairie, glades, roadsides, open areas; nearly statewide, less common in the Delta Region.

Remarks: Formerly known as *Mimosa quadrivalvis* var. *nuttallii* and *Schrankia uncinata*. The leaflets have sensitive hairs that trigger the leaflets to close when touched, hence the common name. Seeds from this plant contain a purgative and have been used in laxatives. Bobwhite quail are known to eat the seeds, and wild turkey feed on the leaves. This plant is also appropriately named Devil's Shoestrings by rural children running barefoot through the prickly stems. Powderpuff, *Mimosa strigillosa*, is similar but lacks spines; southern counties.

OHIO HORSE MINT
Blephilia ciliata
Mint Family (Lamiaceae)

Description: Plants with square stems covered with downy hair, up to 2' tall. The leaves are opposite, without stalks, up to 2½" long, broadest below the middle and tapering to the base, with fine hairs on the underside and small scattered teeth along the margins. The basal leaves remain green through the winter. The pink flowers are packed in a tight cluster, with up to 4 clusters stacked one above another. The flowers are hairy, with 2 lips, the lower lip with 3 lobes and reddish spots.

May—July

Habitat/Range: Open woods, old fields, roadsides; Ozark Region and Crowley's Ridge.

Remarks: Also called Pagoda Plant. The Cherokee used a preparation of the fresh leaves for headaches. The aromatic leaves can be used as tea when steeped in hot water. Another species, Wood Mint, *Blephilia hirsuta*, has leaf stalks up to 1" long, base of leaf rounded, edges of leaves noticeably toothed, and the stem usually with 2 or more branches; found in moist woods; reported from Crittenden County.

FIELD MILKWORT
Polygala sanguinea
Milkwort Family, (Polygalaceae)

Description: Small annual plants less than 12" tall, usually with a single, angled stem. The leaves are alternate, widely spaced, narrow, and up to 1¾" long and ⅛" wide. The flowers are in a dense, cylindrical cluster at the tops of branches. The flowers vary from pink to rose-purple to white or greenish and are less than ¼" long. The flowers have 5 sepals, and 3 small petals that are united into a small tube.

May—October

Habitat/Range: Prairies, dry open woods, fields, sandy ground; nearly statewide, less common in the Delta and Coastal Plain regions.

Remarks: There are 9 species of milkwort in the genus *Polygala* in Arkansas.

CURLY MILKWEED
Asclepias amplexicaulis
Milkweed Family (Asclepiadaceae)

Description: Single, unbranched stems, up to 30" long, often curve upwards instead of being totally erect. The plants are smooth with up to 5 pairs of leaves. Leaves are up to 6" long and 3" wide, often with wavy or curly margins. There are typically 1, sometimes 2 flower clusters on each plant, each with 20 to 40 flowers on long stalks. The flowers are typically green and pink-or-purple tinged. The fruit is smooth and 4 to 6" long.

May—July

Habitat/Range: Upland prairies, sand prairies, glades, and dry woods; scattered across the state but absent from the Delta Region.

Remarks: The loose cluster of flowers on long stalks gives the resemblance to a starburst fireworks display.

COMMON MILKWEED
Asclepias syriaca
Milkweed Family (Asclepiadaceae)

Description: A robust plant, up to 5' tall, with a stout stem, large leaves, and large flower clusters. The stem is unbranched, with fine hairs and milky sap. The leaves are opposite, thick, leathery, oval, hairy, on short stalks, up to 8" long, and 4" wide, with pinkish veins. The flowers are in large rounded clusters at the tops of the stems and in the upper leaf axils. Each dark pink flower is about ¼" across, with 5 reflexed petals surrounding 5 spreading hoods, each with a tiny, pointed horn arising from it. The fruits are pods up to 4" long, with soft spines on the surface and filled with numerous seeds, each with silky hairs at one end.

May–August

Habitat/Range: Old fields, pastures, degraded prairie, and along roadsides; reported from a few northwestern and northeastern counties but likely to be found in other parts of the state.

Remarks: Native American Indians used root tea as a laxative and as a diuretic to expel kidney stones and dropsy (an abnormal accumulation of blood in the body; edema). The milky latex was applied to warts, moles, and ringworm. Common Milkweed was also used by early American physicians for treating asthma and rheumatism.

EVERLASTING PEA
Lathryus latifolius
Pea Family (Fabaceae)

Description: A sprawling or climbing plant, up to 3' long, with broadly winged stems. The leaves are alternate, divided into 2 leaflets, with a tendril that emerges from between the leaflets. The leaflets are up to 4" long, narrow, with pointed tips. There are several flower clusters arising from the axils of the leaves. The pink to rose pink flowers are up to 2" across and pea-shaped with 5 petals.

May–September

Habitat/Range: Escaped from cultivation along roadsides, fencerows, and old homesites; native to Europe; scattered across the state.

Remarks: The common name of this plant refers to its long blooming period. As the vine continues to grow, it produces new flowers along the lengthening stem. A related species, Singletary Pea, *Lathryus hirsutus*, has 1–3 flowers in a cluster, with smaller flowers; *April–July*; nearly statewide.

FAME FLOWER
Phemeranthus calycinus
Purslane Family (Portulacaceae)

Description: Small, succulent plants, up to 1' tall. The leaves are numerous, fleshy, round in diameter, up to 2½" long, and arising from the base. A thin, wand-like stalk supports several showy pink to rose-purple flowers, about ½" across, with 5 petals and 30 or more stamens. The flowers do not open until late in the afternoon, hence the alternate common name of Flower-Of-An-Hour.

May—July

Habitat/Range: Thin soil, rocky areas and sandstone glades; Ozark and Ouachita regions.

Remarks: Formerly known as *Talinum calycinum*. A similar species of Fame Flower or Rock Pink, *Phemeranthus parviflorus*, formerly known as *Talinum parviflorum*, has shorter leaves, less than 2" long, smaller flowers, about ⅜" and fewer stamens, usually less than 8; similar habitat; scattered counties across the state except absent from the Delta Region.

SHOWY EVENING PRIMROSE
Oenothera speciosa
Evening Primrose Family (Onagraceae)

Description: A low-growing, either trailing or somewhat upright plant, with stems up to 2' long. The leaves are alternate, narrow, up to 3½" long and 1" wide, with wavy to weakly toothed margins. The flowers emerge on long stalks from the leaf axils. A showy pink to white flower, up to 3" across, with 4 broad petals tinged with yellow at the base and marked with thin, dark pink lines.

May—July

Habitat/Range: Along roadsides, disturbed ground; statewide.

Remarks: Of the 13 species of the genus *Oenothera* in Arkansas, showy evening primrose is the only one with pink to white flowers.

WILD BEAN
Strophostyles helvula
Pea Family (Fabaceae)

Description: A trailing or twining annual vine, up to 5' long, often is branching above. The lowest leaves are usually opposite, the rest are alternate. The leaves are on stalks and divided into 3 rounded leaflets, up to 2½" long, sparsely hairy, usually with a large lobe along one of the margins or on both sides. The flowers are clustered along the vine, and up to ½" long. The pods are narrow and up to 4" long.

May—September

Habitat/Range: Moist rocky woods and thickets, low ground and gravel bars along streams, idle fields, and along roadsides; occasional throughout the state.

Remarks: A smaller Wild Bean, *Strophostyles leiosperma*, has silky-gray stems and leaflets; its leaflets are narrow, lack lobes, and up to 2" long; prairies, dry woods, fields, roadsides; scattered counties across the state. The only perennial Wild Bean, *Strophostyles umbellata*, has somewhat leathery leaflets that lack lobes and hairs; dry woods, stream banks; statewide.

SOAPWORT
Saponaria officinalis
Pink Family (Caryophyllaceae)

Description: Often forming colonies, the stems are typically branched, and up to 2' tall. The leaves are opposite, stalkless, smooth, up to 4" long and 1½" wide, with 3–5 conspicuous veins along the leaves and often with wavy margins. The flowers are fragrant, in open clusters at the top, with each flower about 1" across. Each flower has a long tube and 5 petals that vary from pink to white, with a notch at the end of each petal.

May—September

Habitat/Range: Disturbed ground, roadsides, railroads, and gravel bars along streams; native to Europe and escaped as a garden plant; statewide.

Remarks: Also called Bouncing Bet. A soapy green lather can be made from the plant by rubbing the leaves and stems in water. This natural cleanser, saponin, was used to wash fabrics and tapestries as far back as ancient Greece. Later, Soapwort was also used to produce a "head" on beer. The plant has been used to treat asthma, jaundice, gout, syphilis, rheumatism, coughs, and bronchitis. If taken in large doses or over a prolonged period of time, it can cause severe irritation to the gastrointestinal tract.

ROSE PINK
Sabatia angularis
Gentian Family (Gentianaceae)

PELTON'S ROSE-GENTIAN
Sabatia arkansana
Gentian Family (Gentianaceae)

Description: An annual with single stems up to 10" tall, square stems and alternate branching near the top. The leaves are opposite, do not clasp the stem, narrow, ¼–1¼" long, less than ¼" wide, smooth and lack teeth. The flowers are on individual stalks, up to 1" across, with 5 pink to magenta-pink petals and a yellow inner ring at the center.

June—July

Habitat/Range: Flat, open glades; Saline County

Remarks: This rose-gentian is new to science having been discovered by John Pelton, retired, nature photographer, amateur botanist, and former president of the Arkansas Native Plant Society. A related species, Texas Rose-Gentian, *Sabatia campestris*, differs by being larger, up to 16" tall, leaves up to 1½" long, about ½" wide, and clasp the stem or are rounded at the base; rocky areas, roadsides; occurring in a band across the state from northwest to southeast.

Description: Annual or biennial plants up to 2' tall, with smooth, square stems and opposite branches, giving it a candelabra-like appearance. The leaves are opposite, clasp the stem, stalkless, up to 1½" long and 1" wide, smooth, and lack teeth. The flowers are on individual stalks, up to 1½" across, with 5–6 rose-pink (rarely white) petals with a yellow inner ring at the base.

June—August

Habitat/Range: Dry to moist soil in open woods, pinelands, old fields; statewide.

Remarks: Also known as Marsh Pink. Another species, Narrowleaf Rose-Gentian, *Sabatia brachiata*, has a round stem, opposite branches, narrow leaves that do not clasp the stem; occurs in prairie, open areas, roadsides; Grand Prairie and central counties.

COMMON TEASEL
Dipsacus fullonum
Teasel Family (Dipsacaceae)

Description: A tall, stout biennial with very prickly, branched stems, up to 8' in height. The leaves are opposite and joined around the stem, up to 12" long, toothed, broadest at the base, narrowing to a pointed tip, and lacking prickles except underneath along the midvein. The flowers are densely packed along a cylindrical head at the top of a long stalk. Several stiff, long bracts with prickles curve upward around the flower head. Tiny, tubular pink flowers bloom in rings around the head.

June—September

Habitat/Range: Disturbed soil in fields, pastures, along roadsides; native to Europe; scattered counties in the Ozark Region and Polk County.

Remarks: Formerly called *Dipsacus sylvestris*. Common Teasel is a noxious weed; once established it is hard to eradicate. The flower heads have been used in dried flower arrangements and on spindles to raise the nap of woolen cloth. Another species, Cut-Leaved Teasel, *Dipsacus laciniatus*, has deeply lobed leaves and long hairs, not prickles, on the margins; native to Europe; more limited in occurrence than Common Teasel.

MEADOW BEAUTY
Rhexia virginica
Melastome Family (Melastomataceae)

Description: Short plants growing up to 2' tall, with exotic-looking flowers, gland-tipped hairs, and square stems with wings. The leaves are opposite, stalkless, up to 2½" long and about 1" wide, with 3 veins along the leaf. The flowers are rose-colored, with gland-tipped hairs on the buds and calyx, and about ¾" across. There are 4 broad petals and 8 bright yellow stamens.

June—October

Habitat/Range: Low, wet areas mostly in ravines and valleys; scattered over the lower two-thirds of the state.

Remarks: A similar species, Maryland Meadow Beauty, *Rhexia mariana*, lacks the wings and hairs along the stem, has larger leaves and pale pink flowers; occurs in wet areas in prairies, open areas, and along roadsides; nearly statewide except for northern Ozark Region counties.

WOOD SAGE
Teucrium canadense
Mint Family (Lamiaceae)

Description: Usually unbranched plants, up to 4' tall, with square stems and covered with fine downy hair. The leaves are opposite, stalked, up to 6" long and 2½" wide, widest near the base, tapering to a pointed tip, and with coarse teeth along the margins. The flowers are clustered along a narrow column, with each flower on a short stalk about ⅛" long. Each pinkish flower is about ¾" long, with the small upper lip divided into small lobes while the lower lip is broad and marked with dark red to purple blotches.

June—August

Habitat/Range: Moist soil in low woods, prairies, ditches, pastures, and roadsides; statewide.

Remarks: Also called American Germander. Leaf tea was used to induce menstruation, urination, and sweating. The plant was also used to treat lung ailments, intestinal worms, piles, and, externally, as a gargle and antiseptic dressing.

SMOOTH HEDGE NETTLE
Stachys tenuifolia
Mint Family (Lamiaceae)

Description: Plants are square-stemmed, hairy along the ridges, usually unbranched, and up to 3' tall. Leaves are 2–6" long, about 1" wide, with toothed edges along the margins. Pinkish flowers are in whorls of 6, with several whorls along the upper stem. Flowers are about ½" long, with 2 lips; the lower lip broad, spreading, and 3-lobed.

June—September

Habitat/Range: Moist soil, low woods; in scattered counties across the state.

Remarks: The Meskwaki soaked the leaves and drank the liquid for bad colds.

SPOTTED KNAPWEED
Centaurea stoebe
Aster Family (Asteraceae)

Description: A biennial or short-lived perennial plant, with several stems emerging from the base to 3' tall. The basal leaves are up to 6" long and densely hairy, with shallow to deep lobes. The stem leaves are deeply divided into narrow, fingerlike lobes, with the leaves toward the top simple and undivided. The flower heads are at the ends of loosely arranged branches. The bracts at the base of the flowers have dark spots on their tips. The flowers are pink, with the outer ones enlarged.

June—September

Habitat/Range: Disturbed soil, fields, roadsides; native to Europe; mainly in the Ozark Region.

Remarks: Formerly known as *Centaurea maculosa*. This plant is a noxious weed that overwhelms other plants by emitting toxic sap through its roots. The sap is also being studied for its potential as a possible cancer-causing agent.

ROUGH BUTTONWEED
Diodia teres
Madder Family (Rubiaceae)

Description: Annual plants, somewhat creeping along the ground, with square, branching stems, up to 2' long. The leaves are opposite, stalkless, narrow, up to 1¼" long and ¼" wide, with pointed tips and a pronounced central vein. At the junction of the leaves, there is a pair of whitish, papery stipules (a leaflike appendage) with bristles along the edges. The flowers are small, about ¼" across, stalkless, and attached at the axis of the leaf and the stem. The tubular flower has 4 pink petals and 4 small stamens.

June—September

Habitat/Range: Sandy, open ground, woods, fields, roadsides; statewide.

Remarks: A related species, Large Buttonweed, *Diodia virginiana*, lacks hairs, has white flowers up to ⅜" across; wet woods, swamps, wet ground along streams and ditches; statewide.

SLENDER BUSH CLOVER
Lespedeza virginica
Pea Family (Fabaceae)

Description: A narrow-stemmed plant, up to 3' tall, with hairy, branching stems. The leaves are numerous, stalked, divided into 3 narrow leaflets, each of which is up to 1½" long and less than ¼" wide. The pink to rose-purple flowers are in dense clusters interspersed with leaves on the upper part of the stem. Each flower is about ¼" long with a spreading upper petal, 2 smaller side petals, and a lower protruding lip. The upper petal has a darker red blotch near its base.

June—September

Habitat/Range: Open dry woods, fields, roadsides, sandy soils; statewide.

Remarks: There are 10 species in the genus *Lespedeza* in Arkansas. Slender Bush Clover is eaten by white-tailed deer and cottontail rabbits, and the seeds are food for wild turkeys, and bobwhite quail.

VIOLET BUSH CLOVER
Lespedeza violaceae
Pea Family (Fabaceae)

Description: A bushy plant with weak stems that tend to lean, usually not more than 18" tall. The leaves are alternate, stalked, and divided into 3 somewhat oval leaflets. Each leaflet is about 1½" long and ¾" wide. The flowers are in sparse clusters at the ends of slender branches. Each flower is ¼" to ⅜" long. The seedpods are small, flattened, and with a single seed.

July—September

Habitat/Range: Dry rocky woodlands, prairies, glades; scattered counties across the state.

Remarks: The seeds are eaten by songbirds, ruffed grouse, bobwhite quail, and wild turkey. The plants are eaten by white-tailed deer.

TICK TREFOIL
Desmodium perplexum
Bean Family (Fabaceae)

Description: A slender-stemmed hairy plant, up to 3½' tall, with several branches arising from the base. The leaves are alternate, with 3 leaflets; the middle leaflet is from 1½–2½ times longer than broad and stalked. There are fine hairs flattened on the lower leaf surfaces. The flowers are small, pink, in loose branches, and about ¼" long. The light brown seedpods easily attach to clothing and hair.

July—October

Habitat/Range: Rocky open woods, prairie, glades; statewide.

Remarks: Formerly known as *Desmodium paniculatum* var. *dillenii*. There are 18 species of Tick Trefoils or Beggar's Lice that occur in the state. The seeds are eaten by songbirds, ruffed grouse, bobwhite quail, and wild turkey.

ROUND-LEAVED TICK TREFOIL
Desmodium rotundifolium
Pea Family (Fabaceae)

Description: A plant with trailing stems up to 3' long, with some branching at its base. The distinctive leaves are alternate, stalked, hairy, and divided into 3 nearly round leaflets. The end leaflet is on a long stalk, up to 2½" long and wide, while the side leaflets are on shorter stalks and up to 1½" long and wide. The flowers are in loose clusters on long hairy stalks arising from the leaf axils. Each flower is about ½" long and ranging from pink to pale lavender or white.

July—September

Habitat/Range: Dry woodlands; scattered counties across the state.

Remarks: Also called Dollarleaf for the shape of its round leaves.

WILD ONION
Allium stellatum
Lily Family (Liliaceae)

Description: A perennial up to 1½' tall, arising from a bulb. The grass-like leaves, which usually wither before flowering time, are at the base and are long, narrow (about ⅛" across), and flat. A single, long stalk bears a rounded cluster of dark pink to red, individually stalked flowers. Each flower has 6 petals, with 6 stamens that extend beyond the petals.

July—October

Habitat/Range: Dolomite and limestone glades and prairies; northern Ozark Region.

Remarks: A closely related species, Nodding Wild Onion, *Allium cernuum*, has the upper stem curved sharply, causing the cluster of flowers to nod downward; the flowers are also a lighter pink; occurs on rocky, thin soils, and roadsides; found in western counties.

PALAFOXIA
Palafoxia callosa
Aster Family (Asteraceae)

Description: A slender annual, up to 18" tall, with tiny black glands on the upper branches. The leaves are very thin, up to 2" long, with smooth margins and a pointed tip. The pinkish flower heads are about ¾" across, with 5–12 small flowers per head, giving it a ragged appearance.

August—October

Habitat/Range: Dolomite glades, rocky open and sandy ground along streams, and along roadsides; northern Ozark Region.

Remarks: Also called Spanish Needles named for the shape of several pointed scales on the seed-like fruit. On first glance, the plants, with their pink round flower heads, look like some type of clover. The genus, *Palafoxia*, is named after Jose de Palafox y Melzi, Duke of Saragossa (1776–1847), a Spanish captain-general, in the war against the invading armies of Napoleon.

Blue/Purple Flowers

This section includes flowers ranging from pale blue
to deep indigo and from lavender to violet.
Since purple flowers grade into pink flowers,
that section should also be checked.

Bird's Foot Violet, page 168

ROUND-LOBED HEPATICA
Anemone americana
Buttercup Family (Ranunculaceae)

Description: Stems are absent in this low-growing plant, with basal leaves that overwinter. The leaves are on hairy stalks, 3-lobed, with blunt tips, leathery, and up to 2½" across. The flowers are single, on long somewhat hairy stalks up to 8" tall. Each flower is about 1" across and can vary in color from purple to lavender to white. The 6–10 "petals" are actually sepals.

February—April

Habitat/Range: Moist, rocky wooded slopes and ravine bottoms; northern Ozark Region and three western Ouachita Region counties.

Remarks: Another common name, Liverleaf, refers to the overwintering leaves that turn a deep reddish-brown, the color of raw liver. Formerly known as *Hepatica nobilis* var. *obtusa*. The Chippewas gave root tea from this plant to children who had convulsions. Leaf tea was used for liver ailments, poor indigestion, and as a laxative. A closely related species, Sharp-Lobed Hepatica, *Anemone acutiloba*, formerly *Hepatica nobilis* var. *acuta*, is almost identical except that it has sharp-pointed leaves. It is found in Newton and Stone counties.

STAR VIOLET
Hedyotis crassifolia
Madder Family (Rubiaceae)

Description: A small, mat-forming winter annual, with stems usually less than 4" tall. The leaves are opposite, few in number, mostly at the base, and less than ½" long. The blue flowers are at the ends of stalks, about ½" across, with a tubular shape, 4 pointed lobes, and a purplish center.

February—April

Habitat/Range: Rocky woods, fields, pastures, roadsides, and in open areas with sparse vegetation where there is little competition with other plants; statewide.

Remarks: Formerly known as *Houstonia pusilla*. This small bluet often forms a carpet of blue in yards and cemeteries.

WOOLLY BLUE VIOLET
Viola sororia
Violet Family (Violaceae)

Description: The plant forms a mound of leaves and flowers on usually hairy to densely hairy stalks, less than 6" tall. The leaves are less than 3" across, somewhat rounded, heart-shaped at the base, with rounded teeth along the margins, and often hairy on both surfaces. The flowers are on long, smooth or hairy stalks and up to 2" across, with 5 petals. The base of each petal is white, with a beard of hairs and purple lines.

March—May

Habitat/Range: Rocky or dry open woods, fields, lawns; nearly statewide, less common in the Delta Region.

Remarks: The plants have been used in salads, as cooked greens, soup thickener, tea, and candy. There are 14 species of violets in the genus *Viola* in Arkansas.

BIRD'S FOOT VIOLET
Viola pedata
Violet Family (Violaceae)

Description: Small, sparse violets, up to 6" tall, with leaves and flowers emerging from the same base. The leaves are deeply cut, resembling a bird's foot, and are often further divided into smaller lobes. The bare flower stems extend above the leaves and are sharply curved at the top with a single flower. The flowers are about 1½" across, with 5 petals; the lowest one is white at the base, with purple lines. The orange stamens form a column in the center of the flower. There are two color variations, one with all 5 petals pale lilac or lavender; the other with the upper 2 petals deep, velvety purple and the lower 3 petals pale lilac to lavender.

March—June

Habitat/Range: Dry open woods, rocky soils, open areas; nearly statewide, less common in the Delta Region.

Remarks: The bi-colored form has been considered by some as the most beautiful violet in the world. Bird's Foot Violet sometimes flowers in the fall if conditions are right.

THREE-LOBED VIOLET
Viola palmata
Violet Family (Violaceae)

Description: A stemless plant with leaves and flower stalks emerging from the base. The leaves are hairy or smooth, about 2–4" across on long stalks, and deeply 3–11 lobed with the earliest leaves being more heart-shaped. The flowers are on long stalks, large, up to 1" across, blue-violet to white, or sometimes streaked, or blotched violet and white.

March—June

Habitat/Range: Moist to dry woods, sandy soils; mainly Ozark and Ouachita regions, less common in the Delta and Coastal Plain regions.

Remarks: Three-Lobed Violet is very mucilaginous and has been used in the South to make soup, where it was known as Wild Okra. The bruised leaves were used to soften and soothe the skin.

JOHNNY-JUMP-UP
Viola rafinesquii
Violet Family (Violaceae)

Description: A small, slender, annual, up to 6" tall. The leaves are alternate, the lowermost nearly circular, the upper ones narrower, up to ¾" long, rounded, on long stalks. At the base of each leaf there is a deeply divided leaf-like stipule. The flowers are on stalks arising from the axils of leaves. The flowers are violet, lavender, or white, up to ¾" long, with 5 petals. The base of each petal is white, with a beard of hairs and purple lines.

March—May

Habitat/Range: Disturbed areas, fields, lawns, cemeteries, and along roadsides; native to Europe; statewide.

Remarks: Johnny-Jump-Up, which looks like a miniature pansy, often forms dense carpets in lawns and cemeteries. The common name refers to the quick growth of this plant in the spring.

SAND PHLOX
Phlox bifida
Phlox Family (Polemoniaceae)

Description: A mat-forming plant, up to 6" high, with wiry, hairy stems. The leaves are opposite, very narrow, up to 2" long and less than ¼" wide, hairy, and lack teeth along the margins. The flowers are light blue, up to 1½" across, on slender, hairy stalks. The 5 narrow petals have deep notches at the tips.

March—May

Habitat/Range: Dry, rocky woods, ledges of bluffs; northern two tier of counties in the Ozark Region.

Remarks: Also called Cleft Phlox. This attractive, mat-forming phlox has been successfully grown in rock gardens.

BLUEBELLS
Mertensia virginica
Borage Family (Boraginaceae)

Description: The pale, fleshy stem grows to 2' tall, with alternate blue-green leaves along the stem. The lower leaves are somewhat oval, up to 6" long and 1½" wide, and tapering to the stem. The stem leaves are smaller. The flowers are in loose clusters, hanging from smooth, slender stalks. Each flower is trumpet-shaped, up to 1¼" long, with 5 petals united to form a long tube. The flower buds are initially pink and open to a light blue.

March—June

Habitat/Range: Moist woods, wooded floodplains; northern part of the Ozark Region.

Remarks: Where Bluebells are found, they often grow in dense colonies, carpeting the forest floor with a crisp porcelain blue, but the plants completely disappear by midsummer. White flowering plants are occasionally found.

WESTERN DAISY
Astranthium integrifolium
Aster Family (Asteraceae)

Description: A hairy annual from 2–16" tall, sometimes branching near the base. The leaves are alternate, up to 3" long, and ½" wide, with the basal leaves sometimes withered by blooming time. The flowers vary in width, up to 1½" across; the ray flowers are whitish tinged with lavender, while the disk flowers are yellow.

April—May

Habitat/Range: Open areas, glades, prairies, along streams, roadsides; Ozark and Ouachita regions; also Little River County.

Remarks: An early blooming aster, Western Daisy, often forms dense mats of flowers, especially along roadsides.

DWARF CRESTED IRIS
Iris cristata
Iris Family (Iridaceae)

Description: A showy plant, up to 8" tall with a creeping, rootlike rhizome. The leaves are mostly basal, up to 8" long and 1" wide, usually slightly curved or arching, and light green, with parallel veins. The light violet to purple, rarely white, flowers are 1–2 on a long stalk, about 2½" across, with 3 smaller petals and 3 larger sepals. The sepals each have a 3-ridged yellow crest, bordered with white and outlined with a purple margin.

April—May

Habitat/Range: Lower wooded slopes and lowland woods associated with streams; Ozark and Ouachita regions.

Remarks: Native American Indians used root ointment (prepared in animal fats or waxes) on cancerous ulcers. Root tea was used to treat hepatitis. A similar species, Dwarf Iris, *Iris verna*, lacks crests along the sepals, has leaves about 1" wide, and darker yellow in the petals; Montgomery, Ouachita, Polk, and Saline counties.

BLUE PHLOX
Phlox divaricata
Madder Family (Polemoniaceae)

Description: This plant has finely hairy stems, up to 1½' tall, unbranched, with one to several stems arising from the base. The leaves are opposite, widely spaced, stalkless, broadest at the base and tapering to point, up to 3" long, finely hairy, and lacking teeth along the margins. The blue to blue-violet flowers are on slender stalks in loose clusters at the top of stems. Each flower is up to 1" across, tubular, 5-lobed, with the tips either rounded or notched.

April—June

Habitat/Range: Rocky or moist woods; statewide.

Remarks: Also called Sweet William. In pioneer medicine, leaf tea was used to treat eczema and to purify the blood. Root tea was taken to treat venereal disease. This long-flowering phlox does well in a partially shaded wildflower garden.

BLUETS
Hedyotis caerulea
Madder Family (Rubiaceae)

Description: A small, mat-forming winter annual, with stems usually less than 6" tall. The leaves are opposite, few in number, mostly at the base, spatula-shaped, less than ½" long, and narrowed to a stalk almost as long as the leaf. The flowers are at the ends of stalks, about ½" across, sky blue, tubular, with 4 pointed lobes and a yellow center.

April—June

Habitat/Range: Sandy banks and open areas along streams, open woods, and fields; in counties through the central part of the state in a north to south direction.

Remarks: Formerly known as *Houstonia caerulea*. Bluets does not form mats as dense as Star Violet (See p. 167); the flowers are also larger and have a yellow center.

GROUND IVY
Glechoma hederacea
Mint Family (Lamiaceae)

Description: A creeping mint with branched stems, rooting at the nodes, up to 15" long. The leaves are opposite, stalked, round, up to 1½" across, with rounded teeth along the margins. The flowers emerge from the axil of the stem and leaf. Each flower is up to ¾" long, with 2 lips. The lower lip is much larger than the upper, usually with 1–2 purple blotches on the inside.

April—July

Habitat/Range: Moist soil in low woodlands, in valleys and banks along streams, lawns, fields, and along roadsides; native to Europe; in scattered counties across the state.

Remarks: Also called Gill-Over-The-Ground. Before Germans began using hops, Ground Ivy was the primary seasoning used in brewing ale to flavor, preserve, and clarify. During more superstitious times, garlands and headpieces of Ground Ivy were worn in Midsummer's Eve, June 24, to ward off spells supposedly cast by witches. Europeans used the plant to treat headaches, kidney ailments, and to aid digestion. The fresh shoots and leaves can be added to salads and soups or can be prepared and eaten like spinach.

VIOLET COLLINSIA
Collinsia violacea
Figwort Family (Scrophulariaceae)

Description: A slender, weak-stemmed winter annual, up to 12" tall, often covering large areas. The upper stem leaves are opposite, stalkless, up to 2" long, nearly uniform in width or widest at the middle, tapering to a pointed tip, and somewhat toothed along the margins. The lower stem leaves have stalks, are more rounded, and lack teeth. The flowers emerge in whorls in axils of the stem; each flower is about ½" long, with 2 lips. The upper lip is white with 2 lobes; the lower lip is violet with 3 lobes. The center lower lobe forms a pouch in which the stamens and the pistil are hidden.

April—June

Habitat/Range: Open woods, glades, roadsides; mostly Ozark Region

Remarks: A closely related species, Blue-Eyed Mary, *Collinsia verna*, has leaves widest at the base and with the flower's lower lip colored blue; moist woods in ravines and valley bottoms along streams; northwestern corner of the state.

SHOWY ORCHIS
Galearis spectabilis
Orchid Family (Orchidaceae)

Description: A single, stout stem, up to 10" tall, with a pair of shiny leaves emerging from the base. The leaves are broad and up to 7" long. Up to 10 flowers are located along the upper part of the stem, with each flower about ¾" long. The flowers are two-toned with the upper purple hood being composed of 2 small petals and 3 petal-like sepals, while the lower lip is white with crinkled edges. A stout, white spur projects downward from the base.

April—June

Habitat/Range: Moist woods and wooded ravines; Ozark Region and Crowley's Ridge.

Remarks: Formerly known as *Orchis spectabilis*. The name *Galearis* is from the Greek galea, for "hood" in reference to the combining of the sepals and petals formed above the lower lip.

DWARF LARKSPUR
Delphinium tricorne
Buttercup Family (Ranunculaceae)

Description: A single-stemmed, rather succulent plant, with fine downy hairs, that begins flowering at 6–10" tall but may reach 18" later in the season. The basal and alternate stem leaves are shaped like a hand with 5–7 deep lobes; the basal leaves are on stalks. The flowers are loosely clustered along the top of the stem. Each flower is up to 1½" long, stalked, with 5 showy sepals, one of which is developed into a spur, up to 1" long. The 4 petals are small inconspicuous. The flowers vary from blue to violet to white.

April—May

Habitat/Range: Moist woods, stream banks; Ozark and Ouachita regions, uncommon in the Delta and Coastal Plain regions.

Remarks: Larkspurs are poisonous to cattle and horses. Most poisoning is in the spring when the plants are fresh and green.

HORSEMINT
Monarda bradburiana
Mint Family (Lamiaceae)

Description: A square-stemmed plant, up to 1½' tall, with one to several unbranched stems emerging from the base. The leaves are opposite, hairy, without stalks, up to 2½" long and 1¼" wide, broadest at the base and narrowest at the tip, and slightly toothed along the margins. The flowers are in a round cluster at the top of the stem with flower tubes barely visible. The flowers are up to 1½" long ending in 2 lips, the lower lip broad and recurving, with numerous purple spots; the upper lip is very hairy and arching upward with stamens protruding.

April—June

Habitat/Range: Dry open woods, bluffs, roadsides; Ozark Region and eastern Ouachita Region.

Remarks: Also called Bee Balm. The crushed leaves are aromatic and minty. A tea can be prepared from the leaves. A similar species of Horsemint, *Monarda russeliana*, has narrower leaves, an upper lip that lacks hairs, and a flower tube that extends well beyond the base; western counties of the Ozark and Ouachita regions.

WILD HYACINTH
Camassia scilloides
Lily Family (Liliaceae)

Description: A stout-stemmed plant emerging from a bulb, up to 2' tall. The stem is bare with long, narrow, grass-like leaves, up to 1' long at its base. At the top of the stem there is a cluster of flowers 1¼–2" wide with up to 50 stalked flowers, each about 1" across, that display 6 petals that vary in color from pale blue to lilac and, rarely, pure white.

April—May

Habitat/Range: Prairies and open woodlands; Ozark and Ouachita regions, Grand Prairie, uncommon in the Gulf Coastal Plain Region.

Remarks: A related species, Prairie Hyacinth, *Camassia angusta*, has the flower cluster ¾–1¼" wide; deep lavender to pale purple flowers that begin to flower in May; prairies and open woodlands; Benton, Logan, Saline, and Washington counties.

JACOB'S LADDER
Polemonium reptans
Phlox Family (Polemoniaceae)

Description: Low, weak-stemmed plants, up to 15" tall. The alternate leaves are up to 12" long, with each leaf divided into 3–13 leaflets, which form a "ladder." The leaflets are up to 1½" long, widest in the middle, and tapering at both ends. The flowers are in a loose cluster at the top of the stem. Each bell-shaped flower is about ½" across and often nodding. The 5 pale blue petals are united for about half their length.

April—May

Habitat/Range: Moist woods, slopes, streamsides; primarily the Ozark Region.

Remarks: The Menomini tribe used this plant to treat eczema and skin sores. The Mesquakie and Potawatami used it for treating hemorrhoids. Root tea was used to induce sweating and to treat fevers, snakebites, bowel complaints, and bronchial afflictions.

VENUS' LOOKING GLASS
Triodanis perfoliata
Bellflower Family (Campanulaceae)

Description: A slender, mostly unbranched, annual, up to 18" tall, with stems angled and hairs along the ridges. The leaves are roundish, about as long as broad, and clasp the stem with a heart-shaped base. There are teeth along the margin and the veins are fan-shaped. Several star-shaped, stalkless flowers arise from the leaf axils, each about ½" across, with 5 deep violet to purple petals. Those flowers on the lower stalk do not open but produce the seed.

April—August

Habitat/Range: Disturbed often sandy soil in pastures, old fields, open woodlands and along roadsides; statewide.

Remarks: Formerly known as *Specularia perfoliata*. The Cherokee made a liquid from the root to treat an upset stomach from overeating.

WOODLAND SPIDERWORT
Tradescantia ernestiana
Spiderwort Family (Commelinaceae)

Description: Slender plants, up to 2' tall, with smooth stems and leaves. The leaves are dull green, narrowly lance-shaped, up to 10" long and ½–1½" wide, and pointed at the tip. The flowers are in a cluster at the top of the plant and nested in an upper pair of leaves. The 3 petals vary in deep shades of blue, purple, or rose-red.

April—June

Habitat/Range: Moist rocky slopes of woodlands in valleys and ravines, roadsides; mostly western Ozark and Ouachita regions.

Remarks: A similar plant species, Prairie Spiderwort, or Western Spiderwort, *Tradescantia occidentalis*, has narrower leaves, blue flowers, and flower stalks with densely covered gland-tipped hairs; mostly central and southern part of the state.

OZARK SPIDERWORT
Tradescantia ozarkana
Spiderwort Family (Commelinaceae)

Description: Smooth, slender plants, with slightly zigzag stems, up to 20" tall. Leaves smooth, light green to gray-green, narrow, and up to 12" long, with a whitish coating on the surface that can be rubbed off. The flowers are in a cluster at the top of the plant and nested in an upper pair of leaves. The 3 petals are white or in shades of pink or lavender-blue, with each about ½" long.

April—May

Habitat/Range: Moist, rocky slopes of woodlands in valleys and ravines; occurs in western Ozark Region counties; also Polk and Montgomery counties.

Remarks: The genus *Tradescantia* has an estimated 71 species native to the New World from southern Canada south to Argentina. There are 12 species of spiderworts in Arkansas.

WOOLLEN BREECHES
Hydrophyllum appendiculatum
Waterleaf Family (Hydrophyllaceae)

Description: Plants often forming dense colonies, with hairy stems, often branched, and up to 2' tall. The leaves are up to 6" long and about as wide, with 5–7 shallow lobes, hairy, and coarsely toothed along the margins. The upper surface of the leaves is often mottled gray or light green. The flowers are in loose clusters at the tops of long, hairy stalks. Each flower is up to ½" across, on slender, hairy stalks, with 5 petals and 5 stamens that are equal to or extend just beyond the petals.

April—July

Habitat/Range: Moist woods on lower slopes and valleys; Ozark Region.

Remarks: Also called Great Waterleaf. The nectar and pollen of these showy flowers attract various kinds of bees, including honeybees, bumblebees, Mason bees, Miner bees, Andrenid bees, and Halictid bees (including Green Metallic bees).

VIRGINIA WATERLEAF
Hydrophyllum virginianum
Waterleaf Family (Hydrophyllaceae)

Description: Plants often forming dense colonies, with smooth stems, up to 2' tall. The lower leaves are deeply divided into 5–7 lobes with the lower pair of lobes at the base quite separate from the others. The flowers are in clusters on long stalks, with the heads extending beyond the leaves. Flowers are violet to white, up to ½" long, and shaped like a tiny fluted, narrow bell. The 5 petals are joined together at their bases, with 5 stamens extending well beyond the petals, giving the flowers a rather hairy appearance.

April—July

Habitat/Range: Moist woods at the base of slopes and in valleys; scattered counties in the Ozark Region.

Remarks: Native American Indians used root tea as an astringent (a substance that causes tissue to contract) to stop bleeding and for diarrhea and dysentery. Tea or mashed roots were used to treat cracked lips and mouth sores. The Iroquois used the tender young leaves as greens. A similar species, Browne's Waterleaf, *Hydrophyllum brownei*, has very hairy stems and branches; moist woods; endemic (found only in Arkansas; a few western counties in the Ozark and Ouachita regions.

WILD COMFREY
Cynoglossum virginianum
Borage Family (Boraginaceae)

Description: An attractive plant with large leaves and a hairy, wand-like stem, up to 2½' tall. The basal leaves and lower stem leaves are up to 1' long, on stalks, rough-hairy, and oval. The upper stem leaves are smaller, lack stalks, and clasp the stem. The flowers are on short, branching clusters at the top of the stem. The light blue flowers are about ½" across, with 5 rounded lobes and 5 stamens.

April—June

Habitat/Range: Moist woods, wooded slopes; nearly statewide, less common in the Delta Region except for Crowley's Ridge.

Remarks: Cherokees used root tea for "bad memory," cancer, and milky urine. A related species, Common Hound's Tongue, *Cynoglossum officinale*, is a downy-covered biennial with a branched stem; it is leafy to the top and has lance-shaped leaves, dark purple to reddish-purple flowers, and a musty odor; pastures, fields, roadsides; native to Europe and Asia; Ozark Region.

CANCER WEED
Salvia lyrata
Mint Family (Lamiaceae)

Description: A hairy plant with a single, square stem, up to 2' tall. The basal leaves have long stalks, up to 8" long and 3" wide, with wavy to lobed margins. There is usually 1 smaller pair of stem leaves attached without stalks. The flowers are in a series of whorls on the upper part of the stem, with about 6 flowers in a whorl. Each flower is about 1" long, light blue, with the upper lip shorter than the lower lip.

April—June

Habitat/Range: Moist or rocky, usually open woods, sandy or gravelly soils along streams, roadsides and pastures; statewide.

Remarks: Also called Lyre-Leaved Sage. Native American Indians used the root in salve for sores. Tea from the whole plant was used for coughs, colds, nervous debility, and, taken with honey, for asthma. It was a folk remedy for cancer and warts.

HAIRY PHACELIA
Phacelia hirsuta
Waterleaf Family (Hydrophyllaceae)

Description: A branched, annual plant, up to 14" tall, with densely spreading hairs on the stems and leaves. The leaves are divided into 3–7 segments, with rounded lobes and dense hairs on both surfaces and along the margins. The basal leaves have stalks, but the stem leaves are attached directly to the stem. The flowers are about ¾" across, on short hairy stalks, and in loose clusters at the tops of stems. Each flower has 5 lavender to blue rounded lobes.

April—June

Habitat/Range: Rocky fields, valleys, open woods, along roadsides; nearly statewide, less common in the Delta Region.

Remarks: The name Phacelia is from the Greek *phakelos*, a bundle; relating to the clustered arrangement of the flowers. There are 200 species of annual and perennial Phacelias from the Andes and North America with 7 species occurring in Arkansas. The second most common species, Smooth Phacelia, *Phacelia glabra*, lacks hair; occurs in central and southeastern part of the state.

CELESTIAL LILY
Nemastylis geminiflora
Iris Family (Iridaceae)

Description: A low growing plant with grass-like leaves and a showy sky blue flower. The leaves are up to 12" long and about ¼" wide. The flowers are from 1–2 per stem and up to 2½" across with 6 petals. Each flower opens once around mid-morning and closes by mid-afternoon.

April—May

Habitat/Range: Glades, prairies, rocky sites, pinelands; eastern Ozark Region counties, a few southwest counties, and the Grand Prairie.

Remarks: A similar species, Nuttall's Pleatleaf, *Nemastylis nuttallii*, has a taller stem, up to 8", narrower leaves less than ¼" wide, smaller flowers, less than 2" across, which are more purple in color that open in late afternoon and close during the night; occurs in prairies, glades, dry upland woodland; found in a few Ozark Region counties, also Jefferson County.

BLUE TOADFLAX
Nuttallanthus canadensis
Figwort Family (Scrophulariaceae)

Description: Plants with smooth, slender stems, up to 18" tall, with trailing offshoots at the base that display rosettes of leaves that stay green all winter. The leaves are alternate on the upper stem and opposite or whorled below, narrow, and up to 1" long and ⅛" wide. The light blue flowers are in a loose cluster along the upper part of the stem. Each flower is about ½" long, with 2 lips: the upper has 2 lobes; the lower has 3. A long, down-curved spur emerges from the back of the flower.

April—September

Habitat/Range: Sandy soil in open ground, glades, open woods, old fields; statewide.

Remarks: This plant was formerly known as *Linaria canadensis*. The flowers are pollinated by bumblebees and other long-tongued bees.

BLUE STAR
Amsonia tabernaemontana
Dogbane Family (Apocynaceae)

Description: A branched, smooth plant, up to 3' tall, with milky sap. The leaves are alternate, firm, somewhat leathery, up to 6" long and 2" across, with a dull surface on the upper leaves. Numerous flowers are arranged at the tops of stems. Each flower is star-shaped, light blue, about ½" across, with 5 petals. The narrow seedpods are about 4" long and turn up. The plants turn an attractive pale yellow in autumn.

April—June

Habitat/Range: Woods, low, moist ground, roadsides; Statewide.

Remarks: A similar species, Shining Blue Star, *Amsonia illustris*, has a shiny surface on the upper leaves and has seedpods that hang down; *April—June*; gravel bars along creeks and rivers; northern Ozark Region and a few Delta Region counties.

SAMPSON'S SNAKEROOT

Orbexilum pedunculatum
Pea Family (Fabaceae)

Description: A slender, sparingly branched plant, up to 3' tall. The leaves are alternate, stalked, and divided into 3 leaflets. Each leaflet is up to 3" long and ½" wide, with the center leaflet on a longer stalk. The flowers are in cylindrical clusters at the top of long stalks. Individual flowers are light blue to bluish-purple, about ¼" long, and shaped like other flowers in the pea family.

April—June

Habitat/Range: Dry open woods, pinelands, prairies; nearly statewide, less common in the Gulf Coastal Plain Region.

Remarks: Formerly known as *Psoralea psoralioides*. The Cherokee made root tea for treating colic and indigestion.

BLUE-EYED GRASS

Sisyrinchium angustifolium
Iris Family (Iridaceae)

Description: Small, clump-forming plants, with stems branching at the top, up to 12" tall, with pointed, upright, grass-like leaves. The flower stems are flat, about ⅛" wide with 2 narrow wings. There are several flowers, each on a slender stalk. Each flower is medium to dark blue with a yellow center, about ½" across, with 3 sepals and 3 petals, all looking like petals.

April—June

Habitat/Range: Prairies, rocky open woods, and glades; statewide.

Remarks: There are 9 species of Blue-Eyed Grass that occur in Arkansas. The Cherokee boiled the roots and gave the liquid to children to treat diarrhea.

VIPER'S BUGLOSS
Echium vulgare
Borage Family (Boraginaceae)

Description: Mostly single-stemmed plants, up to 3' tall, with bristly hairs on the stems and leaves. The basal leaves are stalkless, narrow, up to 6" long. The stem leaves are progressively smaller up the stem. The flowers are on the upper stem in crowded, curled spikes. Each flower is funnel-shaped, about ¾" long, with uneven petals. The pink buds turn purple when open.

April—May

Habitat/Range: Open disturbed ground, gravel bars, along roadsides and railroads; native to Europe; reported in the northwestern part of the state but will likely spread.

Remarks: Also called Blueweed. Bugloss is an English word given to several plants of the borage family. Viper refers to the resemblance of the seed to the head of a viper snake. In early folk medicine, a leaf tea was used for fevers, headaches, nervous conditions, and to ease pain from inflammation. The hairs may cause a rash.

DAME'S ROCKET
Hesperis matronalis
Mustard Family (Brassicaceae)

Description: Usually a single, hairy-stemmed plant, up to 4' tall. The leaves are alternate, lance-shaped, hairy above, sharply toothed, with short stalks or stalkless. The purple flowers are fragrant, showy, with 4 petals, each up to 1" long.

May—July

Habitat/Range: Escapes from plantings, where it is grown as an ornamental; a native to Europe and Asia; a few Ozark Region counties, also Pulaski County.

Remarks: Also called Purple Rocket. Dame's Rocket is a well-known flower of old-fashioned gardens and English cottage gardens. Twenty four species are known from the Mediterranean region to central Asia.

SMALL SKULLCAP
Scutellaria parvula
Mint Family (Lamiaceae)

ROUGH SKULLCAP
Scutellaria integrifolia
Mint Family (Lamiaceae)

Description: A single but sometimes branched plant up to 20" tall with fine hairs along the stem and showy bluish flowers. Leaves along the stem are opposite, from ¾–1" long, narrow, lack teeth along the margin, and with smaller leaves clustered in the axils. Flowers are blue and from ¾–1" long, with 2 white markings on the lip.

May–July

Habitat/Range: Open woods; Gulf Coastal Plain Region, also Chicot and Logan counties.

Remarks: Another species, Heartleaf Skullcap, *Scutellaria ovata*, has heart-shaped leaves 2–6" long with rounded teeth; open woods; Ozark and Ouachita regions. Then there's Hairy Skullcap, *Scutellaria elliptica*, with fine hairy stems, leaves to 3" long, broadest below the middle with rounded teeth along the edges and pale violet flowers; woodlands; Ozark and a few Ouachita counties.

Description: A short, slender plant, up to 8" tall, with a hairy, square stem. The leaves are opposite, stalkless, hairy, less than 1" long and about ¼" wide, lance-shaped, rounded at the base, and blunt-tipped. The flowers are opposite each other on short stalks that emerge from the leaf axils. Each violet flower is about ⅜" long with a small, hooded upper lip and a broad, lobed lower lip. The lower lip has a white center with purple spots.

May–July

Habitat/Range: Rocky, open woods, prairies, glades, fields; nearly statewide, less common in the Delta Region.

Remarks: There are 9 Skullcap species in the genus *Scutellaria* in Arkansas. The unusual shape of the upper lip of the flowers accounts for the name "skullcap."

BLUE FALSE INDIGO
Baptisia australis
Pea Family (Fabaceae)

Description: Smooth, branched, shrub-like plants, up to 4' tall. The leaves are alternate, divided into 3 leaflets, each less than 2" long. The flowers are on stalks well above the leaves. Each purple flower is about 1" long, with the upper petal notched, 2 smaller side petals, and a middle keel-shaped lip. The seed pods are black, hairless, about 2" long, with a pointed tip.

May—June

Habitat/Range: Dolomite glades and prairies; northern tier of Ozark Region counties plus Crawford and Sebastian counties.

Remarks: Native American Indians used root tea as an emetic (to induce vomiting) and a purgative (to clear the bowels). Externally, it was used as a wash for inflammation, cuts, wounds, bruises, and sprains, and in a compress for relieving toothaches.

CAROLINA LARKSPUR
Delphinium carolinianum
Buttercup Family (Ranunculaceae)

Description: The stems of this plant are wand-like, with soft hairs, and up to 3½' tall. The stalked leaves are mostly on the lower half of the stem. The leaves are fan-shaped, with 3–7 segments that are often divided once or twice again. The short-stalked flowers are alternately arranged along the upper stem. Each flower is about 1" long and shaped like a cornucopia, consisting of 5 white to blue, petal-like sepals with the upper sepal curved back and upward in a long, tubular spur, 2 lateral, spreading sepals, and 2 lower sepals.

May—June

Habitat/Range: Rocky open woods, prairies, glades, and along roadsides; nearly statewide, less common in the Delta Region.

Remarks: An extract of the seeds of larkspurs, mixed with soap, has been used as a folk remedy to kill head lice. All parts of the plant are poisonous.

WINTER VETCH
Vicia villosa
Pea Family (Fabaceae)

Description: Annual plants with soft hairs on the spreading stems, up to 2' long. The leaves are alternate and divided into 16–24 leaflets with a grasping tendril at the tip. The leaflets are narrow, up to ¾" long, with a small, pointed tip and tapering or rounded at the base. The flowers are on 1-sided stems about 4" long, that arise from the leaf axils. Each flower is up to ½" long, on a short stalk, with 5 violet and white flowers having the typical structure of members of the pea family.

April—June

Habitat/Range: Disturbed ground, fields, roadsides; native to Europe; statewide.

Remarks: There are 3 native and 6 exotic species of vetches in Arkansas.

OHIO SPIDERWORT
Tradescantia ohiensis
Spiderwort Family (Commelinaceae)

Description: Slender plants, up to 3' tall, with smooth, bluish to silvery green stems and leaves. The arching leaves are alternate, up to 15" long, about 1" wide, and tapering to a long point, with a sheath that wraps around the stem. The flowers are in a tight cluster at the top of the stem. Each flower is about 1½" across, with 3 green sepals, 3 blue to purple, rounded petals, and 6 yellow-tipped stamens covered with long purple hairs.

May—July

Habitat/Range: Open woods, prairies, old fields, roadsides and railroads; nearly statewide, uncommon in the Delta Region.

Remarks: The plant was once thought to be a cure for spider bites. Native American Indians used the stems as potherbs. Each showy flower lasts but a day. A similar species, Hairystem Spiderwort, *Tradescantia hirsuticaulis*, has long and short hairs along the stem, somewhat drooping leaves, sepals rose to purple, sparsely to medium hairy; open woodlands, glades; Ouachita and Gulf Coastal Plain regions. Another species, Hairyflower Spiderwort, *Tradescantia hirsutiflora*, has only long hairs along the stem, rather stiff leaves, sepals dull green, very hairy; open woodlands, glades; western Ouachita Region and Gulf Coastal Plain Region.

PURPLE BEARD-TONGUE
Penstemon cobaea
Snapdragon Family (Scrophulareaceae)

Description: A showy plant, up to 2' tall, with fine hairs on the stem and leaves. The leaves are opposite, up to 8" long and 3" wide near the base of the plant, somewhat pointed at the tip, with small teeth scattered along the edges. The upper leaves are smaller and clasp the stem. The flowers are clustered along a column at the top of the stem. Each flower is tubular, about 2" long, with two spreading lips divided into 2 upper lobes and 3 lower lobes. The flowers appear in varying shades of purple, with purple lines and white blotches at the mouth.

May—June

Habitat/Range: Glades, prairies, ledges, and roadsides; northern Ozark Region counties, also Hempstead, Little River, and Sevier counties.

Remarks: Of the 8 species of penstemons in Arkansas, this by far is the showiest. The large tubular flowers are pollinated by bumblebees.

PURPLE MILKWEED
Asclepias purpurascens
Milkweed Family (Asclepiadaceae)

Description: Plants with stout stems, up to 4' tall, with milky sap and opposite leaves. The leaves are thick, up to 6" long, tapering at each end, on short stalks, and with fine hairs on the underside. The smaller side veins are at right angles to the central vein, which is also typically red. The flowers are in large, round clusters at the top of the stem. Each flower has 5 reflexed petals, surrounding 5 spreading hoods, each with a tiny, pointed horn arising from it. The fruit pods are about 6" long and ¾" thick, with fine hairs, and filled with numerous seeds, each with silky hairs at one end.

May—July

Habitat/Range: Open woods, edge of woods, open areas, roadsides; scattered counties throughout the state.

Remarks: Milkweeds have a long medical history, but they have also been used for food. The young shoots were cooked as an asparagus substitute. The flowers, buds, and immature fruits were cooked in boiling water; the water had to be changed to remove the bitter tasting toxins. During World War II, the milky latex was tested as a rubber substitute, and the plumes of the seed heads were collected by schoolchildren and others as part of the war effort. The fluffy material was used as a substitute in life preservers when there was a shortage of kapok, which is the silky down surrounding the seeds of the kapok tree of Africa and tropical American.

WILD BERGAMOT
Monarda fistulosa
Mint Family (Lamiaceae)

Description: The plants have a fragrant aroma and square stems; both characteristics are typical of the mint family. They branch and grow up to 5' tall, with the upper stem usually with fine hairs. The leaves are opposite, on short stalks, up to 5" long, 2" wide, widest towards the base and narrowing to a long pointed tip, with teeth along the margins. The flowers are numerous in dense round heads, at the top of the stem. The tubular, lavender flowers have 2 long lips: the upper narrow, arching upward and hairy, with stamens protruding; the lower broad and 3-lobed.

June—August

Habitat/Range: Dry woods, prairies, fields, and roadsides; statewide.

Remarks: Many Native American tribes made tea from the flower heads and leaves to treat colds, fevers, whooping cough, abdominal pain, headaches, and as a stimulant. The Lakotas wrapped boiled leaves in a soft cloth and placed it on sore eyes overnight to relieve pain. Chewed leaves were placed on wounds under a bandage to stop the flow of blood. Wild Bergamot is still used in herbal teas.

WILD PETUNIA
Ruellia humilis
Acanthus Family (Acanthaceae)

Description: Plants with hairy, squarish stems, often branched, usually less than 12" tall. The leaves are opposite, on very short stalks or stalkless, about 2" long and 1" wide, with long hairs along the veins and leaf margins. The showy, light lavender to purple flowers emerge from the leaf axils on the upper half of the plant. Each flower is up to 2½" long, tubular, and flaring to 5 broad lobes. The mouth of the flower is often marked with dark purple lines.

May—October

Habitat/Range: Dry or rocky woods, prairies, glades; statewide.

Remarks: A similar species, Smooth Wild Petunia, *Ruellia strepens*, has sparsely hairy stems and leaves, short stalks, and stems up to 3' tall; grows in moist or lowland woods, and borders of streams; nearly statewide, less common in Gulf Coastal Plain Region. Another species of Wild Petunia, *Ruellia pedunculata*, has single flowers on long stalks with a reduced pair of leaves; dry to moist woods, glades, banks of streams; statewide.

PALE PURPLE CONEFLOWER
Echinacea pallida
Aster Family (Asteraceae)

Description: A stout-stemmed, showy plant, up to 3' tall, with coarse, bristly hairs on the stems and leaves. The leaves at the base are on long stalks, up to 10" long and 1½" wide, tapering at both ends with parallel veins running along the length of the blade. The stem leaves are few, smaller, with short stalks. The flower heads are single on long stems, with several drooping, pale purple petal-like ray flowers, each about 3½" long surrounding a purplish-brown, dome-shaped central disk. The pollen on the anthers is white.

May—July

Habitat/Range: Rocky open woods, prairies, pinelands; nearly statewide, less common in the Delta Region.

Remarks: Native American Indians used the root to treat snakebites, stings, spider bites, toothaches, burns, hard-to-heal wounds, flu, and colds. It is widely used today in pharmaceutical preparations. A similar species, Glade Coneflower, *Echinacea simulata*, has petals that are a deeper purple and droop less than pale purple coneflower; the pollen is yellow; dolomite glades; northern Ozark Region counties.

CALAMINT
Clinopodium arkansanum
Mint Family (Lamiaceae)

Description: A sparse, low-growing mint, with smooth, branching, square stems, up to 12" tall and very fragrant. The stem leaves are opposite, stalkless, slender, less than ½" long, often with a smaller pair of leaflike bracts emerging from each leaf axil. The basal leaves are round and rose-purple underneath. The flowers are on stalks attached at the leaf axils. Each light purple flower is tubular, about ⅜" long, with 2 lips. The upper lip has 2 small lobes; the lower lip is larger with 3 lobes.

May—August

Habitat/Range: Rocky ground, glades, ledges; Ozark Region and a few Ouachita Region counties.

Remarks: Formerly known as *Calamintha arkansana* and *Satureja arkansana*. A leaf tea has been used for colds, fevers, coughs, indigestion, kidney and liver ailments, and headaches. The essential oil, which can be lethal if taken internally, has been used as an insect repellant but may cause dermatitis.

SMOOTH PHLOX
Phlox glaberrima
Phlox Family (Polemoniaceae)

Description: Smooth, hairless plants, up to 3' tall, but usually less than 2' in height. The leaves are stalkless, smooth, opposite on the stem, up to 5" long, ⁵⁄₈" wide, broadest at the base and gradually tapering to a pointed tip. The bright magenta flowers are tubular and open into 5 broad lobes, about ½" across.

May—June

Habitat/Range: Moist prairies, low areas in woods; mostly the lower two-thirds of the state.

Remarks: Smooth Phlox is the only tall phlox to bloom in the spring. The name phlox means flame, in reference to the bright colors of the blooms. The species name *glaberrima* means "very smooth."

LEATHER FLOWER
Clematis versicolor
Buttercup Family (Ranunculaceae)

Description: A vine that can climb to a height of 8'. The leaves are divided into from 2–4 leaflet pairs. The bell-shaped flowers vary from pale lavender to reddish purple with yellow toward the tips.

May—September

Habitat/Range: Woodland edges; Ozark Region; also Polk and Saline counties.

Remarks: A related species, Bluebill, *Clematis pitcheri*, has a reddish stem, leaflets with 3–5 pairs, more oval and thicker, and flowers that are lavender and vase shaped. Found in woodland edges and thickets; scattered counties in the Ozark and Ouachita regions. Another related species, Blue Jasmine, *Clematis crispa*, has 2–4 leaflet pairs; flowers blue to purple with wavy margins; woodland edges, slopes and banks, and roadsides; southern half of the state.

PURPLE POPPY MALLOW
Callirhoe involucrata
Mallow Family
(Malvaceae)

Description: A low lying plant with spreading hairy stems, up to 30" long. The leaves are 1½–3" long, 1–3" wide, and divided into 3–7 lobes. The flowers are solitary on stalks up to 8" long. The 5 petals are rose to purple and 1–2½" long with numerous stamens that are united into a column.

May—August

Habitat/Range: Prairies, roadsides, grassy open places; scattered in a few counties in the Ozark Region; also Logan and Pulaski counties.

Remarks: Another species, Bush's Poppy Mallow, *Callirhoe bushii*, has upright stems to 2½' tall and leaves with broader lobes. Found along roadsides, edges of glades, open areas; occurs in a few scattered Ozark Region counties; rare. *May—August*

FRINGED POPPY MALLOW
Callirhoe digitata
Mallow Family
(Malvaceae)

Description: A smooth, widely-branching, spindly plant, up to 5' tall, with a whitish coating on the stems that can be rubbed off. The leaves are alternate, stalked, and divided into 5–7 narrow, deep, finger-like lobes. Each lobe can be further divided and is usually less than ¼" across. The flowers are on long stalks, with each flower 1½–2" across. The 5 petals are bright magenta with ragged outer edges and a central column containing the stamens and style.

May—August

Habitat/Range: Prairies, dolomite glades, open areas; Ozark and Ouachita regions.

Remarks: The Dakota used poppy mallow root for internal pains and smoke from the dried root to bathe aching body parts.

NARROW-LEAVED VERVAIN
Verbena simplex
Vervain Family (Verbenaceae)

Description: Short, slender plants, 12–18" tall, with ridges along the stem. The leaves are opposite, stalkless, narrow, up to 3½" long and 1" wide, with sparse teeth, and tapering at both ends. The flowers are crowded along a spike at the top of the stem. Each flower is lavender to purple, small, about ¼" across, with a short tube and 5 spreading petals.

May—September

Habitat/Range: Prairies, glades, fields, along roadsides, disturbed soil; primarily the Ozark Region.

Remarks: Another species, Creeping Vervain, *Verbena bracteata*, is shorter, stems spreading or sprawling, with leaves deeply lobed; disturbed soil; statewide.

HOARY VERVAIN
Verbena stricta
Vervain Family (Verbenaceae)

Description: Stout, densely hairy plants, up to 4' tall, branching in the upper half. The leaves are opposite, with very short stalks, gray-hairy, broadly rounded, up to 4" long and 2½" wide, and toothed along the margins. The flowers are crowded along 1 to several narrow spikes at the top of the plant. Each purple flower is about ¼" across, with 5 spreading, rounded lobes.

May—September

Habitat/Range: Open areas, old fields, roadsides, disturbed soil; Ozark Region, Crowley's Ridge and a few Ouachita counties.

Remarks: There are 7 native and 5 nonnative species in the genus *Verbena* in Arkansas and around 3,000 worldwide, with most occurring in the tropics.

MUSK THISTLE
Carduus nutans
Aster Family (Asteraceae)

Description: A sturdy biennial with a spiny, winged-stem, up to 7' tall. First year's leaves spread over the ground, radiating out from a central core and overwinter, sending up branching stems the second year. Leaves are up to 10" long, 4" wide, smooth, deeply lobed with spiny tips. The flower heads are about 2" across, solitary, nodding at the ends of very long stalks, with numerous reddish-purple flowers.

May—October

Habitat/Range: Pastures, fields, roadsides, and other disturbed places; native to Europe; scattered locations across the state and will likely keep spreading.

Remarks: Also called Nodding Thistle, this is an aggressive, noxious weed that is hard to eradicate once established. The fluffy seeds can be carried long distances by the wind.

CHICORY
Cichorium intybus
Aster Family (Asteraceae)

Description: A branched, hairy plant, up to 3' tall, with milky sap and ridges along the stem. The leaves are alternate, lobed or toothed along the margins, with the upper leaves clasping the stem. The flower heads are up to 1½" across, lack stalks, and emerge all along the stem. Each head has blue (sometimes white or pink), petal-like ray flowers with 5 notches at the tip of each narrow ray.

May—October

Habitat/Range: Disturbed soil, roadsides, fields, pastures; native to Europe; northern counties and will likely continue to spread.

Remarks: Chicory was used as a medicinal herb, vegetable, and salad plant in ancient Egyptian, Greek, and Roman times. Since the 17th century, dried, roasted, ground roots have been used as a coffee substitute. Chicory is a gentle, but effective bitter tonic, which increases the flow of bile and is used to treat gallstones.

PASSION FLOWER
Passiflora incarnata
Passion Flower Family (Passifloraceae)

Description: A vine, up to 20' long, that climbs or sprawls with the help of tendrils. The leaves are alternate, with 3 broad, toothed lobes, usually smooth, and up to 5" across. The unusual flowers are single, arising on stalks from the axils of leaves. Individual flowers are up to 3" across, with several petals and a purple fringe. There are 5 drooping stamens around the pistil, which has 3–4 curved stigmas. The fruit is oval, smooth, yellow when ripe, up to 2" long, and contains many seeds with gelatinous coverings.

May—September

Habitat/Range: Edge of woods; ditch banks, fencerows, and along roadsides and railroads; statewide.

Remarks: Also known as Maypops, which comes from children in the South stomping on the fruit to make it pop. Native American Indians used the root to treat boils, cuts, earaches, and inflammation. A tea was made from the plant to soothe the nerves. The fruit is edible.

PURPLE PRAIRIE CLOVER
Dalea purpurea
Pea Family (Fabaceae)

Description: Slender, leafy plants, up to 2' tall, with 1 to several stems arising from a common base. The leaves are divided into 3–9 shiny, narrow leaflets, each about 1" long and ⅛" wide. The flowers are densely packed in a cylindrical head at the tops of the branches, with the flowers opening in a circle around the head from bottom to top. Each flower is about ¼" long, with a large petal and 4 smaller petals, with 5 orange stamens.

May—August

Habitat/Range: Rocky open woods, prairies, glades; northern Ozark counties and western Gulf Coastal Plain counties.

Remarks: Formerly known as *Petalostemum purpureum*. Sensitive to overgrazing, Purple Prairie Clover is an indicator of high-quality habitat. Native American Indians used the plant medicinally by applying a tea made from the leaves to open wounds. The Pawnee took root tea as a general preventive medicine. Settlers mixed the bark from white oak trees together with the flowers of Purple Prairie Clover to make a drink used for diarrhea. Native American Indians gathered the tough, elastic stems to make brooms.

SPIKED LOBELIA
Lobelia spicata
Bellflower Family (Campanulaceae)

Description: Slender, smooth, single-stemmed plants, up to 3' tall, with milky sap and ridges along the stem that is very hairy on the lower part. The leaves are alternate, narrow, up to 3½" long and 1" wide, with teeth along the margins. The pale blue to nearly white flowers are on short stalks that alternate along the stem. There is a small leaf-like bract at the base of each flower stalk. The flowers are less than ½" long, with 2 lips; the small upper lip has 2 lobes that are stiffly erect; the broad lower lip has 3 larger spreading lobes.

May—July

Habitat/Range: Dry woods, prairies, glades; nearly statewide, less common in the Delta Region.

Remarks: Native American Indians used a tea of the plant to induce vomiting. Root tea was used to treat trembling by applying the tea to scratches made in the affected limb. A similar species, *Lobelia appendiculata*, has the lower stem smooth to slightly hairy; nearly statewide, less common in the Ozark Region. Then, Indian Tobacco, *Lobelia inflata*, has the base of the flower inflated and hair on the lower stem; nearly statewide, less common in the Delta and Gulf Coastal Plain. And, Downy Lobelia, *Lobelia puberula*, has larger, much darker blue flowers, usually along one side of the stem that is covered with fine hairs; damp areas; nearly statewide except for the northern one-quarter.

DAY FLOWER
Commelina erecta
Spiderwort Family (Commelinaceae)

Description: A perennial plant, up to 3' tall, with branching, upright stems. The leaves are lance-shaped with parallel veins, up to 6" long and 1½" wide, and clasping the stem. The flowers emerge from a boat-like sheath, one at a time. Each flower, which lasts but a day, is up to 1" across, with 2 rounded blue petals and 1 smaller white petal. There are 6 yellow-tipped stamens.

May—September

Habitat/Range: Moist or dry sandy soil along streambanks, rocky wooded slopes, roadsides; statewide.

Remarks: Another species, Common Dayflower, *Commelina communis*, is annual, has smaller leaves and flowers, and shorter, sprawling stems, up to 2' long, which often root at the nodes; native to Asia; disturbed moist sites; statewide. Another, Small Dayflower, *Commelina diffusa*, has the lower petal blue; moist woodlands and disturbed ground; scattered across the state.

WINGED LOOSESTRIFE
Lythrum alatum
Loosestrife Family (Lythraceae)

Description: A smooth, loosely branching plant to 2' tall, with squarish stems that may support shallow wings or flaps of tissue. The leaves are opposite on the lower stem and alternate above, narrow, up to 2" long, progressively smaller toward the top; broadly rounded at the base and pointed at the tip. The pale lavender to reddish-purple flowers are up to ½" across and arise singly from the upper leaf axils. Each flower has a narrow tube with 6 petals.

June—September

Habitat/Range: Wet, open areas in marshes, prairies, margins of streams, ponds, and ditches; scattered across the state.

Remarks: The genus, *Lythrum*, is Greek for "gore," as in the blood-and-guts kind that would be seen in battle; the species, *alatum*, is Latin for "winged." Winged Loosestrife should not be confused with Purple Loosestrife, which is a taller plant with flowers arranged in clusters along an end spike.

PURPLE LOOSESTRIFE
Lythrum salicaria
Loosestrife Family (Lythraceae)

Description: A multi-branched plant with a 4-sided stem, up to 5' tall with opposite leaves or in whorls of 3. The leaves are stalkless, narrow to lance-shaped, 1–4" long. The reddish-purple flowers are in clusters at the tips of stems from 4–16" long. The flowers are ½–1" across with 6 petals.

June—September

Habitat/Range: Moist areas along edges of marshes, ponds, roadsides; native to Europe; reported in northeastern Arkansas.

Remarks: Purple Loosestrife often occurs in dense stands that shade out native flora. The plant was introduced to the east coast of North America in the early 1800s by immigrants as an ornamental and herb. It spread into the Midwest in the 1880s. Difficult to eradicate, each plant can produce 1000s of seeds a year that can lay dormant in the soil for many years. It can also reproduce from roots and broken stems. Its planting as an ornamental should be discouraged.

BUTTERFLY PEA
Clitoria mariana
Pea Family (Fabaceae)

Description: A smooth, twining but not climbing plant, up to 3' long. The leaves are stalked and divided into 3 leaflets with the center leaflet on a long stalk. The leaflets are up to 3½" long, broadest at the base and tapering to a pointed tip. There are 1–3 flowers on short stalks attached along the stem. The showy lavender to pale blue flowers are about 2" long with purple markings along the center of the large, flat petal (the standard). The central keel points downward.

June—August

Habitat/Range: Dry woods; not common; nearly statewide.

Remarks: Flowers late in the season may pollinate without opening. There are 35 species in the genus *Clitoria*, mostly native to warm regions of the world. A similar species, Spurred Butterfly Pea, *Centrosema virginianum*, are smaller, up to 1¼" long, with a white patch in the center of the large, flat petal (the standard); central keel points upward; similar flowering dates and habitat; mainly Gulf Coastal Plain Region.

MONKEY FLOWER
Mimulus alatus
Figwort Family

Description: Smooth, often branched plants, up to 3' tall, with squarish stems or at least a ridge down the sides. The stems are also winged with strips of green tissue. The leaves are opposite, stalked, up to 4" long, broadest toward the base, tapering at the tip, and toothed. The flowers are on stalks arising from the leaf axils. Each blue flower is about 1" long, with 2 lips: the upper small, the lower broad with 3 lobes.

June—September

Habitat/Range: Wet ground along streams, spring branches, and ponds, and in low wet woods; statewide.

Remarks: The common name refers to the flower's resemblance to a grinning monkey's face. Another species, of Monkey Flower, *Mimulus ringens*, has leaves without stalks, blue flowers up to 1½" long, and angles of the stem without wings; habitat similar; Baxter, Fulton, and Sharp counties.

TALL BELLFLOWER

Campanulastrum americanum
Bellflower Family (Campanulaceae)

Description: A tall, slender, annual plant, up to 6' in height, with ridges along the stem. The leaves are alternate, stalked, up to 6" long, lance-shaped, with fine teeth along the margins. The flowers emerge at the leaf axils and are about 1" across, with 5 pointed, spreading petals. A white ring is present at the base of the petals. The style is long and curves upwards.

June—September

Habitat/Range: Moist open woods and borders of woods, wooded streamsides, and thickets; nearly statewide, rare in the Gulf Coastal Plain Region.

Remarks: Also called American Bellflower, and formerly known as *Campanula americana*. The Mesquakie used leaf tea to treat coughs and tuberculosis, and the crushed root to treat whooping cough.

PURPLE CONEFLOWER

Echinacea purpurea
Aster Family (Asteraceae)

Description: A showy plant, up to 4' tall, with branching stems and with rough hairs on the stems and leaves. The basal leaves, on long stalks, are up to 6" long, broadest at the base, tapering to a pointed tip, and coarsely toothed. The stem leaves are alternate, smaller, on shorter stalks, and coarsely toothed. The large flower heads are at the ends of long stalks and up to 5" across. The 10–20 petal-like reddish-purple ray flowers surround a cone-shaped central disk. The cones are golden red when in flower.

June—September

Habitat/Range: Open woods, edges of woods, wooded floodplains; nearly statewide, less common in the Delta and Gulf Coastal Plain regions.

Remarks: Plains Indians used the root to treat snakebites, bee stings, headaches, stomach cramps, toothaches, and sore throats, and for distemper in horses. Some tribes discovered that the plant was like a burn preventative, enabling the body to endure extreme heat. They used the plant's juice in sweat baths and for ritual feats such as immersing hands in scalding water or holding live coals in the mouth. Coneflowers are widely used today in pharmaceutical preparations.

BLUE HEARTS
Buchnera americana
Snapdragon Family (Scrophulariaceae)

Description: Usually a single-stemmed plant, up to 3' tall. Leaves are from 2–4" long, opposite, lance-shaped, with a few coarse teeth along the margins. Flowers are along a spike at the tip of the stem, reddish-purple, about ½" long tubular with 5 widely spreading lobes.

June—September

Habitat/Range: Prairies, dolomite glades; a few scattered counties in the Ozark Region, Grand Prairie, and Ashley County

Remarks: The genus name, *Buchnera*, is in honor of Johann Gottfried Buchner, an 18th century German botanist.

BLUE SAGE
Salvia azurea
Mint Family (Lamiaceae)

Description: A slender, sometimes branched plant, up to 5' tall, with short hairs along the square stem. The leaves are widely spaced along the stem, opposite, short-stalked, narrow, up to 4" long and 1" wide, with a few teeth along the margins. The flowers are in whorls along the upper stem, with up to 8 flowers in a whorl. Each flower is blue, with a white center, tubular, about 1" long, with 2 lips: the upper lip is narrow and hooded, the lower lip is broad with 2 lobes.

June—October

Habitat/Range: Prairies, glades, open areas; Ozark and Ouachita regions.

Remarks: The attractive blue flowers are pollinated by bumblebees.

IVYLEAF MORNING GLORY
Ipomoea hederacea
Morning Glory Family (Convolvulaceae)

Description: An annual vine, up to 6' long, with twining or climbing hairy stems. The leaves are alternate, hairy, stalked, usually deeply 3-lobed with a heart-shaped base, without teeth, and up to 5" long. From 1–3 flowers appear opposite each leaf. Flowers are funnel-shaped, stalked, blue, up to 1½" long, with 5 united petals.

June—October

Habitat/Range: Cultivated and idle fields, open areas, and along railroads; native to tropical America; statewide.

Remarks: The flowers are open only for a short time in the morning and each flower lasts but a day. There are 2 native and 7 nonnative species of morning glory in the genus *Ipomoea* in Arkansas.

MISSOURI IRONWEED
Vernonia missurica
Aster Family (Asteraceae)

Description: A densely hairy, single-stemmed plant, up to 6' tall. Leaves are up to 8" long and 2½" wide, with long crooked hairs on the lower surface. The flower heads are in clusters on several branches at the top of the stem. There are 34–55 purple flowers in each flower head.

July—September

Habitat/Range: Low, open woods, prairies, roadsides, fields; nearly statewide, less common in the Ozark Region.

Remarks: Another similar species, Texas Ironweed, *Vernonia texana*, has leaves rapidly decreasing in size going up the stem with the upper leaves merely bracts; open woods, roadsides, fields; Gulf Coastal Plain Region.

ARKANSAS IRONWEED
Vernonia arkansana
Aster Family (Asteraceae)

Description: From 1 to several stems arise from the base to a height of 4', with willow-like leaves. The leaves are alternate, stalkless, up to 6" long and ½" wide, gradually tapering at both ends, and with small teeth along the margins. The reddish-purple flower heads are few in number but large, with each head containing over 55 small flowers. The bracts at the base of the flower head are long and curled.

July—October

Habitat/Range: Rocky open woods, prairies, glades, and along gravel and sandbars of streams; Ozark Region and Crittenden County.

Remarks: Formerly known as *Vernonia crinita*. There are 8 species of ironweed in Arkansas.

WESTERN IRONWEED
Vernonia baldwinii
Aster Family (Asteraceae)

Description: Hairy plants up to 5' tall, with alternate leaves up to 7" long and 2½" wide. The leaves are broadest near the middle and tapering at both ends, densely hairy underneath, and toothed along the margins. The flower heads are numerous, up to ½" across, with about 30 small purple flowers in each head. Each flower head is surrounded at the base with a cup of small, overlapping bracts with pointed, spreading tips.

July—September

Habitat/Range: Dry or rocky wooded slopes, fields, pastures, along roadsides; nearly statewide, less common in the Delta and Gulf Coastal Plain regions.

Remarks: Another species, Tall Ironweed, *Vernonia gigantea* (formerly *V. altissima*), up to 7' tall, has the lower surface of leaves with sparse hairs, the bracts along the cup of the flower heads blunt instead of pointed and less than 30 small flowers per flower head; moist soil, low woods; statewide.

GROUNDNUT
Apios americana
Pea Family (Fabaceae)

Description: A climbing or sprawling vine with milky sap and widely spaced, stalked, alternate, divided leaves. The leaves have 3–7 leaflets on short stalks, each up to 3" long, with smooth edges along the margins, broadly rounded bases and pointed tips. Flowers are in dense clusters on short stalks emerging at the bases of leaves. The flowers are brownish-purple, fragrant, up to ½" long, with an upper hooded petal, 2 smaller side petals, and a strongly curved, keel-like lower petal. The fruits are wavy pods 2–4" long.

July—September

Habitat/Range: Moist soil, borders of marshes, ponds, lakes, and, streams; statewide.

Remarks: Groundnuts were important food sources of the Osage, Pawnee and many other tribes. The Osage gathered them in late summer and fall and stored them in caches for winter use. Also an important food of New England colonists, the pilgrims were dependent on the potato-like tuber for their survival that first winter. The tubers can be used in soups or stews, or fried like potatoes with 3 times the protein of the latter. The seeds in summer can be eaten cooked like peas.

INDIAN HELIOTROPE
Heliotropium indicum
Borage Family (Boraginaceae)

Description: An upright, coarsely hairy annual from 1–3' tall. The leaves are from 1½–4" long, broadest below the middle, abruptly narrowed at the base, with a wrinkled surface. The flowers appear on one side of the stem that uncurls as the flowers mature. Flowers are 5-lobed, small, less than ¼" across, and lavender blue.

June—October

Habitat/Range: Moist, disturbed areas; native to Asia; statewide.

Remarks: Also called Turnsole from the Latin *tourner*, to turn, and *sol*, the sun, a name for plants such as heliotropes and sunflowers whose flowers turn towards the sun.

MISTFLOWER
Conoclinium coelestinum
Aster Family (Asteraceae)

Description: Downy, branching, purplish stems, up to 18" tall, which can spread by underground runners. The leaves are opposite, on short stalks, oval to triangular, with large teeth along the margins. The flower heads are in flat-topped clusters at the tops of stems. Each head has 35–70 bright blue or purplish disk flowers.

July—October

Habitat/Range: Moist ground along streams, spring branches, ditches, and low areas in pastures; Statewide.

Remarks: Formerly known as *Eupatorium coelestinum*. Another name, Wild Ageratum, relates to its similarity to the annual ageratum grown in gardens. From a distance the color and density of the flower clusters resembles low-lying foggy mist.

CLAMMY CUPHEA
Cuphea viscosissima
Loosestrife Family (Lythraceae)

Description: A sparsely branched annual, up to 2' tall, with sticky, purplish hairs. The stalked leaves are opposite on the stem, broadest below the middle, and from ¾"–2" long. There are 1–2 small, reddish-purple flowers arising at the junctions of the upper stem and leaves. The flowers have 6 petals, with the upper 2 larger than the lower 4.

July—October

Habitat/Range: Dry soil in open areas; Ozark Region and a few Ouachita Region counties.

Remarks: Formerly called *Cuphea petiolata*, Clammy Cuphea or Blue Waxweed was once used to treat infant cholera in the late 1800s. This plant has recently been tested for its potential cancer fighting properties.

PURPLE JOE PYE WEED
Eupatorium purpureum
Aster Family (Asteraceae)

Description: A tall, slender plant, sometimes growing to a height of 10'. The stem is solid, not hollow, and green, but it may be tinged with purple, especially at the nodes where the leaves are attached. The large, thin leaves are in whorls of 3–4, on short stalks, and up to 12" long and 3" wide, tapering at both ends with numerous small teeth along the margins. The tiny fragrant flower heads are in large domelike clusters 6" across or more. Each cylindrical flower head contains 3–7 petal-like ray flowers that vary from pink to purple to almost white.

July—September

Habitat/Range: Woodlands; northern two-thirds of the state.

Remarks: Legend has it that Joe Pye, a Native American Indian herb doctor of the Massachusetts Bay Colony, used this plant to cure fevers. The Iroquois and, more recently, people in some areas of Appalachia, used parts of these plants to treat urinary disorders. Chippewa mothers bathed fretful children in a tea made from this plant to bring restful sleep. It was also traditional for Mesquakie men to nibble the leaves to ensure success in courtship. Another species, Hollow Joe Pye Weed, *Eupatorium fistulosum*, has hollow purplish stems and leaves often more than 4 in a whorl; found in low, wet ground; most frequent in northcentral and southwestern counties.

DITTANY
Cunila origanoides
Mint Family (Lamiaceae)

Description: A low, much-branched, wiry plant, up to 12" tall, sometimes with fine hairs along the square stem. Leaves are opposite, stalkless, hairless, up to 1½" long, broadest at the base, tapering to a pointed tip, and usually with a few teeth along the margins. The rose-purple flowers are in clusters arising from the leaf axils. Each flower has 2 lips: the smaller upper lip has 2 lobes, and the larger lower lip has 3. The lips have purplish dots.

July–October

Habitat/Range: Dry, rocky or open woods, sandstone cliffs; nearly statewide, uncommon in the Delta Region.

Remarks: In late fall, during hard freezes, dittany produces "frost flowers." These are ribbons of ice oozing out of cracks at the base of the stem. Sap from still-active roots freezes as it emerges from the dead stem, growing like a white ribbon as more fluid is pumped out.

BLUE LETTUCE
Lactuca floridana
Aster Family (Asteraceae)

Description: Tall, slender plants, up to 7' tall, with milky sap. The leaves are up to 12" long, hairless, have deep lobes, with the tip broadly triangular, and the base tapering to a stalk edged with leafy tissue. The flower heads are numerous, on widely branching stems, light blue, small, and about ½" across. Each head has 11–16 petal-like ray flowers.

July—October

Habitat/Range: Woods, woodland borders, roadsides; Ozark and Ouachita regions, less common in the Gulf Coastal Plain and Delta regions except for Crowley's Ridge.

Remarks: The young leaves have been eaten in salads and as cooked greens. The milky sap is bitter.

ROUGH BLAZING STAR
Liatris aspera
Aster Family (Asteraceae)

Description: A single-stemmed plant that is hairy or smooth, up to 4' tall, arising from a corm. The basal leaves are short-stalked and up to 16" long and 2" wide. The stem leaves are progressively shorter upwards on the stem. The flower heads are alternately arranged and loosely spaced along a wand-like spike, up to 1½' long. The bracts on the head are rounded with white to purplish, papery tips. The heads are up to 1" across, with 15–25 small, purple disk flowers, each with 5 lobes.

July—October

Habitat/Range: Prairies, open areas; nearly statewide, less common in the Delta Region.

Remarks: The Mesquakies used the plant for bladder and kidney troubles. The Pawnees boiled the leaves and root together and fed the tea to children with diarrhea. Root tea was used as a folk remedy for kidney and bladder ailments, gonorrhea, and colic, and was gargled for sore throats. The root was mashed and applied to snakebites.

PRAIRIE BLAZING STAR
Liatris pycnostachya
Aster Family (Asteraceae)

SCALY BLAZING STAR
Liatris squarrosa
Aster Family (Asteraceae)

Description: Often hairy, single-stemmed plants to 2½' tall, with narrow, somewhat rigid leaves. The lower leaves are up to 10" long and ½" wide but are progressively smaller upward along the stem. The flower heads are few to solitary, each about ½" across, and emerging from the upper leaf axils. The bracts below the flower head overlap with spreading pointed tips that look spine-like or scaly. Each flower head has 20–40 small, purple, disk flowers that are tubular with 5 lobes. The top flower head tends to be larger with more disk flowers.

July—September

Habitat/Range: Rocky or dry open woods, prairies, glades; nearly statewide, less common in the Delta and Gulf Coastal Plain divisions.

Remarks: Scaly Blazing Star was used as a diuretic, a tonic, and a stimulant. It was also used to treat gonorrhea, kidney trouble, and uterine disease.

Description: Hairy, slender, unbranched, spikes up to 5' tall, arising from a corm. The leaves are alternate, stalkless, and numerous, with the lower leaves sometimes over 12" long and up to ½" wide, gradually reducing in size up the stem. The flowers heads are in a long dense spike, often over 12" long, at the top of the plant. Each small head is about ¼" across, with small, hairy, outward curving purple bracts. There are 5–10 disk flowers in each head, each with 5 lobes.

July—October

Habitat/Range: Prairies, open ground, roadsides; statewide.

Remarks: Also called Gayfeather. Cultivated varieties of Prairie Blazing Star are grown for the cut-flower market. The flowering spikes can be air-dried for use in winter arrangements. A similar species, Pinkscale Blazing Star, *Liatris elegans*, is shorter, up to 4' tall with large lavender-pink petal-like bracts, about ½" long surrounding the disk flowers; sandy or rocky open areas; mainly southwestern Arkansas.

GARDEN PHLOX
Phlox paniculata
Phlox Family (Polemoniaceae)

Description: A showy, late-blooming phlox, up to 5' tall. The leaves are opposite, stalkless, up to 6" long and 2" wide, broadest along the middle and narrowing at both ends, with the side veins prominent. The flowers are often in large, pyramidal clusters at the tops of the stems. The reddish-purple (sometimes white) flowers are on short stalks, up to ¾" across, with a short-hairy tube, 5 lobes, and with 1 of the yellow stamens extending just beyond the mouth of the flower.

July—September

Habitat/Range: Moist woods, edge of woods, low woods along streams and in valleys; Ozark Region.

Remarks: Also called Perennial Phlox. Garden Phlox is so named because of its popularity as a garden plant and the many horticultural varieties that have been developed from it.

GREAT BLUE LOBELIA
Lobelia siphilitica
Bellflower Family (Campanulaceae)

Description: Unbranched plants, up to 3' tall, with milky sap. The leaves are alternate, stalkless, up to 6" long and 1½" wide, widest in the middle and tapering at both ends, with teeth along the margins. The flowers are crowded along the upper part of the stem. Each flower is ¾–1½" long, deep blue, with pale stripes along the tube and with 2 lips. The upper lip is split into 2 upright lobes, and the lower lip into 3 spreading lobes with a white base.

July—October

Habitat/Range: Wet ground in woodlands, along streams, gravel bars, roadsides; Ozark Region, Crowley's Ridge, uncommon in Ouachita Region.

Remarks: The Mesquakies finely chopped the roots and mixed them into food of a quarrelsome couple without their knowledge. This, they believed, would avert divorce and make the pair love each other again. Other tribes used root tea for syphilis and leaf tea for colds, fevers, upset stomachs, worms, coup, and nosebleeds.

FIELD THISTLE
Cirsium discolor
Aster Family (Asteraceae)

Description: A robust biennial plant, up to 6' tall with a hairy, ridged stem. The leaves are deeply divided into stiff, narrow, spiny lobes. The leaves are 4–8" long with dense white woolly hairs below. The flower heads are 1–1½" long with spine-tipped bracts below the rose-purple heads.

July—October

Habitat/Range: Fields, pastures, roadsides, open woods, degraded prairies; scattered across the state.

Remarks: Also called Pasture Thistle. A similar looking species, Bull Thistle, *Cirsium vulgare*, differs by having the upper stem and branches winged by a wavy strip of prickly green leafy tissue running from the base of the leaf down the stem. This thistle comes from Europe and is a noxious weed. It is found in disturbed soil; scattered throughout the state. Another species, Yellow Thistle, *Cirsium horridulum*, has pale yellow or pale purplish flower heads about 2" across; leaves large and spiny; rocky open areas, fields, roadsides; mainly the Gulf Coastal Plain Region.

TALL THISTLE
Cirsium altissimum
Aster Family (Asteraceae)

Description: A tall, branching biennial to short-lived perennial plant, up to 8' in height. The alternate, deep green leaves grow to 12" long. The leaves are not lobed but have coarse teeth along the leaf margins that end in spines. The undersides of the leaves have whitish woolly hairs. The flower heads are at the ends of long stalks, up to 2' tall, with a short spine at the end of each bract. Each rose-purple flower is tubular, about 1" long, with 5 narrow lobes, each about ⅜" long.

August—September

Habitat/Range: Dry, open, or rocky woodland, borders of woods, disturbed soil, and along roadsides; scattered across the state.

Remarks: The fluffy down from mature thistle heads is a favorite nest lining for American goldfinches. Another species, Soft Thistle, *Cirsium carolinianum*, is widely branching with few upper leaves and long bare flower stalks; flower heads bright reddish-purple; open woodlands, idle land, roadsides; mainly in central and southern counties.

SLENDER FALSE FOXGLOVE
Agalinis tenuifolia
Figwort Family (Scrophulariaceae)

Description: A much-branched annual plant, less than 2' tall, with narrow ridges along the main stem. The leaves are opposite, very narrow, up to 3" long and often less than $\frac{1}{8}$" wide, with smooth edges. The upper leaves have smaller leaves emerging from the same axils. Single flowers arise from the leaf axils on stalks longer than the calyx. Each rose-purple flower is less than $\frac{1}{2}$" long and funnel-shaped, with a short tube opening to 5 rounded lobes. There are purple spots and 4 hairy stamens in the mouth of the flower.

July—September

Habitat/Range: Dry or moist open woodlands, borders of streams; northcentral and southwestern counties and Crowley's Ridge.

Remarks: Formerly called *Gerardia tenuifolia*. Another species of False Foxglove, *Agalinis(Gerardia) fasciculata*, is up to 3' tall, with deep reddish-purple flowers about 1" long, with flower stalks shorter than the calyx; open areas, roadsides; lower three-fourths of the state.

CAMPHORWEED
Pluchea camphorata
Aster Family (Asteraceae)

Description: An annual or short-lived perennial from 1–5' tall with a camphor-like odor. Leaves are alternate, lance-shaped to oval, toothed and taper at the base. Flowers are pinkish-purple, without ray flowers and clustered at the tips of branches.

August—November

Habitat/Range: Wet woods, borders of swamps, sloughs, streams; also idle, sometimes disturbed land; nearly statewide, less frequent in the northern Ozark Region counties.

Remarks: Also known as Marsh Fleabane. Another species, Stinkweed, *Pluchea foetida*, has leaves that clasp the stem and whitish to yellowish flowers; Gulf Coastal Plain.

BLUE CURLS
Trichostema dichotomum
Mint Family (Lamiaceae)

Description: A much-branched, annual plant, up to 2' tall, with square stems, and covered with dense, gland-tipped hairs. The leaves are opposite, broadest in the middle, up to 2½" long and ¾" wide, with usually smooth margins, and tapering at the base to a short stalk about ½" long. The flowers are about ¾" long with the lower lip with a patch of white and purple spots. The 4 stamens are long and curve downward.

August—September

Habitat/Range: Rocky open woods, glades, open areas, sandy soil along streams; nearly statewide, less common in the Delta Region.

Remarks: The attractive small flowers with their lavender-blue corolla and long curving stamens must be viewed up-close to be appreciated.

BEEFSTEAK PLANT
Perilla frutescens
Mint Family (Lamiaceae)

Description: An annual, up to 3' tall with coarse hairs along the 4-sided purple stem. Leaves are opposite, stalked, toothed along the margins, up to 4" long and 3" wide, and purple-green to entirely purple below with hairs along the veins. The flowers emerge along an expanding purple, hairy stalk, 6–10" long. The purple flowers are small, hairy, with a 3-lobed upper lip and a single-lobed lower lip.

August—October

Habitat/Range: Disturbed ground in low areas, especially along streams; native to Asia; statewide.

Remarks: All parts of the plant are fragrant and have been used as a culinary herb by some Oriental cultures; also to treat a variety of ailments from diarrhea to morning sickness and various nervous conditions. Perilla oil is used in food products and also in making lacquers and finishes for wood. It is a less expensive substitute for linseed oil.

SOUTHERN PRAIRIE ASTER
Eurybia hemispherica
Aster Family (Asteraceae)

Description: A smooth stemmed plant from 8–30" tall, with alternate, grass-like leaves up to 8" long. Flowers emerge from leaf axils, from 1–2" across, with 15–35 blue or violet rays. Disk flowers are yellow.

August—October

Habitat/Range: Prairies, sandy to rocky soils; mainly in the southern two-thirds of the state.

Remarks: Formerly known as *Aster paludosus* subspecies *hemisphericus*. The showy flowers are noticeably larger than what might be expected for a plant this size.

AROMATIC ASTER
Symphyotrichum oblongifolium
Aster Family (Asteraceae)

Description: Fragrant, hairy plants, up to 2½' tall, with spreading branches. The leaves are alternate, crowded, hairy, up to 3" long and less than 1" wide, with clasping bases and a rough surface. The flower heads are at the end of short branches, with numerous, small, leaf-like bracts along their length. Each flower head is 1" across and has 20–40 purple, petal-like ray flowers surrounding the yellow disk flowers.

August—November

Habitat/Range: Dry open woods, glades; Ozark and Ouachita regions, also Crittenden County.

Remarks: Formerly known as *Aster oblongifolius*. Aromatic Aster takes on a shrublike look with hundreds of attractive flowers when grown in the garden and given full sun. It continues to flower well after the first frost.

STIFF-LEAVED ASTER
Ionactis linariifolia
Aster Family (Asteraceae)

Description: Plants with more than 1 stem emerging from a base, less than 2' tall, with stiff, roughish, minutely hairy leaves. The leaves are alternate, stalkless, up to 1½" long and ⅛" wide, and tapering to fine points. Several flowers are at the tops of stems on short individual stalks. Each flower head is up to 1¼" wide, with 10–15 satiny purple, petal-like ray flowers surrounding a yellow disk.

August—October

Habitat/Range: Rocky open woods, prairies, glades; west half of Ozark Region, also Ouachita Region.

Remarks: Also called Flax-Leaved Aster. Formerly known as *Aster linariifolius*. Stiff-Leaved Aster is easily identified by its low stature, its crowded, stiff, narrow leaves, and its few to solitary flower heads.

BLUE ASTER
Symphyotrichum anomalum
Aster Family (Asteraceae)

Description: Plants with stiff, erect stems, up to 4' tall. The leaves are alternate, the lower leaves lance-shaped, up to 3½" long and 1½" wide, heart-shaped at the base, with a wing of tissue along the leaf base. The upper leaves are lance-shaped, smaller, and without leaf stalks. The flower heads are ½" across, with numerous bracts at the base that curve downward. Each flower head has 30–45 bright lavender, petal-like ray flowers surrounding a yellow disk.

August—October

Habitat/Range: Rocky open woods; Ozark and Ouachita regions, also Crittenden and Mississippi counties.

Remarks: Also called Woodland Aster. Formerly known as *Aster anomalus*. The flowers and fruits of Blue Aster are eaten by wild turkey, and the leaves by white-tailed deer.

NEW ENGLAND ASTER
Symphyotrichum novae-angliae
Aster Family (Asteraceae)

Description: Showy plants, with hairy branching stems, up to 6' tall. The leaves are alternate, numerous, up to 4" long and 1" wide, hairy, with pointed tips and leaves that clasp the stem. Several flower heads are clustered along the upper stems. Each head is about 1½" across, with over 40 bright purple, petal-like ray flowers surrounding a yellow disk. The flowers can also be pinkish-purple or pale lavender.

August—October

Habitat/Range: Low open areas in valleys and along streams, roadsides; scattered across the Ozark Region, also Clark and Nevada counties.

Remarks: Formerly known as *Aster novae-angliae*. This aster is quite easily grown in gardens. The Mesquakie burned the plant and blew the smoke up the nose of an unconscious person to revive him or her. Other tribes used root tea for diarrhea and fevers.

SKY BLUE ASTER
Symphyotrichum oolentangiense
Aster Family (Asteraceae)

Description: This species has rough, slightly hairy stems, up to 3' tall. The leaves are alternate, thick, sandpapery on both sides, and lack teeth along the margins. The basal leaves have long stalks, heart-shaped leaf bases, lance-shaped, and up to 5" long and 2" wide. The stem leaves are much smaller and lack stalks. The flower heads are in spreading clusters at the tops of stems. Each head is about 1" across, with 10–25 blue petal-like ray flowers surrounding a yellow disk.

August—November

Habitat/Range: Rocky open woods, prairies; Ozark Region, also western Ouachita Region.

Remarks: Formerly known as *Aster oolentangiensis* and *Aster azureus*.

SPREADING ASTER
Symphyotrichum patens
Aster Family (Asteraceae)

Description: This plant has slender, hairy, somewhat brittle stems, up to 2½' tall. The leaves are alternate, sandpapery, hairy, lance-shaped, up to 2" long and 1" wide, with bases clasping the stem. The flower heads are single on branches arising from the leaf axils. Each head is about 1" across, with about 15–25 blue, petal-like ray flowers surrounding a yellow disk.

August—October

Habitat/Range: Open woods; statewide.

Remarks: Formerly known as *Aster patens*. Spreading Aster is one of 26 species of asters that occur in Arkansas.

SOAPWORT GENTIAN
Gentiana saponaria
Gentian Family (Gentianaceae)

Description: Unbranched stems, with a soapy sap, up to 2½' tall, with stalkless leaves that are opposite along the stem. The upper leaves are usually the largest, up to 4" long and 1½" wide. The flowers occur in 1–3 clusters along the stem with leaf-like bracts below each cluster. Each flower is about 1½" long, deep blue to nearly purple, with petals that remain closed at the tip.

September—November

Habitat/Range: Moist woods, open sandy areas; a few central to eastern Ozark counties and several counties in the Ouachita Region.

Remarks: Also known as Closed Gentian, for the condition of the flowers. Bumblebees are the primary pollinators because they are strong enough to pry open the flowers to get to the nectar.

DOWNY GENTIAN
Gentiana puberulenta
Gentian Family (Gentianaceae)

STIFF GENTIAN
Gentianella quinquefolia
Gentian Family (Gentianaceae)

Description: Annual or biennial plants, up to 16" tall, with 4-sided stems, and several upper branches. The leaves are opposite, stalkless, up to 2½" long and 1" wide, broadest at the base and abruptly tapering to a pointed tip. The flowers are lilac to pale lavender-blue, tubular, upright, up to 1" long, and mostly closed at the top, with 5 bristle-tipped lobes.

August—October

Habitat/Range: Moist open wooded slopes; central Ozark Region and Crittenden County.

Remarks: Formerly known as *Gentiana quinquefolia*. Root tea was once used as a bitter tonic to stimulate digestion and weak appetite. Also used for headaches, hepatitis, jaundice, and constipation.

Description: A plant with stout, unbranched stems, up to 12" tall, with shiny, pointed, opposite leaves. The leaves are without stalks, broadest toward the base, up to 2" long and 1" wide. The showy flowers are in dense clusters of 3–10. Each flower is deep blue to bluish-purple, up to 1½" long and about as wide, with 5 spreading lobes.

September—October

Habitat/Range: Dry to moist prairies, glades; Benton, Prairie, Saline, and Washington counties.

Remarks: This is one of the last flowers to bloom in the fall, even surviving the first frosts. The Winnebagos and Dakotas took root tea as a tonic. The Mesquakies used the root to treat snakebite.

Green Flowers

This section includes green flowers and flowers that have a greenish cast. Since green flowers grade into white flowers, that section should also be checked.

American Columbo, page 226

ALUMROOT
Heuchera americana
Saxifrage Family (Saxifragaceae)

Description: Hairy plants with tall, leafless, flowering stalks, up to 2½' high, arising from a base of long-stalked leaves. The leaves are round, up to 4" across, with shallow lobes and toothed edges, and a heart-shaped leaf base. Small flowers are arranged along the top half of a long flowering stem. The flowers are somewhat bell-shaped and droop on individual short stalks that branch from the main flower stalk. Each flower is up to ¼" long, with 5 green sepals and 5 petals that are barely visible. The stamens are tipped with brilliant orange and extend beyond the petals.

April—June

Habitat/Range: Rocky, open woods and bluff ledges; occurs in the Ozark and Ouachita regions and Crowley's Ridge.

Remarks: Also called Rock Geranium. Native American Indians and early settlers used a root powder as an astringent to close wounds and to treat diarrhea and sore throats. The Mesquakie used the leaves as a dressing for open sores.

BLUE COHOSH
Caulophyllum thalictroides
Barberry Family (Berberidaceae)

Description: A low spreading plant from 1–2' tall with one large leaf that is divided into many small leaflets and a smaller many divided leaf just below the flowers. The leaflets are 1–3" long, smooth, and irregularly lobed above the middle. The flower clusters arise above the leaves on 1–2 stalks, with 6 yellowish-green, petal-like sepals. The six gland-like petals are inconspicuous. The round fleshy fruit is a deep iridescent blue.

March—May

Habitat/Range: Moist woods on slopes and along streams; uncommon in the Ozark and Ouachita Regions.

Remarks: Cohosh is an Algonkin word meaning "rough," referring to the rhizome with its many old stem scars. A root tea was used extensively by North American Indians to aid in labor, treat menstruation, abdominal cramps, urinary tract infections, lung ailments and fevers. It is a folk remedy for rheumatism, cramps, epilepsy, and inflammation of the uterus.

GREEN TRILLIUM
Trillium viridescens
Lily Family (Liliaceae)

Description: Unbranched plants, up to 20" tall, with a whorl of 3 leaves at the top of a stout, smooth stem. The leaves are attached to the stem without stalks, smooth, broadest at the base or middle, up to 5" long, and 2½" wide, tip pointed, with the upper surface green and not or only slightly mottled. The flowers arise directly from the stem, with the 3 green sepals widely spreading and the 3 green to yellowish-green sometimes tinged with purple petals upright, each up to 3" long. The purple stamens are also upright.

April—May

Habitat/Range: Moist woods in ravines or valleys; Ozark and Ouachita regions; also western Gulf Coastal Plain Region

Remarks: This is the tallest of the 5 trilliums known to occur in Arkansas. The aroma emitted from the flowers is reminiscent of rotting apples.

fruit

GREEN DRAGON
Arisaema dracontium
Arum Family (Araceae)

Description: A single, highly dissected leaf with deep, narrow lobes is attached to a smooth green stalk, up to 3' tall. The leaf is divided into 5–15 segments; each segment is lance-shaped, up to 10" long and 4" wide, smooth, and lacking teeth along the margins. The flower branches off the leaf stalk near the base on its own bare stalk, up to 6" long. The flowers are wrapped in a tubular green sheath called a *spathe*. Inside the *spathe*, the flowers are crowded together along a column called a *spadix* and at the top emerges a green, tail-like, cylindrical column, up to 7" long. In the fall, a cluster of shiny orange-red fruit is arranged along a thick head.

April—June

Habitat/Range: Moist rocky slopes and wooded ravines; statewide.

Remarks: Native American Indians first dried the bulblike corm and used it for food. Fresh corms, however, contain calcium oxalate crystals, which cause intense burning in the mouth and throat; boiling the corms neutralizes the crystals.

WOOD SPURGE
Euphorbia commutata
Spurge Family (Euphorbiaceae)

Description: Several stems may arise from the base, up to 16" tall, with milky sap and light green leaves. The leaves are alternate, stalkless, smooth, oval, and rounded at the tip. The leaves just below the flowers are often joined at the base. The tiny flowers are nested in a cup of small leaves.

April—June

Habitat/Range: Wooded slopes, along streams, and in gravelly soils; Ozark Region and some Ouachita Region counties.

Remarks: There are 11 species in the genus *Euphorbia* that occur in Arkansas.

GREEN VIOLET
Hybanthus concolor
Violet Family (Violaceae)

Description: Hairy, unbranched plants, up to 2' tall, often in large colonies. The dark green leaves are alternate, hairy, lance-shaped, up to 4" long and 1¼" wide, tapering at both ends, and usually lacking teeth along the margins. There are 1–3 flowers arising from the leaf axils. Each flower is about ⅜" long, green, attached to a drooping stalk, with 5 green, narrow sepals and 5 greenish-white petals. One petal is wider than the others and swollen at the base.

April—June

Habitat/Range: Moist woods; Ozark and Ouachita Regions, also Lee County.

Remarks: Although belonging to the violet family, this plant looks nothing at all like any of the other 14 violets in Arkansas.

TALL GREEN MILKWEED
Aclepias hirtella
Milkweed Family (Asclepiadaceae)

Description: Stout-stemmed plants, up to 3' tall, with milky sap. The leaves are mostly alternate, hairy, and narrow, up to 6" long and 1" wide, with pointed tips. Several flower clusters arise on stalks from the upper leaf axils. Each flower is up to ½" long and pale greenish, with 5 petals bent backwards and sometimes white-tinged or purple tipped, with 5 green structures called hoods. The seedpods are smooth, slender, and up to 4" long and 1" thick.

May—August

Habitat/Range: Prairies, glades, old fields; scattered counties and absent from the Delta Region except for the Grand Prairie.

Remarks: Formerly known as *Ascerates hirtella* and *Asclepias longifolia* subsp. *hirtella*. Although not as showy as some of the other milkweeds, this tall, narrow-leaved milkweed exhibits a stately appearance.

GREEN-FLOWERED MILKWEED
Asclepias viridis
Milkweed Family (Asclepiadaceae)

Description: A large, somewhat sprawling plant, up to 2' tall, with thick stems and milky sap. The leaves are alternate, fleshy, up to 5" long and 2" wide, with wavy margins. The flowers appear in a large cluster, up to 5" across, at the top of the stem. Each flower is up to 1" across, with 5 green petals spread upward. Inside the flower are 5 purple structures called hoods. The seedpods are up to 6" long and 1" thick, with each seed tipped with a tuft of long white hairs.

April—July

Habitat/Range: Prairies, glades, along roadsides; in scattered counties across the state.

Remarks: Also called Spider Milkweed, it has the largest flowers of the 15 species of milkweeds known to occur in Arkansas.

GREEN MILKWEED
Asclepias viridiflora
Milkweed Family (Asclepiadaceae)

Description: Plants with unbranched, hairy stems, up to 2' tall, with milky sap and opposite leaves. The leaves are thick and vary from narrow to broadly oval, up to 5" long and 2½" wide, with wavy margins. There are from 1 to several dense flower clusters arising from the leaf margins. Each greenish flower is about ½" long, with 5 petals bent backwards and 5 structures called hoods. The smooth, narrow seedpods are up to 6" long and 1" wide.

May—August

Habitat/Range: Prairies, sandy and gravelly soils, old fields; scattered counties and absent from the Delta Region except for the Grand Prairie.

Remarks: Formerly known as *Acerates viridiflora*. The Lakota gave the pulverized roots to children with diarrhea. The Blackfeet chewed the root to relieve sore throat and also applied the root to swellings and rashes.

leaves

AMERICAN COLUMBO
Frasera caroliniensis
Gentian Family (Gentianaceae)

Description: Stiff, smooth plants, with single purple stems, up to 8' tall. The large leaves are whorled at the base and along the stem, broadest at the tip, narrowing towards the stem, and up to 16" long. The whitish-green flowers are in a large cluster at the top of the stem. Each flower is up to 1" across, with brownish-purple dots and a large gland on each of the 4 petals.

May—June

Habitat/Range: Rocky open woods, sandy woods; central and eastern Ozark Region and Ouachita Region.

Remarks: Also known as *Swertia caroliniensis*. The plant produces large basal leaves for several years before sending up a flowering stem. After blooming, the plant dies and spreads its seed to begin new plants. A root tea was formerly used for colic, cramps, dysentery, diarrhea, stomachaches, lack of appetite, nausea, and as a general tonic.

leaves

AMERICAN AGAVE
Manfreda virginica
Agave Family (Agavaceae)

Description: Tall, smooth, slender plants, up to 6' in height, with fleshy, dark green leaves at the base. The basal leaves are thick, smooth, and succulent, up to 16" long and 2" wide, pointed at the tip, and often purple-blotched across the surface. The stem leaves are much reduced in size. The flowers are arranged along a long spike at the top of a wand-like stem. Each green, tubular flower is about 1" long, with large, green to brown stamens extending well beyond the flower.

May—July

Habitat/Range: Sandstone outcrops and glades; dry woods; occasional; nearly statewide, less common in the south central counties.

Remarks: Also called False Aloe and formerly known as *Agave virginica* and *Polianthes virginica*. The flowers are fragrant, similar to Easter lilies. Native Americans used a root tea for dropsy and a wash for snakebites.

POKEWEED

Phytolacca americana
Pokeweed Family (Phytolaccaceae)

Description: Tall, smooth, red-stemmed plants, up to 10' in height. The leaves are smooth, up to 12" long and 3" wide, with long stalks. The small, greenish-white flowers are arranged along a long stalk with each flower individually stalked. The flowers are about ¼" across, lack petals but have 5 greenish sepals and from 5–30 stamens. The purple to black berries have a juice that stains.

June—October

Habitat/Range: Disturbed soil in woods, fields, farm lots, and around dwellings; statewide.

Remarks: Also called Pokeberry. The leaves of young plants are cooked and served as "poke salad." The purple juice has been used for coloring foods such as frostings, candies, and beverages, and also as a red dye and ink. The root and stem are poisonous. The berries are quickly eaten by birds.

GIANT RAGWEED

Ambrosia trifida
Aster Family (Asteraceae)

Description: A branched, hairy, annual plant, up to 15' tall, sometimes forms dense stands in disturbed sites. The leaves are opposite, stalked, deeply 3-lobed, rough, toothed along the margins, with the lower leaves up to 12" across. The upper leaves are unlobed and smaller. The flowers are arranged on long stalks with the pollen-producing male flowers much more numerous than the female flowers, which are nearly hidden in leaf axils.

July—October

Habitat/Range: Moist soils in low woods, along floodplains and streams, fields, disturbed sites, and along roadsides; statewide.

Remarks: The seed of Giant Ragweed has been found in several archaeological sites where it is thought to have been cultivated as a food source. The seeds are an important food for wildlife. Ragweed pollen is a major contributor to hay fever. Another similar species, Lanceleaf Ragweed, *Ambrosia bidentata*, has alternate, lance-shaped leaves with lobes lacking; statewide. And Common Ragweed, *Ambrosia artemisiifolia*, is up to 2½' tall with leaves divided into numerous small leaflets; found in disturbed soil; statewide.

Brown Flowers

This section includes brown flowers that grade into maroon.
Brown flowers may also grade into green,
so that section should also be checked.

Purple Trillium, page 232

WILD GINGER
Asarum canadense
Birthwort Family (Aristolochiaceae)

Description: A low-growing plant, up to 6" tall, with 2 leaves emerging on hairy stalks from the base. The dark green leaves are round, heart-shaped, as much as 7" across when fully grown, hairy, and leathery with a shiny surface. A single reddish-brown flower, up to 1" across, emerges from the base of the 2 leaves on a hairy stalk. The flower is bell-shaped, lacks petals, but has 3 pointed sepals that curve backwards.

April—May

Habitat/Range: Moist woods; sometimes forming dense colonies; Ozark Region, some Ouachita region counties and Crowley's Ridge.

Remarks: The Mesquakie considered the root of wild ginger to be one of the most important native seasonings. They also thought its use eliminated danger of poisoning when eating an animal that had died of unknown causes. They also chewed the root and spit it upon bait to improve the chances of catching fish. Settlers used the root as a spice substitute for tropical ginger. In frontier medicine it was used for the treatment of several ailments.

fruit

JACK-IN-THE-PULPIT
Arisaema triphyllum
Arum Family (Araceae)

Description: This plant has a leaf divided into 3 leaflets, which is attached to a smooth green stalk, up to 18" tall. Each leaflet is lance-shaped, smooth, up to 7" long, and lacks teeth along the margins. The flower stalk branches off from the leaf stalk near the base. The flowers are wrapped in a tubelike green sheath called a *spathe*, which folds over at the top. The underside of the hood or flap is typically brown with white stripes. Inside the spathe the flowers are crowded together along the lower end of a cylindrical brown or green column called a *spadix*. In the fall, a cluster of shiny orange-red fruit is arranged along a thick head.

March—May

Habitat/Range: Moist woods; statewide.

Remarks: The Chippewas used the bulblike underground stem, called a corm, to treat sore eyes, and the Pawnee applied a powder made from the corm to the head or temples for headache. The corm was also used to treat snakebite, ringworm, stomach gas, rheumatism, and asthma; it was also boiled or baked for food. If eaten raw, however, the corm's calcium oxalate crystals render it poisonous.

SESSILE TRILLIUM
Trillium sessile
Lily Family (Liliaceae)

Description: Plants with smooth, stout stems, up to 10" tall, with a whorl of 3 leaves at the tip. The leaves are oval, rounded or pointed at the tip, rounded at the base, smooth, up to 4" long, without stalks, and usually mottled on the surface. A single stemless flower arises just above the leaves to 1½" long. The 3 green sepals are spreading and up to 1" long, while the 3 purplish-brown petals point upwards enclosing the 6 stamens.

March—May

Habitat/Range: Moist woods; Ozark and Ouachita regions.

Remarks: Also called Wake Robin. The term "sessile" in sessile trillium refers to the leaves lacking stalks. Sessile Trillium has had much the same uses as Purple Trillium.

PURPLE TRILLIUM
Trillium recurvatum
Lily Family (Liliaceae)

Description: Unbranched, stout-stemmed plants, up to 18" tall, with a whorl of 3 leaves at the top. The leaves are broadest in the middle and tapering at both ends, up to 4" long, smooth, and mottled on the surface. The bases of the leaves are stalked. The single flower is attached to the top of the stem without a stalk. The 3 green sepals are curved down, while the 3 reddish-brown (sometimes yellow) petals are upright and surround the 6 stamens.

March—May

Habitat/Range: Moist woods; statewide.

Remarks: Also called Purple Wake Robin. Several North American tribes used the root to treat open wounds and sores, menstrual disorders, menopause, and internal bleeding; to induce childbirth; and as an aphrodisiac. Frontier physicians used the crushed fresh leaves to treat snakebites, stings, and skin irritations.

SPRING CORAL ROOT ORCHID
Corallorhiza wisteriana
Orchid Family (Orchidaceae)

Description: Single-stemmed, brown to purplish, up to 16" tall and lacking green color. Leaves are reduced to 3 alternating, sheathing scales along the stem. There are 5–25 purplish-brown flowers. The flower lip is white with purple spots and a wavy margin.

April—May

Habitat/Range: Moist or rocky open woods; scattered counties across the state.

Remarks: Orchids in the genus *Corallorhiza* have coral-shaped roots as the name implies. Lacking green chlorophyll, the plants must obtain their nutrients from decaying organic matter.

LARGE WHORLED POGONIA
Isotria verticillata
Orchid Family (Orchidaceae)

Description: A stout single stem arises from 8–12" tall to a whorl of 5–6 leaves and a single flower. The leaves are from 1–2" inches long and expand while the flower blooms. The flower has 3 purplish, spreading sepals, up to 2½" long. The pale yellow-green petals extend forward and cover most of the 3-lobed lip that is white with purple edges.

April—May

Habitat/Range: Open acid woods, damp ground near springs; lower Ozark Region, Ouachita and Gulf Coastal Plain regions and Crowley's Ridge.

Remarks: This orchid grows in colonies by sending out long, horizontal roots that give rise to new stems. The flowers are pollinated by small bees.

CLIMBING MILKWEED
Matelea decipiens
Milkweed Family (Asclepiadaceae)

Description: A climbing or trailing hairy vine, with opposite, heart-shaped leaves up to 5" long. The maroon flowers are in clusters on stalks that arise from the leaf of axils. Each flower has 5 upright petals with each petal up to ¾" long. The seed pods are up to 4" long and ¾" thick, with numerous short projections along the surface.

May–June

Habitat/Range: Rocky open woods, edges of glades, and along streams; in scattered counties statewide.

Remarks: Formerly known as *Gonolobus decipiens*. Another Climbing Milkweed, *Matelea gonocarpa*, has narrower leaves and lacks hairs; scattered across the state. A white flowering, Climbing Milkweed, *Matelea baldwyniana*, is hairy with broad leaves; western Arkansas and Lawrence County.

TWAYBLADE ORCHID
Liparis lilifolia
Orchid Family (Orchidaceae)

Description: A smooth, hairless plant, from 4–8" tall, with a pair of glossy green leaves arising from the base. Sterile plants have a single leaf. The leaves are broadest at or below the middle, about 4" long and 3" wide, with smooth margins and parallel veins. The flowers are purplish-brown, from 5–20, with a broad, showy lip that is somewhat translucent, about ⅜" long, and pointed at the tip. Two thread-like petals hang below the lip.

May–July

Habitat/Range: Moist woods, streambanks; a few scattered counties in the northern half of the state.

Remarks: Also called Large Twayblade, it is closely related to Loesel's Twayblade, *Liparis loeselii*, which has a yellowish lip less than ¼" long and yellowish lateral petals; found in wetland habitats of low woods, seep springs; Garland County.

leaf

PUTTY ROOT ORCHID
Aplectrum hyemale
Orchid Family (Orchidaceae)

Description: This orchid has a leafless stem, up to 1½' tall, and produces one leaf, emerging from the root, that withers away by flowering time. The evergreen leaf appears from September through early May. The leaf is broadest at the middle and narrowing at both ends, up to 6" long and 3" wide, blue-green, and strongly ribbed or pleated. The flowers are stalked and attached along the upper 8" of the stem. Each greenish-maroon flower is about ½" long, with 3 sepals and 3 petals. The lower petal is a 3-lobed lip with a wavy edge.

May—June

Habitat/Range: Moist woods; reported from Garland, Logan, Madison, Newton, Pope and Stone counties.

Remarks: The name for putty root is derived from the sticky juice from the corm (bulblike underground structure), which was once used to glue broken pottery. Another common name, Adam-And-Eve, comes from the plant's production of a new corm every year that is connected by a slender branch to the old one. Native American Indians mashed the corm and applied it to boils. Root tea was formerly used for bronchial troubles.

FIGWORT
Scrophularia marilandica
Figwort Family (Scrophulariaceae)

Description: A stout, square-stemmed plant, up to 7' tall, with multiple branches. The leaves are opposite, long-stalked, lance-shaped, up to 6" long and 3" wide, with teeth along the margins. The tiny flowers are in a loose cluster. Each flower is shaped like a scoop, with 2 brown lips, the upper lip larger and forming the scoop.

July—October

Habitat/Range: Low moist woods; Ozark and Ouachita regions and Crowley's Ridge.

Remarks: Also called Carpenter's Square, for the grooved, 4-angle stem. Native American Indians used root tea to treat fevers and piles, and as a diuretic and tonic. It is also a folk remedy for treating sleeplessness in pregnant women, restlessness, anxiety, and cancer.

FALSE HELLEBORE
Melanthium woodii
Lily Family (Liliaceae)

Description: Plants with long slender stems, up to 6' tall, with ribbed or pleated basal leaves. The basal leaves are broadest at the middle and tapering at both ends, up to 12" long; about 3" wide, and somewhat clasping the stem. The stem leaves are few and narrow. The upper stem is widely branched, hairy, with several flowers on short stalks. Each flower has 5 purplish-brown petals up to ¾" across.

July—August

leaves

Habitat/Range: Mostly north and east wooded slopes; restricted to a few western counties.

Remarks: Formerly known as *Veratrum woodii*. It is a perennial that can go for several years without flowering. All parts of the plant are considered highly toxic. Most grazing animals avoid the plant because of its sharp burning taste. A similar species has been used in pharmaceutical drugs to slow the heart rate, lower blood pressure, and to treat arteriosclerosis.

COMMON HORSE GENTIAN
Triosteum perfoliatum
Honeysuckle Family (Caprifoliaceae)

Description: Stems with gland-tipped hairs, up to 3' tall, with dark green, thick leaves that encircle the stem. The hairy leaves are opposite, stalkless, up to 10" long, broadly lance-shaped, with those in the middle of the stem distinctly fiddle-shaped. The flowers emerge at the leaf axils on short stalks. Each cluster typically has 3–4 purplish-brown flowers that are tubular, up to ¾" long, with 5 overlapping petals. The fruit resembles little oranges in color and shape.

May—July

Habitat/Range: Dry open woodlands; Ozark and Ouachita regions.

Remarks: Native American Indians made a tea of this plant for treating fevers. The roots were mashed and applied to painful swellings. The Pennsylvania Dutch collected the orange fruits and dried the seeds, then roasted and ground them as a coffee substitute. Another species, Early Horse Gentian, *Triosteum aurantiacum*, has hairs without gland tips and leaf bases that narrow and do not encircle the stem; dry open woods; occasional throughout the state. Another species, Yellow-Flowered Horse Gentian, *T. angustifolium*, has yellow flowers and leaves up to 6" long that are narrowed at the base but do not encircle the stem; dry open woodlands; Ozark Region, scattered counties elsewhere.

leaves

CRANE-FLY ORCHID
Tipularia discolor
Orchid Family (Orchidaceae)

Description: A thin, delicate plant, up to 2' tall that is easily overlooked. A basal leaf emerges in mid-summer, overwinters, and withers by the following May. The leaf is dark green above with purple spots, purple beneath and from 2–4" long. In mid-summer, a stalk emerges with 20–30 light brown or tan flowers tinged with green and purple. The flowers are thin, less than 1" long and resemble a crane-fly.

July—September

Habitat/Range: Upland or rich damp acid woodlands; mostly in the southern half of the state and Crowley's Ridge.

Remarks: The plant is pollinated by noctuid moths, by means of the flowers which incline slightly to the right or left, so the pollen sack can attach to one of the moth's eyes.

FALL CORAL ROOT ORCHID
Corallorhiza odontorhiza
Orchid Family (Orchidaceae)

Description: Single-stemmed, brown to purplish, up to 1' tall and lacking green color. Leaves are reduced to 3 alternating, sheathing scales along the stem. There are 5–15 flowers that alternate along the stem. Each small purplish-brown flower has a conspicuous lower lip that is white with small purple dots and crinkled along the margin.

August—October

Habitat/Range: Moist or rocky open woods; north central counties and two southwestern counties.

Remarks: Also called Autumn Coral Root Orchid. This is one of the smallest-flowered orchids in Arkansas. Orchids in the genus *Corallorhiza* have coral-shaped roots as the name implies. Lacking green chlorophyll, the plants must obtain their nutrients from decaying organic matter.

Selected Reading

Arkansas Vascular Flora Committee. 2006. *Checklist of the Vascular Plants of Arkansas*. Fayetteville: University of Arkansas. This is a checklist of all the plants known to occur in the state and is an initial step toward publication of the state's first vascular flora.

Foster, Steven, and James A. Duke. 1990. *A Field Guide to Medicinal Plants*. New York: Houghton Mifflin. Provides illustrations and descriptions of medicinal plants and their uses.

Hunter, Carl G. 1999. *Wildflowers of Arkansas*. 9th Edition. Little Rock, Arkansas: Ozark Society Foundation. The first book published on the wildflowers of the state.

Kaye, Connie, and Neil Billington. 1997. *Medicinal Plants of the Heartland*. Vienna, Illinois: Cache River Press. Provides illustrations and descriptions of medicinal plants and their uses.

Kindscher, Kelly. 1987. *Edible Wild Plants of the Prairie*. Lawrence: University Press of Kansas. Discusses many edible plants and their preparation, use, and history.

Kindscher, Kelly. 1992. *Medicinal Wild Plants of the Prairie*. Lawrence: University Press of Kansas. Discusses many medicinal plants and their historic uses.

Ladd, Doug, and Frank Oberle. 1995. *Tallgrass Prairie Wildflowers*. Helena, Montana: Falcon Publishing. A field guide that can be used in the prairie region of Arkansas.

Peterson, Lee Allen. 1977. *A Field Guide to Edible Wild Plants*. New York: Houghton Mifflin. Provides illustrations and descriptions of edible plants and their preparation and uses.

Smith, Edwin B. 1994. *Keys to the Flora of Arkansas*. Fayetteville, Arkansas: The University of Arkansas Press. A technical key used to identify plants based on their distinguishing features.

Glossary

Alternate leaves: Leaves located singly at intervals along the stem (see Opposite Leaves).

Annual: A plant growing from seed to fruit in one year, then dying.

Anther: The pollen-bearing part of a stamen

Basal: Leaves located at the base of a plant at ground level.

Biennial: A plant growing for two years, blooming the second year, and then dying.

Bract: A reduced or modified leaf, generally situated below a flower or flower cluster.

Bulb: An underground, enlarged portion of a stem that is covered with scales or modified leaves, and in layers like an onion (see Corm).

Calyx: The outer set of flower parts composed of the sepals, which are usually green and found beneath the petals.

Compound leaf: A leaf that is divided into two or more leaflets (see Simple leaf).

Corm: A fleshy bulblike base of a stem, underground, that is solid (see Bulb).

Corolla: All the petals of a flower.

Disk flower: Small, tubular flowers in the central portion of the flower head of many plants in the aster family.

Filament: The slender stalk of a stamen below the anther.

Fruit: The seed-containing part of a plant.

Lanceolate: Shaped like a spear, much longer than wide and widest below the middle

Lobe: A part of a flower or leaf that extends beyond the main body.

Margin: The edge of a leaf.

Mesic: Moderately moist.

Node: The portion of the stem where one or more leaves are attached.

Opposite leaves: Leaves located directly across from each other on the stem (see Alternate Leaves).

Ovary: The portion of the flower where the seeds develop.

Perennial: A plant that normally lives for three or more years.

Petal: A part of the corolla, often brightly colored.

Pistil: The seed producing or female, part of a flower consisting of the ovary, style, and stigma.

Pollen: Fine dust-like grains discharged from the anther of a stamen and typically necessary for seed production.

Ray flower: The outer, petal-like flowers found in the flower head of many plants in the aster family.

Rhizome: An underground stem, usually lateral, that produces roots and shoots.

Seed: The propagative part of a plant developed from an ovule in the fruit.

Sepal: An individual part of the calyx; typically green but sometimes enlarged and brightly colored.

Simple leaf: A leaf composed of a single blade (see Compound leaf).

Stamen: The pollen-producing part of a flower, consisting of anther and filament.

Stigma: The top of the pistil that receives the pollen.

Stipule: A structure at the base of a leaf stalk, usually attached to the stem.

Style: The slender stalk that connects the stigma to the ovary.

Subspecies: Abbreviated "ssp." Similar to variety (see Variety), but used to denote a discreet portion of the range of a species.

Tendril: A slender, coiled or twisted filament with which climbing plants attach to other objects.

Variety: Abbreviated "var." Plants within a species that has a distinct range, habitat, or set of characteristics (see Subspecies).

Whorled: Three or more leaves attached at the same point along a stem and often surrounding the stem.

Winter annual: A plant that germinates in the fall, produces rudimentary leaves, overwinters, and resumes growing in the spring to produce flowers, then seeds and dies.

Index

A

Acerates
  hirtella 224
  viridiflora 224
Achillea millefolium 50
Actaea
  pachypoda 27
  racemosa 42
Adam-And-Eve 235
Agalinis
  fasciculata 212
  tenuifolia 212
Agave, American 227
Agave virginica 227
Ageratina altissima 69
Ageratum, Wild 205
Argimonia
  parviflora 126
  rostellata 126
Agrimony
  Beaked 126
  Swamp 126
Aletris farinosa 32
Alexanders, Golden 91, 96
Alliaria petiolata 33
Allium
   canadense
      var. *canadense* 148
      var. *mobilense* 148
   cernuum 165
   mutabile 148
   stellatum 165
Aloe, False 227
Alumroot 220
  Arkansas 74
  Late 74
Ambrosia
  artemisiifolia 228
  bidentata 228
  trifida 228
American Agave 227
American Bellflower 200
American Columbo 226
American Germander 161
American Ipecac 44
Amianthium muscaetoxicum 30
Amsonia
  illustris 181
  tabernaemontana 181

Anemone
  Carolina 14
  False Rue 13
  Rue 13
  Southern 14
  Tall 23
Anemone
  acutiloba 167
  americana 167
  berlandieri 14
  caroliniana 14
  virginiana 23
Anemonella thalictroides 13
Angelica, Hairy 50
Angelica venenosa 50
Antennaria parlinii 22
Apios americana 204
Aplectrum hyemale 235
Apocynum
  androsaemifolium 54
  cannabinum 54
Aquilegia canadensis 135
Arabis
  canadensis 16
  laevigata 16
Aralia racemosa 36
Arenaria patula 33
Arisaema
  dracontium 222
  triphyllum 231
Arkansas
  Alumroot 74
  Beardtongue 34
Arnoglossum
  atriplicifolium 58
  muhlenbergii 58
  plantagineum 58
  reniforme 58
Aromatic Aster 214
Arrow-Leaved Aster 76
Artichoke, Jerusalem 126
Aruncus dioicus 41
Asarum canadense 230
Asclepias
  amplexicaulis 155
  hirtella 224
  longifolia ssp. *hirtella* 224
  purpurascens 188
  quadrifolia 24

  syriaca 156
  tuberosa 139
  variegata 35
  verticillata 35
  viridiflora 225
  viridis 225
Aster
  Aromatic 214
  Arrow-Leaved 76
  Blue 215
  False 73
  Flax-Leaved 215
  Golden 117
  Hairy 75
  New England 216
  Sky Blue 216
  Southern Prairie 214
  Spreading 217
  Stiff-Leaved 215
  Woodland 215
Aster
  anomalus 215
  azureus 216
  cordifolius 76
  linariifolius 215
  novae-angliae 216
  oblongifolius 214
  oolentangiensis 216
  paludosus ssp. *hemisphericus* 214
  patens 217
  pilosus 75
  sagittifolius 76
Astragalus
  canadensis 29
  crassicarpus var. *trichocalyx* 83
  mexicanus 83
Astranthium integrifolium 171
Atlantic Mock Bishop's Weed 47
Aureolaria
  flava 128
  grandiflora 128
  pectinata 128
  pedicularia 128
Avens, White 44

B

Balm, Bee 175
Baneberry, White 27
Baptisia
  alba var. *macrophylla* 48

australis 185
bracteata var. *leucophaea* 102
leucantha 48
leucophaea 102
nuttalliana 102
sphaerocarpa 89
Barbarea vulgaris 88
Bean, Wild 158
Beard, Goat's 41, 97
Beardtongue
   Arkansas 34
   Foxglove 45
   Pale 34
   Purple 187
   Tubed 45
   White Wand 45
Bear's Foot 52
Beauty
   Maryland Meadow 160
   Meadow 160
   Spring 12
Bedstraw 52
Bee Balm 175
Beechdrops 75
Beefsteak Plant 213
Beggar's Ticks 132
Belamcanda chinensis 141
Bellflower
   American 200
   Tall 200
Bellwort
   Large-Flowered 86
   Small 86
Bergamot, Wild 189
Bet, Bouncing 158
Betony
   Swamp Wood 85
   Wood 85
Bidens aristosa 132
Bindweed, Hedge 39
Bird's Foot Trefoil 111
Bird's Foot Violet 168
Bishop's Weed
   Atlantic Mock 47
   Mock 47
   Ozark Mock 47
Bitterweed 110
Blackberry Lily 141
Black-Eyed Susan 107
Blanket, Indian 137
Blanketflower 137
Blazing Star
   Pinkscale 209

   Prairie 209
   Rough 208
   Scaly 209
Blephilia
   ciliata 154
   hirsuta 154
Bloodroot 16
Bluebells 170
Bluebill 191
Blue-Eyed Grass 182
Blue-Eyed Mary 173
Blue Hearts 201
Bluets 172
   Long-Leaved 25
Blueweed 183
Boltonia
   asteroides 73
   diffusa 73
Boneset
   Common 67
   False 67
   Late 78
   Tall 67, 78
Bouncing Bet 158
Bradburiana pilosa 117
Brassica
   nigra 88
   rapa 88
Brickellia eupatorioides 67
Breeches
   Dutchman's 17
   Woolen 178
Brier, Sensitive 154
Brown-Eyed Susan 107
Buchnera americana 201
Buckley's Goldenrod 120
Buckwheat, Climbing 70
Bugloss, Viper's 183
Bunchflower 56
Bundleflower, Illinois 59
Bush Clover
   Round-Headed 64
   Slender 163
   Violet 163
Bush's Poppy Mallow 192
Buttercup
   Bristly 81
   Hairy 89
   Harvey's 81
Butterfly Pea 199
   Spurred 199
Butterfly Weed 139
Butterweed 93

Buttonweed
   Large 162
   Rough 162

C

Cacalia
   atriplicifolia 58
   muhlenbergii 58
   plantaginea 58
   tuberosa 58
Calamint 190
Calamintha arkansana 190
Callirhoe
   bushii 192
   digitata 192
   involucrata 192
Calopogon
   oklahomensis 149
   pulchellus 149
   tuberosus 149
Calystegia sepium 39
Camas, Death 30
Camassia
   angusta 175
   scilloides 175
Campanula americana 200
Campanulastrum americanum 200
Camphorweed 212
Campion, Starry 60
Canada Goldenrod 130
Cancer-Root, One-Flowered 23
Cancer Weed 179
Cardamine
   bulbosa 15
   concatenata 15
   rhomboidea 15
Cardinal Flower 142
Carduus nutans 194
Carolina Anemone 14
Carolina Elephant's Foot 73
Carolina Larkspur 185
Carolina Puccoon 94
Carpenter's Square 236
Carpenter's Weed 122
Carrot, Wild 38
Cassia
   fasciculata 117
   marilandica 118
   nictitans 177
Castilleja coccinea 135
Catchfly, Royal 142
Caulophyllum thalictroides 220
Ceanothus americanus 42

Celandine Poppy 87
Celestial Lily 180
Centaurea
  maculosa 162
  stoebe 162
Centrosema virginianum 199
Chaerophyllum
  procumbens 20
  tainturieri 20
Chamaechrista
  fasciculata 117
  nictitans 117
Chelone
  glabra 65
  obliqua var. *speciosa* 65
Chervil, Wild 20
Chickweed, Common 14
Chicory 194
Chrysanthemum leucanthemum 51
Chrysopsis pilosa 117
Cicely, Sweet 24
Cichorium intybus 194
Cicuta maculata 49
Cimicifuga racemosa 42
Cinquefoil
  Common 95
  Rough-Fruited 95
Cirsium
  altissimum 211
  carolinianum 211
  discolor 211
  horridulum 211
  vulgare 211
Clammy Cuphea 205
Claytonia virginica 12
Cleavers 52
Cleft Phlox 170
Clematis
  crispa 191
  pitcheri 191
  versicolor 191
Climbing False Buckwheat 70
Climbing Milkweed 234
Clinopodium virginianum 190
Clitoria mariana 199
Clover
  Crimson 136
  Purple Prairie 195
  Round-Headed Bush 64
  Slender Bush 163
  Violet Bush 163
  White Prairie 48
  White Sweet 37, 101

Yellow Sweet 101
Cohosh
  Black 42
  Blue 220
Colic Root 32
Collinsia, Violet 173
Collinsia
  verna 173
  violaceae 173
Columbine 135
Columbo, American 226
Comandra
  richardsiana 34
  umbellata 34
Comfrey, Wild 179
Commelina
  communis 197
  diffusa 197
  erecta 197
Compass Plant 123
Coneflower
  Glade 190
  Gray-Headed 111
  Large 107
  Long-Headed 140
  Pale Purple 190
  Purple 200
  Sweet 121
  Yellow 108
Conium maculatum 40
Conoclinium coelestinum 205
Convolvulus sepium 39
Conyza
  canadensis 60
  ramosissima 60
Coral Root Orchid
  Spring 233
  Fall 240
Corallorhiza
  odontorhiza 240
  wisteriana 233
Coreopsis
  Lance-Leaved 94
  Large-Flowered 94
  Plains 115
  Prairie 114
  Tall 115
Coreopsis
  grandiflora 94
  lanceolata 94
  palmata 114
  pubescens 94
  tinctoria 115

  tripteris 115
Corn Salad 21
  Long-Flowered 21
  Ozark 21
Coronilla varia 153
Corydalis
  Pale 84
  Small-Flowered 84
Corydalis
  flavula 84
  micrantha 84
Cowbane 70
Crane-Fly Orchid 239
Cream Wild Indigo 102
Creeping Lady's Sorrel 96
Creeping Vervain 193
Cress, Spring 15
Crimson Clover 136
Cross, Widow's 149
Croton, Woolly 61
Croton
  capitatus 61
  monanthogynus 61
Crown Vetch 153
Crownbeard
  White 76
  Yellow 109
Crested Iris, Dwarf 171
Culver's Root 61
Cunila origanoides 207
Cup Plant 122
Cuphea, Clammy 205
Cuphea
  petiolata 205
  viscosissima 205
Curls, Blue 213
Cuscuta spp. 62
Cynoglossum
  officinale 179
  virginianum 179
Cynthia, Two-Flowered 92
Cypripedium
  kentuckiense 90
  parviflorum
    var. *parviflorum* 90
    var. *pubescens* 90

D

Daisy
  Doll's 73
  Ox-Eye 51
  Western 171
Daisy Fleabane 49

Dalea
   candida 48
   purpurea 195
Dame's Rocket 183
Dandelion
   Dwarf 92
   False 99
   Potato 92
Dasistoma macrophylla 114
Daucus carota 38
Day Lily, Orange 138
Dayflower 197
   Common 197
   Small 197
Dead Nettle, Purple 145
Death Camas 30
Delphinium
   carolinianum 185
   tricorne 174
Dentaria laciniata 15
Deptford Pink 150
Desmanthus illinoiensis 59
Desmodium
   paniculatum var. *dillenii* 164
     perplexum 164
     rotundifolium 164
Devil's Grandmother 73
Devil's Shoestrings 154
Dianthus armeria 150
Dicentra cucullaria 17
Digitalis purpurea 45
Diodia
   teres 162
   virginiana 162
Dipsacus
   fullonum 160
   laciniatus 160
   sylvestris 160
Dittany 207
Dock, Prairie 122
Dodder 62
Dodecatheon
   frenchii 146
   meadia 146
Dogbane, Spreading 54
Dogtooth Violet 12
   Prairie 12
   White 12
   Yellow 82
Doll's Daisy 73
Doll's Eyes 27
Dollarleaf 164
Draba brachycarpa 11

Dragon, Green 222
Dragonhead
   False 153
   Narrow-Leaved False 153
Drummond's Goldenrod 131
Dutchman's Breeches 17

E

Echinacea
   pallida 190
   paradoxa 108
   purpurea 200
   simulata 190
Echium vulgare 183
Elephant's Foot, Carolina 73
Elephantopus
   carolinianus 73
   tomentosa 73
Elm-Leaved Goldenrod 129
Enemion biternatum 13
Epifagus virginiana 75
Erechtites hieracifolia 71
Erigenia bulbosa 11
Erigeron
   annuus 49
   canadensis 60
   philadelphicus 22
   pulchellus 22
   strigosus 49
Eryngium yuccifolium 64
Erythronium
   albidum 12
   mesochoreum 12
   rostratum 82
Eupatorium
   altissimum 67, 78
   coelestinum 205
   eupatorioides 67
   fistulosum 206
   perfoliatum 67
   purpureum 206
   rugosum 69
   serotinum 78
Euphorbia
   bicolor 79
   commutata 223
   corollata 51
Eurybia hemispherica 214
Evening Primrose 118
   Showy 157
Everlasting, Sweet 71
Everlasting Pea 156

F

Fallopia scandens 70
Fame Flower 157
Fern-Leaved Foxglove 128
Field Milkwort 155
Field Mustard 88
Field Thistle 211
Figwort 236
Fire Pink 136
Fireweed 71
Firewheel 137
Flax
   Small Yellow 113
   Wild 113
Fleabane
   Annual 49
   Daisy 49
   Dwarf 60
   Marsh 212
   Philadelphia 22
Flower
   Cardinal 142
   Fame 157
   Leather 191
   Monkey 199
   Passion 195
   Pencil 106
   Yellow Passion 106
Flowering Spurge 51
Flower-Of-An-Hour 157
Fly Poison 30
Fog Fruit 38
Foot
   Bear's 52
   Carolina Elephant's 73
Four-O'clock
   White 151
   Wild 151
Foxglove
   False 212
   Fern-Leaved False 128
   Mullein 114
   Slender False 212
   Smooth False 128
   Yellow False 128
Foxglove Beardtongue 45
Fragaria virginiana 25
Frasera caroliniensis 226
Frog Fruit 38
Frostweed 76
French's Shooting Star 146
Fruit

Fog 38
Frog 38

G

Gaillardia
  aestivalis 137
  pulchella 137
Galearis spectabilis 174
Galium aparine 52
Garden Phlox 210
Garlic
  False 19
  Wild 148
Garlic Mustard 33
Gaura
  Biennial 62
  Demaree's 62
Gaura
  demareei 62
  longiflora 62
Gayfeather 209
Gentian
  Closed 217
  Common Horse 238
  Downy 218
  Early Horse 238
  Pale 74
  Soapwort 217
  Stiff 218
  Yellow-Flowered Horse 238
Gentiana
  alba 74
  flavida 74
  puberulenta 218
  quinquefolia 218
  saponaria 217
Gentianella quinquefolia 218
Geranium, Wild 145
Geranium maculatum 145
Gerardia
  fasciculata 212
  tenuifolia 212
Germander, American 161
Geum canadense 44
Giant Ragweed 228
Gill-Over-The-Ground 173
Gillenia stipulata 44
Ginger, Wild 230
Ginseng 57
Glade Coneflower 190
Glandularia canadensis 144
Glechoma hederacea 173
Gnaphalium obtusifolium 71

Goat's Beard 41, 97
Goat's Rue 147
Golden Alexanders 91, 96
Golden Aster 117
Golden Ragwort 93
Goldenglow 121
Goldenrod
  Blue-Stem 129
  Buckley's 120
  Canada 130
  Cliff 131
  Drummond's 131
  Elm-Leaved 129
  Gray 120
  Old Field 120
  Tall 130
  Woodland 120
Goldenseal 28
Gonolobus decipiens 234
Goodyera pubescens 66
Grandmother, Devil's 73
Grass
  Blue-Eyed 182
  Yellow Star 84
Grass Pink Orchid 149
  Oklahoma 149
Gray-Headed Coneflower 111
Great Plains Ladies' Tresses 77
Green-Flowered Milkweed 225
Grindelia lanceolata 132
Groundcherry, Longleaf 116
Ground Ivy 173
Ground Plum 83
Groundnut 204
Groundsel, Round-Leaved 92
Gumplant 132

H

Hairy Angelica 50
Hairy Buttercup 89
Hairyflower Spiderwort 186
Hairystem Spiderwort 186
Harbinger Of Spring 11
Harvey's Buttercup 81
Hawkweed
  Hairy 105
  Long-Bearded 105
Hearts, Blue 201
Heart-Leaved Meadow Parsnip 91
Hedge Bindweed 39
Hedge Nettle, Smooth 161
Hedge Parsley 55
  Japanese 55

Hedyotis
  caerulea 172
  crassifolia 167
  longifolia 25
Helenium
  amarum 110
  autumnale 133
  flexuosum 110
Helianthus
  annuus 125
  divaricatus 124
  grosseserratus 125
  hirsutus 124
  maximilianii 125
  mollis 124
  tuberosus 126
Heliopsis helianthoides 101
Heliotrope 59
Heliotrope, Indian 204
Heliotropium
  indicum 204
  tenellum 59
Hellebore, False 237
Hemerocallis fulva 138
Hemlock
  Poison 40
  Water 49
Hemp, Indian 54
Henbit 144
Hepatica
  Round-Lobed 167
  Sharp-Lobed 167
Hepatica
  nobilis
    var. *acuta* 167
    var. *obtusa* 167
Hesperis matronalis 183
Heterotheca pilosa 117
Heuchera
  americana 220
  parviflora 74
  villosa var. *arkansana* 74
Hieracium
  gronovii 105
  longipilum 105
Hoary Vervain 193
Hogwort 61
Horse Gentian
  Common 238
  Early 238
  Yellow-Flowered 238
Horse Mint 119, 175
  Ohio 154

Horse Nettle 37
Horsetail Milkweed 35
Horseweed 60
Hound's Tongue, Common 179
Houstonia
   caerulea 172
   longifolia 25
   pusilla 167
Hyacinth
   Prairie 175
   Wild 175
Hybanthus concolor 223
Hydrastis canadensis 28
Hydrophyllum
   appendiculatum 178
   brownei 178
   virginianum 178
Hymenocalis
   liriosome 55
   occidentalis 55
Hymenopappus
   artemisaefolius 46
   scabiosaeus 46
Hypericum
   gentianoides 116
   perforatum 113
   punctatum 113
Hypoxis hirusta 84

I

Illinois Bundleflower 59
Impatiens
   capensis 140
   pallida 112
Indian Blanket 137
Indian Heliotrope 204
Indian Hemp 54
Indian Paintbrush 135
Indian Physic 44
Indian Pink 137
Indian Pipe 78
Indian Plantain
   Pale 58
   Prairie 58
Indian Tobacco 196
Indigo
   Blue False 89, 185
   Cream Wild 102
   Long-Bracted Wild 102
   Nuttall's 102
   White Wild 48
   Yellow Wild 89
Ionactis linariifolius 215

Ipecac, American 44
Ipomoea
   hederacea 202
   pandurata 40
Iris
   Dwarf 171
   Dwarf Crested 171
Iris
   cristata 171
   verna 171
Ironweed
   Arkansas 203
   Missouri 202
   Tall 203
   Texas 202
   Western 203
   Yellow 131
Isopyrum biternatum 13
Isotria verticillata 233
Ivy, Ground 173
Ivyleaf Morning Glory 202

J

Jack-In-The-Pulpit 231
Jacob's Ladder 176
Jasmine, Blue 191
Jerusalem Artichoke 126
Jewel-Weed 140
Joe Pye Weed
   Hollow 206
   Purple 206
Johnny-Jump-Up 169

K

Kentucky Lady's-Slipper Orchid 90
Knapweed, Spotted 162
Krigia
   biflora 92
   dandelion 92
   virginica 92

L

Lactuca
   canadensis 127
   floridana 208
   scariola 127
   serriola 127
Ladder, Jacob's 176
Ladies' Tobacco 22
Ladies' Tresses
   Great Plains 77
   Little 77
   Nodding 77

Shining 47
Slender 77
Spring 47
Lady's-Slipper Orchid 90
   Large Yellow 90
   Kentucky 90
   Small Yellow 90
Lady's Sorrel, Creeping 96
Lamium
   amplexicaule 144
   purpureum 145
Lanceleaf Ragweed 228
Lance-Leaved Coreopsis 94
Laportea canadensis 63
Large-Flowered Bellwort 86
Large-Flowered Coreopsis 94
Larkspur
   Carolina 185
   Dwarf 174
Lathryus
   hirsutus 156
   latifolius 156
Leafcup 52
Leather Flower 191
Lespedeza, Sericea 68
Lespedeza
   capitata 64
   cuneata 68
   violaceae 163
   virginica 163
Lettuce
   Blue 208
   Prickly 127
   Tall White 72
   Wild 127
Leucanthemum vulgare 51
Liatris
   aspera 208
   elegans 209
   pycnostachya 209
   squarrosa 209
Lilium
   michiganense 141
   superbum 141
Lily
   Blackberry 141
   Celestial 180
   Michigan 141
   Orange Day 138
   Turk's Cap 141
   Yellow Trout 82
Linaria canadensis 181
Linum

medium var. *texanum* 113
  sulcatum 113
Liparis
  lilifolia 234
  loeselii 234
Lithospermum
  canescens 94
  caroliniense 94
Liverleaf 167
Lobelia
  Downy 196
  Great Blue 210
  Spiked 196
Lobelia
  cardinalis 142
  inflata 196
  puberula 196
  siphilitica 210
  spicata 196
Loesel's Twayblade 234
Long-Bearded Hawkweed 105
Long-Bracted Wild Indigo 102
Long-Flowered Corn Salad 21
Long-Headed Coneflower 140
Longleaf Groundcherry 116
Long-Leaved Bluets 25
Looking Glass, Venus' 176
Loosestrife 104
  Fringed 104
  Narrow-Leaved 104
  Purple 198
  Winged 198
Lotus corniculatus 111
Lousewort 85
Ludwigia alternifolia 109
Lyre-Leaved Sage 179
Lysimachia
  ciliata 104
  lanceolata 104
  nummularia 105
  quadriflora 104
Lythrum
  alatum 198
  salicaria 198

M

Maianthemum racemosum 30
Manfreda virginica 227
Marbleseed 43
Marigold, Swamp 132
Marsh Fleabane 212
Marsh Pink 159
Marsh Spiderlily, Western 55

Master, Rattlesnake 64
Mary, Blue-Eyed 173
Maryland Meadow Beauty 160
Matelea
  baldwyniana 234
  decipiens 234
  gonocarpa 234
Maximilian Sunflower 125
Mayapple 19
Maypops 195
Meadow Beauty 160
  Maryland 160
Meadow Parsnip 91
  Hairy 91
  Heart-Leaved 91
Meadow Rue
  Early 53
  Purple 53
  Waxy 53
Medic, Black 83
Medicago lupulina 83
Melanthium
  virginicum 56
  woodii 237
Melilotus officinalis 37, 101
Mertensia virginica 170
Mexican Hat 140
Michigan Lily 141
Milfoil, Common 50
Milkweed
  Climbing 234
  Common 156
  Curly 155
  Green 225
  Green-Flowered 225
  Horsetail 35
  Purple 188
  Spider 225
  Tall Green 224
  Variegated 35
  White 35
  Whorled 24
Milkwort, Field 155
Mimosa
  nuttallii 154
  quadrivalvis var. *nuttallii* 154
  strigillosa 154
Mimulus
  alatus 199
  ringens 199
Mint
  Hairy Mountain 63
  Ohio Horse 154

Slender Mountain 63
Wood 154
Minuartia patula 33
Mirabilis
  albida 151
  nyctaginea 151
Missouri Ironweed 202
Missouri Primrose 100
Mistflower 205
Mock Bishop's Weed 47
Monarda, Dotted 119
Monarda
  bradburiana 175
  fistulosa 189
  punctata 119
  russeliana 175
Moneywort 105
Monkey Flower 199
Monotropa uniflora 78
Morning Glory, Ivyleaf 202
Moth Mullein 39, 98
Mountain Mint
  Hairy 63
  Slender 63
Mullein
  Moth 39, 98
  Woolly 108
Mullein Foxglove 114
Musk Thistle 194
Mustard
  Black 88
  Field 88
  Garlic 33

N

Narrow-Leaf Rose-Gentian 159
Narrow-Leaved False Dragonhead 153
Narrow-Leaved Loostrife 104
Narrow-Leaved Vervain 193
Needles, Spanish 165
Nemastylis
  geminiflora 180
  nuttallii 180
Neptunia lutea 112
Nettle
  Horse 37
  Purple Dead 145
  Smooth Hedge 161
  Stinging 63
  Wood 63
New England Aster 216
New Jersey Tea 42
Nodding Ladies' Tresses 77

250

Nodding Pogonia 72
Nodding Thistle 194
Nodding Wild Onion 165
Nothoscordum bivalve 19
Nuttall's Pleatleaf 180
Nuttall's Sedum 87
Nuttall's Wild Indigo 102
Nuttallanthus canadensis 181

O

Obedient Plant 153
Oenothera
   biennis 118
   macrocarpa 100
   missouriensis 100
   pilosella 100
   speciosa 157
Ohio Horse Mint 154
Ohio Spiderwort 186
Oklahoma Grass Pink Orchid 149
One-Flowered Cancer-Root 23
Onion
   Nodding Wild 165
   Wild 148, 165
Onosmodium molle 43
Opuntia
   compressa 103
   humifusa 103
   macrorhiza 103
Orbexilum pedunculatum 182
Orchid
   Autumn Coral Root 240
   Crane-Fly 239
   Fall Coral Root Orchid 240
   Grass Pink 149
   Kentucky Lady's-Slipper 90
   Large Lady's-Slipper 90
   Large Twayblade 234
   Oklahoma Grass Pink 149
   Putty Root 235
   Ragged 36
   Small Lady's-Slipper 90
   Spring Coral Root 233
   Three-Birds Orchid 72
   Twayblade 234
   Yellow Fringed 119
Orchis, Showy 174
Orchis spectabilis 174
Ornithogalum umbellatum 26
Orobanche uniflora 23
Osmorhiza
   claytonii 24
   longistylis 24

Ox-Eye Daisy 51
Ox-Eye Sunflower 101
Oxalis
   corniculata 96
   dillenii 96
   stricta 96
   violaceae 146
Oxypolis rigidior 70
Ozark Corn Salad 21
Ozark Mock Bishop's Weed 47
Ozark Spiderwort 177
Ozark Trillium 18
Ozark Wake Robin 18

P

Packera
   aurea 93
   glabella 93
   obovata 92
   plattensis 92
   tomentosa 92
Pagoda Plant 154
Paintbrush, Indian 135
Palafoxia 165
Palafoxia callosa 165
Pale Purple Coneflower 190
Palmer's Saxifrage 17
Panax quinquefolius 57
Parsley
   Hedge 55
   Japanese Hedge 55
   Prairie 90
Parsnip
   Hairy Meadow 91
   Heart-Leaved 91
   Meadow 91
   Wild 99
Parthenium integrifolium
   var. *hispidum* 43
   var. *integrifolium* 43
Partridge Pea 117
   Sensitive 117
Passiflora
   incarnata 195
   lutea 106
Passion Flower 195
   Yellow 106
Pastinaca sativa 99
Pea
   Butterfly 199
   Everlasting 156
   Partridge 117
   Sensitive Partridge 117

Singletary 156
Pear
   Common Prickly 103
   Plains Prickly 103
Pedicularis
   canadensis 85
   lanceolata 85
Pelton's Rose-Gentian 159
Pencil Flower 106
Penstemon
   arkanansus 34
   cobaea 187
   digitalis 45
   pallidus 34
   tubiflorus 45
Perennial Phlox 210
Perilla frutescens 213
Persicaria pensylvanica 152
Petalostemon
   candidum 48
   purpureum 195
Petunia
   Smooth Wild 189
   Wild 189
Phacelia
   Hairy 180
   Smooth 180
Phacelia
   glabra 180
   hirsuta 180
Phemeranthus
   calycinus 157
   parviflorus 157
Philadelphia Fleabane 22
Phlox
   Blue 172
   Cleft 170
   Downy 147
   Garden 210
   Perennial 210
   Sand 170
   Smooth 191
Phlox
   bifida 170
   divaricata 172
   glaberrima 191
   paniculata 210
   pilosa 147
Phyla lanceolata 38
Physalis longifolia 116
Physic, Indian 44
Physostegia
   angustifolia 153

virginiana 153
Phytolacca americana 228
Pimpernel, Yellow 96
Pineweed 116
Pink
   Deptford 150
   Fire 136
   Indian 137
   Marsh 159
   Rock 157
   Rose 159
Pinkweed 152
Pipe, Indian 78
Plains Coreopsis 115
Plains Prickly Pear 103
Plainsman, Old 46
Plant
   Beefsteak 213
   Compass 123
   Cup 122
   Compass 123
   Gum 132
   Obedient 153
   Pagoda 154
Plantain
   Pale Indian 58
   Prairie Indian 58
   Rattlesnake 66
   Robin's 22
Plantanthera ciliaris 119
Platanthera lacera 36
Pleatleaf, Nuttall's 180
Pluchea
   camphorata 212
   foetida 212
Plum, Ground 83
Podophyllum peltatum 19
Pogonia
   Large Whorled 233
   Nodding 72
Poison, Fly 30
Poison Hemlock 40
Pokeberry 228
Pokeweed 228
Polemonium reptans 176
Polianthes virginica 227
Polygala
   sanguinea 155
   senega 41
Polygonatum biflorum 31
Polygonum
   pensylvanicum 152
   scandens 70

Polymnia
   canadensis 52
   uvedalia 52
Polytaenia nuttallii 90
Poppy, Celandine 87
Poppy Mallow
   Bush's 192
   Fringed 192
   Purple 192
Porteranthus stipulatus 44
Potentilla
   recta 95
   simplex 95
Potato Dandelion 92
Potato Vine, Wild 40
Powderpuff 154
Prairie Aster, Southern 214
Prairie Blazing Star 209
Prairie Clover
   Purple 195
   White 48
Prairie Coreopsis 114
Prairie Dock 122
Prairie Hyacinth 175
Prairie Indian Plantain 58
Prairie Parsley 90
Prairie Ragwort 92
Prairie Spiderwort 177
Prairie Sundrops 100
Prairie Tea 61
Prenanthes altissima 72
Prickly Lettuce 127
Prickly Pear
   Common 103
   Plains 103
Primrose
   Evening 118
   Missouri 100
   Showy Evening 157
Prunella vulgaris
   ssp. *lanceolata* 150
   ssp. *vulgaris* 150
Pseudognaphalium obtusifolium 71
Psoralea psoralioides 182
Ptilimnium
   capillaceum 47
   nuttallii 47
Puccoon
   Carolina 94
   Orange 94
Purple-Headed Sneezeweed 110
Pussytoes 22

Putty Root Orchid 235
Pycnanthemum
   pilosum 63
   tenuifolium 63
Pyrrhopappus carolinianus 99

Q

Queen Anne's Lace 38
Quinine, Wild 43

R

Ragweed
   Common 228
   Giant 228
   Lanceleaf 228
Ragwort
   Golden 93
   Lanceleaf
   Prairie 92
   Woolly 92
Ranunculus
   harveyi 81
   hispidus 81
   sardous 89
Ratibida
   columnaris 140
   columnifera 140
   pinnata 111
Rattlesnake Master 64
Rattlesnake Plantain 66
Rattlesnake Root 72
Rattle Weed 29
Rhexia
   mariana 160
   virginia 160
Robin
   Purple Wake 232
   Wake 232
Robin's Plantain 22
Rock Geranium 220
Rockcress, Smooth 16
Rocket
   Dame's 183
   Purple 183
   Yellow 88
Rock Pink 157
Root
   Colic 32
   Culver's 61
Rose-Gentian
   Pelton's 159
   Texas 159
Rose Pink 159

Rose Verbena 144
Rose Vervain 144
Rosinweed, Starry 123
Rough-Fruited Cinquefoil 95
Round-Headed Bush Clover 64
Round-Leaved Groundsel 92
Round-Leaved Tick Trefoil 164
Round-Lobed Hepatica 167
Royal Catchfly 142
Rudbeckia
   grandiflora 107
   hirta 107
   laciniata 121
   subtomentosa 121
   triloba 107
Rue
   Early 53
   Goat's 147
   Purple Meadow 53
   Waxy Meadow 53
Rue Anemone 13
   False 13
Ruellia
   humilis 189
   pedunculata 189
   strepens 189

S

Sabatia
   angularis 159
   arkansana 159
   brachiata 159
   campestris 159
Sage
   Blue 201
   Lyre-Leaved 179
   Wood 161
Salvia
   azurea 201
   lyrata 179
Sampson's Snakeroot 182
Sand Phlox 170
Sandwort, Slender 33
Sanguinaria canadensis 16
Saponaria officinalis 158
Satureja arkansana 190
Saxifraga
   palmeri 17
   texana 17
Saxifrage 17
   Palmer's 17
Sawtooth Sunflower 125
Scaly Blazing Star 209

Schrankia uncinata 154
Scrophularia marilandica 236
Scutellaria
   elliptica 184
   integrifolia 184
   ovata 184
   parvula 184
Seal, Solomon's 31
   False 30
Securigera varia 153
Sedum
   Nuttall's 87
   Yellow 87
Sedum
   nuttallianum 87
   pulchellum 149
   ternatum 18
Seedbox 109
Selenia 86
Selenia aurea 86
Self-Heal 150
Seneca Snakeroot 41
Senecio
   aureus 93
   glabellus 93
   obovatus 92
   plattensis 92
   tomentosa 92
Senna, Wild 118
Senna marilandica 118
Sensitive Brier 154
Sensitive Partridge Pea 117
Sericea Lespedeza 68
Sessile Trillium 232
Seymeria macrophylla 114
Sharp-Lobed Hepatica 167
Shining Blue Star 181
Shining Ladies' Tresses 47
Shoestrings, Devil's 154
Shooting Star 146
   French's 146
Showy Evening Primrose 157
Showy Orchis 174
Sicklepod 16
Silene
   regia 142
   stellata 60
   virginica 136
Silphium
   astericus 123
   integrifolium 123
   laciniatum 123
   perfoliatum 122

   terebinthinacium 122
Singletary Pea 156
Sisyrinchium angustifolium 182
Skullcap
   Hairy 184
   Heartleaf 184
   Rough 184
   Small 184
Sky Blue Aster 216
Slender Sandwort 33
Small-Flowered Corydalis 84
Small-Fruited Whitlow Grass 11
Small Skullcap 184
Smallanthus uvedalius 52
Smilacena racemosa 30
Snakeroot
   Black 42
   Sampson's 182
   Seneca 41
   White 69
Sneezeweed 133
Sneezeweed, Purple-Headed 110
Snow-On-The-Prairie 79
Soapwort 158
   Gentian 217
Solanum carolinense 37
Solidago
   altissima 130
   buckleyi 120
   caesia 129
   canadensis 130
   drummondii 131
   nemoralis 120
   petiolaris 120
   ulmifolia 129
Solomon's Seal 31
   False 30
Sorrel
   Creeping Lady's 96
   Violet Wood 146
   Yellow Wood 96
Southern Prairie Aster 214
Spanish Needles 165
Specularia perfoliata 176
Spider Milkweed 225
Spiderlily
   Northern 55
   Western Marsh 55
Spiderwort
   Hairyflower 186
   Hairystem 186
   Ohio 186
   Ozark 177

Prairie 177
Western 177
Woodland 177
Spigelia marilandica 137
Spiked Lobelia 196
Spikenard 36
Spiranthes
   cernua 77
   lacera 77
   lucida 47
   magnicamporum 77
   tuberosa 77
   vernalis 47
Spreading Aster 217
Spreading Dogbane 54
Spring Beauty 12
Spring Coral Root Orchid 233
Spring Cress 15
Spring Ladies' Tresses 47
Spurge
   Flowering 51
   Wood 223
St. John's Wort
   Common 113
   Spotted 113
Stachys tenuifolia 161
Star
   Blue 181
   French's Shooting 146
   Pinkscale Blazing 209
   Prairie Blazing 209
   Rough Blazing 208
   Scaly Blazing 209
   Shining Blue 181
   Shooting 146
   Violet 167, 172
Star Grass, Yellow 84
Star Of Bethlehem 26
Starry Campion 60
Starry Rosinweed 123
Stellaria media 14
Stiff Gentian 218
Stiff-Leaved Aster 215
Stinkweed 212
Stonecrop, Wild 18
Strawberry, Wild 25
Strophostyles
   helvula 158
   leiosperma 158
   umbellata 158
Stylophorum diphyllum 87
Stylosanthes biflora 106
Sundrops, Prairie 100

Sunflower
   Ashy 124
   Bristly 124
   Common 125
   Downy 124
   Maximilian 125
   Ox-Eye 101
   Sawtooth 125
   Tickseed 132
   Woodland 124
Susan
   Black-Eyed 107
   Brown-Eyed 107
Swamp Agrimony 126
Swamp Wood Betony 85
Sweet William 172
Swertia caroliniensis 226
Symphyotrichum
   anomalum 215
   novae-angliae 216
   oblongifolium 214
   oolentangiense 216
   patens 217
   pilosum 75
   urophyllum 76

T

Taenidia integerrima 96
Talinum
   calycinum 157
   parviflorum 157
Tea
   New Jersey 42
   Prairie 61
Teasel
   Common 160
   Cut-Leaved 160
Tephrosia virginiana 147
Teucrium canadense 161
Texas Ironweed 202
Texas Rose-Gentian 159
Thalictrum
   dasycarpum 53
   dioicum 53
   revolutum 53
   thalictroides 13
Thaspium
   barbinode 91
   trifoliatum 91
Thimbleweed 23
Thistle
   Bull 211
   Field 211

   Musk 194
   Nodding 194
   Soft 211
   Tall 211
   Yellow 211
Three-Birds Orchid 72
Three-Lobed Violet 169
Tick Trefoil 164
   Round-Leaved 164
Ticks, Beggar's 132
Tickseed
   Star 94
   Tall 115
Tickseed Sunflower 132
Tipularia discolor 239
Toadflax
   Blue 181
   False 34
Tobacco, Indian 196
Toothwort 15
Torilis
   arvensis 55
   japonica 55
Touch-Me-Not
   Pale 112
   Spotted 140
Tradescantia
   ernestiana 177
   hirsuticaulis 186
   hirsutiflora 186
   occidentalis 177
   ohiensis 186
   ozarkana 177
Tragopogon
   dubius 97
   pratensis 97
Trefoil
   Bird's Foot 111
   Round-Leaved Tick 164
   Tick 164
Tresses
   Great Plains Ladies' 77
   Little Ladies' 77
   Nodding Ladies' 77
   Slender Ladies' 77
   Spring Ladies' 47
Trichostema dishotomum 213
Trifolium incarnatum 136
Trillium
   Green 221
   Ozark 18
   Purple 232
   Sessile 232

White 18
Trillium
  flexipes 18
  pusillum var. *ozarkanum* 18
  recurvatum 232
  sessile 232
  viridescens 221
Triodanis perfoliata 176
Triosteum
  angustifolium 238
  aurantiacum 238
  perfoliatum 238
Triphora trianthophora 72
Trout Lily
  White
  Yellow 82
Turnsole 204
Turtlehead
  Rose 65
  White 65
Twayblade
  Large 234
  Loesel's 234
Twayblade Orchid 234
Two-Flowered Cynthia 92

U
Uvularia
  grandflora 86
  sessilifolia 86

V
Valerianella
  longiflora 21
  ozarkana 21
  radiata 21
Variegated Milkweed 35
Venus' Looking Glass 176
Veratrum
  virginicum 56
  woodii 237
Verbascum
  blattaria 39, 98
  thapsus 108
Verbena, Rose 144
Verbena
  bracteata 193
  canadensis 144
  simplex 193
  stricta 193
Verbesina
  alternifolia 131
  helianthoides 109
  virginica 76

Vernonia
  altissima 203
  arkansana 203
  baldwinii 203
  crinita 203
  gigantea 203
  missurica 202
  texana 202
Veronicastrum virginicum 61
Vervain
  Creeping 193
  Hoary 193
  Narrow-Leaved 193
  Rose 144
Vetch
  Crown 153
  Winter 186
Vicia villosa 186
Viola
  palmata 169
  pedata 168
  pensylvanica 82
  primulifolia 20
  pubescens 82
  rafinesquii 169
  sororia 168
  striata 20
Violet
  Bird's Foot 168
  Collinsia 173
  Dogtooth 12
  Green 223
  Pale 20
  Prairie Dogtooth 12
  Star 167, 172
  Three-Lobed 169
  White 20
  White Dogtooth 12
  Wood Sorrel 146
  Yellow 82
  Yellow Dogtooth 82
  Woolly Blue 168
Viper's Bugloss 183
Virginia Waterleaf 178

W
Wake Robin 232
  Ozark 18
  Purple 232
Water Hemlock 49
Waterleaf
  Browne's 178
  Great 178
  Virginia 178

Waxweed, Blue 205
Waxy Meadow Rue 53
Weed
  Butterfly 139
  Cancer 179
  Rattle 29
Western Daisy 171
Western Ironweed 203
White Lettuce, Tall 72
Whitlow Grass, Small-Fruited 11
Whorled Milkweed 24
Whorled Pogonia, Large 233
Widow's Cross 149
Wild Indigo, Cream 102
Wild Stonecrop 18
  Yellow 89
William, Sweet 172
Winged Loosestrife 198
Wingstem 109
Winter Vetch 186
Wood Betony 85
  Swamp 85
Wood Mint 154
Wood Nettle 63
Wood Sage 161
Wood Sorrel
  Yellow 96
  Violet 146
Wood Spurge 223
Woodland Aster 215
Woodland Goldenrod 120
Woodland Spiderwort 177
Woollen Breeches 178
Woolly Blue Violet 168
Woolly Croton 61
Woolly Mullein 108
Woolly-White 46
Wort
  Common St. John's 113
  Spotted St. John's 113

Y
Yarrow 50
Yellow-Flowered Horse Gentian 238
Yellow Fringed Orchid 119
Yellow-Puff 112

Z
Zigadenus nuttallii 30
Zizia
  aptera 91
  aurea 91, 96

About The Author

After completing masters' degrees in botany and zoology from Southern Illinois University, Carbondale, Don Kurz spent the next 30 years working to inventory, acquire, protect, and manage natural areas, endangered species sites, and other special features. Growing up in Illinois, some of his early jobs included working for the Illinois Environmental Protection Agency, the Illinois Natural Areas Inventory, and the Natural Land Institute. Later, he was employed by the Missouri Department of Conservation, where he held various supervisory positions in the Natural History Division, including that of Natural History chief.

For over 30 years, Don has been writing about nature and photographing landscapes, wildlife, and plants. His work has appeared in several calendars and magazines and in numerous wildflower books including Falcon Publishing's *Tallgrass Prairie Wildflowers*. He is also author of Falcon's *Scenic Driving the Ozarks, including the Ouachita Mountains* and *Ozark Wildflowers*, as well as *Shrubs and Woody Vines of Missouri*, *Shrubs and Woody Vines of Missouri Field Guide*, *Trees of Missouri*, and *Trees of Missouri Field Guide*, all published by the Missouri Department of Conservation. Additionally, *Illinois Wildflowers* and *Missouri's Natural Wonders Guidebook*, are published by Tim Ernst Publishing/Cloudland.net.